Beyond Golgotha

Margaret Horsfield
Peter Horsfield

Brechin Books
1993

Published by
BRECHIN BOOKS
P.O. Box 1021, Station A, Nanaimo,B.C. V9R 5Z2
Phone / Fax: 604-753-4638

Typeset by The Vancouver Desktop Publishing Centre
Printed in Canada by Hignell Printers
Cover design Paul Gelinas

Canadian Cataloguing in Publication Data

Horsfield, Margaret.
Beyond Golgotha

Includes bibliographical references and index.
ISBN 0-9697008-0-6

1. Jesus Christ—Crucifixion—Biblical teaching. 2. Jesus Christ—Resurrection—Biblical teaching. 3. Bible. N.T. Gospels—Criticism, interpretation, etc. 4. Bible. N.T.—Relation to the old testament.
I. Horsfield, Peter, 1919- II. Title.
BT431.H67 1993 232.96 C93-091266-7

For Phyllis, with love

The Middle East

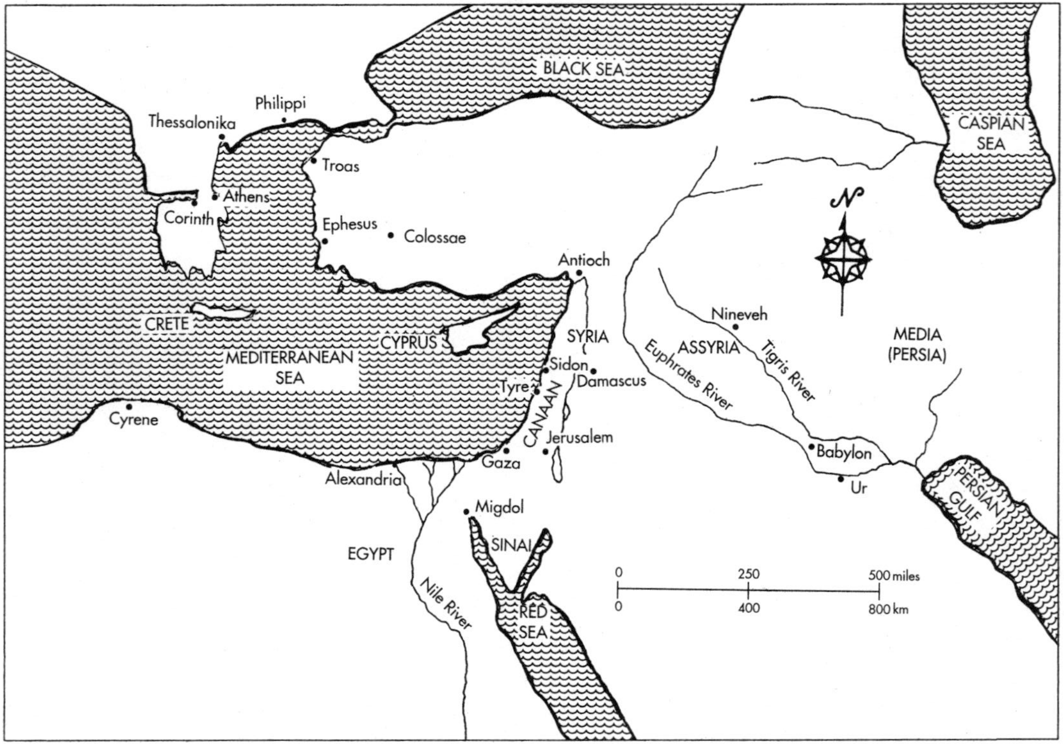

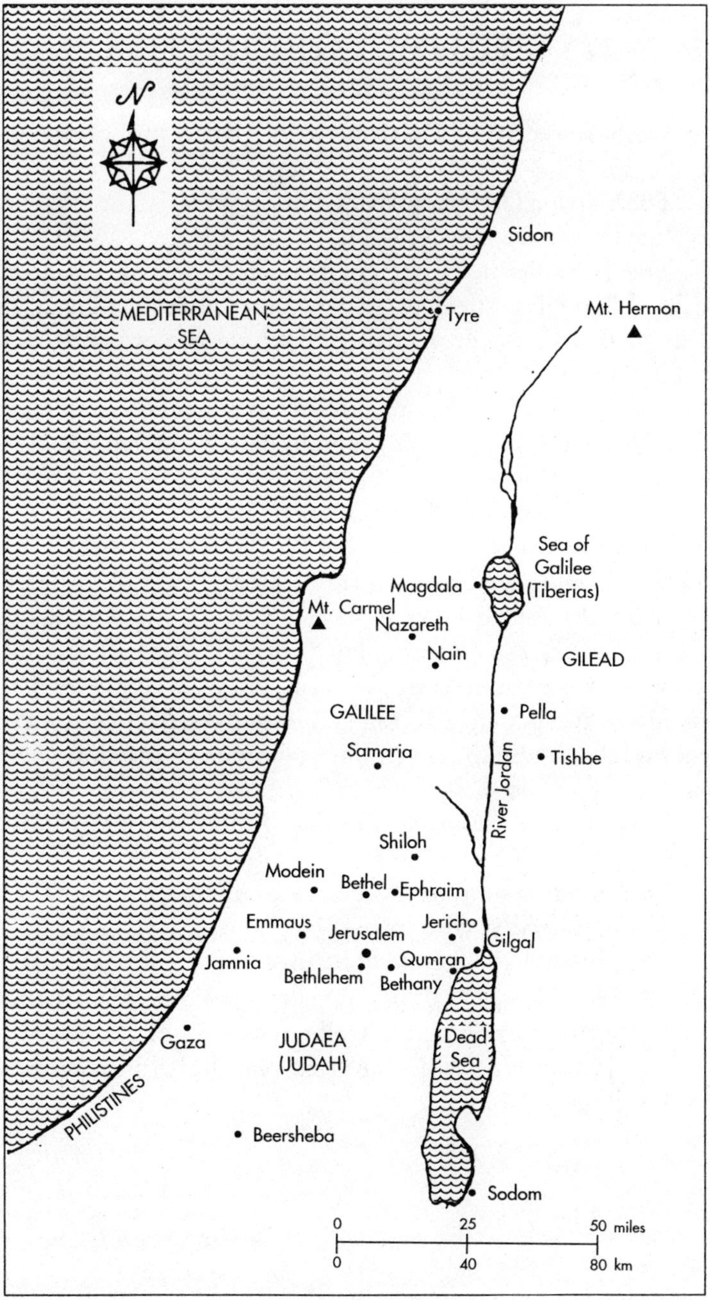
N
Sidon
MEDITERRANEAN SEA
Tyre
Mt. Hermon
Sea of Galilee (Tiberias)
Magdala
Mt. Carmel
Nazareth
Nain
GILEAD
GALILEE
Pella
Samaria
Tishbe
River Jordan
Shiloh
Modein
Bethel
Ephraim
Emmaus
Jericho
Jerusalem
Gilgal
Jamnia
Qumran
Bethlehem
Bethany
Gaza
JUDAEA (JUDAH)
Dead Sea
PHILISTINES
Beersheba
Sodom
0
25
50 miles
0
40
80 km

Palestine

Acknowledgements

We have received help from many quarters in writing this book.

The Canada Council provided financial assistance that was invaluable. We are most grateful.

The Benedictine Sisters in Nanaimo, British Columbia enabled Peter Horsfield to give a lecture series exploring the ideas in this book. From that, the whole project grew. Our thanks to all the sisters.

Then on CBC Radio, the IDEAS documentary series presented Margaret Horsfield's programmes "Crucified, Dead and Buried". For that, we thank Bernie Lucht and Alison Moss.

Our warm thanks to Elizabeth Hart and the staff at the library of the Vancouver School of Theology; to Lloyd Gaston, Michael Goulder and Kim Murray who kindly read the manuscript for us; and to Peter Horsfield's many students, whose interest has been so encouraging.

We are grateful to Carol Heaton, in London, England, for her advice and patience; to Liz Hammond-Kaarremaa, on Protection Island, who has been our computer counsellor; and to Sandra Gwyn and Gail Singer in Toronto.

Very special thanks to Gordon Elliott for his help and friendship over the years.

Our greatest support has been Anne Horsfield. We thank her wholeheartedly, with love.

This book has been written in many locations, both in Canada and in England. It has travelled between us by rowboat and ferry, by bicycle and wheelbarrow, by jet aircraft, float plane and fibre-optic cable. It has travelled hopefully. We hope this continues.

Margaret Horsfield
Peter Horsfield

Protection Island
April 1993

Contents

Introduction

In the telling of stories, nothing ever comes from nothing; all stories draw on other earlier stories for form, for narrative structure, sometimes for theme and content. This is true of newspaper stories, folk stories, and biblical stories alike.

Here we are looking at biblical stories. We start with the stories associated with the death of Jesus at the place called Golgotha, just outside Jerusalem. The stories surrounding this death are told in the New Testament of the Bible. They are nearly 2000 years old, and they are part of a storytelling tradition that was ancient when they were written. Within this tradition, stories are often very closely interrelated. The stories of the death of Jesus and its aftermath are no exception. They reflect and echo many other earlier stories.

In our first book *Beyond Bethlehem* we looked at the stories of the birth of Jesus and their links with other stories. Because the birth stories so clearly and openly reflect earlier stories, in *Beyond Bethlehem* we found ourselves in what we called a "looking glass world" of text. Here with the stories of the death and resurrection of Jesus, we are in different territory. Rather than a looking glass world we find ourselves in what seems to be a hall of mirrors. Reflections of many ancient stories appear in the stories of the death and resurrection of Jesus in complex, sometimes bewildering ways, like images and fragments of images being mirrored from one surface to another. Sometimes these reflections can be seen directly, sometimes they are glimpsed indistinctly and distantly. In story after story about the death and resurrection of Jesus, the language and images, ideas and themes of earlier material are reflected in such variety and in so many ways that it becomes uncertain where or when the original ideas or images arose.

Most of the ancient material we will be looking at comes from the Hebrew Scriptures. Here are the stories, the poems, the songs, the prophecies, the prayers that inform the later accounts about Jesus. Here is the rich web of language, images, ideas, and themes later echoed in the New Testament. In this book we want to seek out and examine the connections between the stories of Jesus and this earlier material. This process sets before our eyes details of the settings that we might otherwise miss. It lets us hear nuances of vocabulary that we might otherwise not hear. Above all it introduces a large cast of characters in dozens of closely connected stories; heroes and villains, honest people and dishonest, patriots and traitors, all of them supporting characters either directly or indirectly in the stories of the death and resurrection of Jesus.

In the New Testament there are so many stories about the death and resurrection of Jesus that we cannot look at them all in close detail. We have simply tried to include the best known of these. With the other, older material the process of selection has been more complex. There are countless stories from the Hebrew Scriptures and from Jewish writings near the time of Jesus that can be understood to bear some relation to the stories of the death and resurrection of Jesus. From this wealth of material, we have had to make a relatively small selection. Our choice has been made in part by following up the direct quotations from these older stories that appear in the New Testament stories of Jesus, and in part by following indirect allusions and echoes. The death and resurrection stories are rich with such allusions to other material. Some are clearly and readily evident, while others are a matter of personal perception. We have tried to follow up the clearest of these, and for the rest we have allowed ourselves an element of personal preference. Sometimes we choose to follow up allusions or connections that may seem very faint or even slightly odd. Inevitably, not everyone will agree with our choice of material. A connection between two stories or images that seems very clear to one person may be obscure to another. What we hope our choice will show is the great variety of ways in which the stories of Jesus's death and resurrection can be understood to reflect other material. We hope our choice of material is helpful in its variety; that in different ways the older writings will be seen to illuminate the later ones about Jesus and will give a sense of the background against which the stories of the death and resurrection were written.

We make no pretence in this book to address the question of "what really happened?" in the stories of the death and resurrection of Jesus. We do not claim to know what really happened, nor do we believe the biblical stories about Jesus are designed to tell us what really happened. To insist on demanding hard facts from these stories is simply frustrating. Even in recent history it is difficult to know exactly what has happened, be it in a news story or in our own lives. With these two thousand year old stories about Jesus, the historical details are virtually impossible to know. What we can know, however, is more about the nature of the stories we are told about Jesus; what influenced them, how they are structured and where their roots lie. But while this may affect our attitude to these stories, while it may change our expectations and alter our understanding of the material, this approach will not and cannot provide hard and fast conclusions about what really happened.

There are always difficulties in approaching the stories of Jesus's death and resurrection. Although these are very widely known, they are on the whole very narrowly understood. For instance, vast numbers of people know the stories about Jesus rising from the dead after he was executed. Some people believe these accounts and some do not. Amongst those who believe them, many are thrown into an emotional fervour by the stories. Amongst those who do not believe them, many are scornful of the stories. The nature of the stories can be completely overshadowed by clamorous statements of belief or disbelief. We do not intend to contribute to such statements. We intend instead to focus closely on the stories themselves, and on what we understand to be their background.

It is not our purpose here to comment on the religious beliefs people may hold about these stories, other than to say that we cannot allow the religious viewpoints of others to intimidate us. The viewpoints of academic specialists must be treated in a similar fashion. However much respect we have for the often outstanding work of academics who have studied these stories, we cannot allow their theories or findings or beliefs to dictate to us.

We are very aware of the strong reactions that these stories about Jesus can and do provoke. We are very aware that over many centuries contradictory and confusing theories and theologies have mushroomed, cloud-like, from the stories of Jesus's death and resurrection. We are very aware that these stories are often treated as if they are the property of special interest groups, committed Christians on the one hand, or academic specialists on the other. But although we are aware of all this, we also are convinced that no one, neither priest nor professor, holds the final key to understanding these stories. They are open to all of us to approach and to try to understand.

Throughout this book, academics may wonder if we are academic enough, committed Christians may wonder if we are Christian enough, journalists and critics may wonder if we are sternly analytical enough. They all probably will conclude that we are not. In writing this book, neither of us lays claim to any superior knowledge or authority. We are not biblical scholars, nor are we specialists in ancient languages. All we can claim is a keen interest in biblical research, and a love for biblical stories.

What we are proposing is a way of exploring the stories of the death and resurrection of Jesus. We start this book from the premise that most people know great and good stories when they hear them, and that the great and the good stories of any culture or civilisation or religion are worth telling and retelling, considering and reconsidering from many different angles and viewpoints. This premise has led us to develop a particular approach to the stories about Jesus, and for us this has been both a surprise and a pleasure. This surprise and pleasure lie in seeing how the well-known stories of the death and resurrection of Jesus are so closely connected to older, often less well known stories, and in finding ourselves able to look at all of these in a new light. This is only one of many ways to approach this material. It is one we have come to know well and to enjoy enormously.

Notes to the Reader

A few practical points may be helpful before going any further:

- The first three chapters of this book provide general background about the writers of the New Testament. From Chapter 4 onwards, we follow the stories of the last days of Jesus, relating these to other older stories. Anyone wishing to go directly to the stories may prefer to skip the first three chapters.

- Every chapter is, we hope, self-contained. This means that some stories and biblical passages are cited more than once. We have done this intentionally, in order to make each chapter a complete unit. The best way to see the cumulative effect of all the interrelated stories is to read the chapters in sequence, but it is perfectly feasible to read them in random order.

- As far as possible, we have used the gospel of Mark as our primary text in telling stories about Jesus. We explain our reasons for doing this in Chapter 3. When we reach the stories of the resurrection of Jesus in Chapters 16 and 17, we have to abandon this practice because of the radical differences in how the different gospel writers tell their stories. In the final chapter we return to Mark's gospel.

- About Bibles and abbreviations, a few points. We take all biblical passages from the New Jerusalem Bible (NJB) unless otherwise noted. Other Bibles we refer to include the following: King James Bible, also called the Authorised Version (AV), Revised Version (RV), Scofield Reference Bible, Revised

Standard Version (RSV), Good News Bible, New International Version (NIV), New English Bible (NEB), Revised English Bible, New Revised Standard Version (NRSV). For publication data see the bibliography.

- When we quote from the Bible we follow the chapter and verse indications given in the New Jerusalem Bible. Versification can vary from one version of the Bible to another.

- All Bibles start with the Hebrew Scriptures, also known as the Old Testament. Throughout this book we use the term Hebrew Scriptures rather than Old Testament.

- About the Apocrypha. We refer to its various books from time to time. The Apocrypha is a loosely defined collection of Jewish writings often added to the Hebrew Scriptures. Most of these writings date between the third century BCE and the first century CE, and they were written in Greek rather than in Hebrew. The Apocrypha is not included in all Bibles, but it appears in many good modern translations. Sometimes it is in a special section, and sometimes its books are salted throughout the Hebrew Scriptures. It is important to have a Bible that includes the Apocrypha, if only because these writings tell a great deal about the political and religious developments of their time.

- When giving dates in this book, we use the letters CE (Common Era) and BCE (Before the Common Era). These are used increasingly to replace the notations of AD (anno domini) and BC (before Christ).

- One final point is that any and all mistakes in this book are our own. We hope their number is few.

CHAPTER ONE

Expectations

Stories about Jesus were first told amongst small groups of Christians in Jewish synagogues scattered throughout the Mediterranean world from Rome to the Persian Gulf. These stories were told for many years before they were recorded in any systematic way. By the time the stories were being written down, Jesus had been dead for several decades. The end of the first century CE was in sight, and Christianity was emerging as a distinct religion, separate from its parent Jewish religion.

Throughout the middle years of the first century as the Christian movement gained strength within certain Jewish communities and synagogues, early Christians were defining themselves and asserting their beliefs. This meant they were increasingly setting themselves apart from the practices and beliefs of the synagogues within which their new movement was taking shape.

The separation between Christianity and Judaism was slow and painful. It was the result of many years of steadily accumulating hostilities and mistrust on both sides. Awkwardly, and in an atmosphere of increasing strain, the Christian sect of Judaism became transformed into a distinct and separate religion. This process of separation was the single strongest influence on the early development of Christian churches, and it had a great influence on how stories were told about Jesus.

Most of the first Christians and their leaders were Jews. In the process of identifying themselves and their beliefs, these early Jewish Christians naturally made use of the language and traditions they knew. In this way the language and traditions of Judaism were used to define Christianity. Stories about Jesus followed the storytelling traditions of the Hebrew Scriptures; Christian rituals followed many of the practices of temple and synagogue.

The synagogues of the Mediterranean world in the first century were much more than mere religious assemblies, they were centres for communication and education, alive with the social and political concerns of the day. Often the local government of the Jewish community was entrusted to the synagogue authorities by whatever secular government was in power. This meant amongst other things that Jewish leaders were responsible for law and order within their communities. Because of this, Christian groups at first lived within the religious and secular jurisdiction of their synagogues. Through the synagogue communities they kept in touch with all the fashions and foibles of thought that swayed the minds of Jews of the period. Just as Christian ideas were evolving at that time, so were Jewish ideas, and conflict between the two ideologies grew. This did not bode well for the Christians, because by the last half of the first century, when the stories about Jesus were being recorded, Christians were increasingly seen as troublemakers by the synagogue authorities, who did not hesitate to wield their power. This is evident in the writings of early Christians in the New Testament of the Christian Bible. It is equally evident that the early Christians probably were troublemakers. They challenged the established authorities, declared controversial religious beliefs, and formed their own groups. Not surprisingly, the synagogues wanted to be rid of them.

It was against such a background that the stories of the life and death of Jesus were first told or read aloud to gatherings of Christians. These stories were designed to give the embattled Christians hope for better things to come. The stories reassured them that they were on the right track; that their leader Jesus was indeed that mysterious figure in the Hebrew Scriptures known as the Messiah, the leader who would come to save the world, the leader who would set up a new age of peace and justice.

The Christians of the first, and even of the early second century lived in almost daily expectation that Jesus would return as Messiah. When he did return they would be proven right, their beliefs would be vindicated, and they would be the ones to find honour and favour. A new kingdom, a new realm, a new age would come to birth, both in this world and in the next. The "end times", as they were called, would precede this new order of things. The end times would be full of strife, leading to widespread bloodshed and destruction in the great and final battle between the forces of good and evil.

A useful story to illustrate the atmosphere in which early Christians lived is told by Mark in Chapter 13 of his gospel.[1] This is not a popular passage. For the last hundred years or so it has been out of favour with many scholars because it appears to be independent of the rest of the gospel, and it has been ignored to this day by many churches because it is told in such strange, uneasy language.

In this story, Jesus has recently come into Jerusalem from Galilee to celebrate the Passover and he has been talking to the people who gathered from day to day in the temple courtyards and porticoes. One day as he comes out of the temple one of his disciples says to him, "Master, look at the size of those stones! Look at the size of those buildings!". Jesus is quoted as replying, "You see these great buildings? Not a single stone will be left on another; everything will be pulled down.".

This is interesting because by the time Mark was writing, the massive temple in Jerusalem was either in the process of being destroyed in a terrible war, or it recently had been destroyed. Anyone hearing Mark's story would have known about this. It was a blow that struck at the very heart of the Jewish religion, for the temple was revered and esteemed as the most sacred site of Jewish worship and sacrifice. In the aftershock of its destruction, Jews in synagogues from Rome to Babylon were trying to redefine what it meant to be Jewish.

1 There are similar passages in MT.24 and LK.21.

This often meant identifying in a clear way with one or other of the different sectarian groups within Judaism. This process of identifying with one group necessarily involved opposing other groups. In many places this meant that Jews identified themselves vis-a-vis the Christians who were either a nearby group that had recently split off from the synagogue or were a sect still in their midst.

For first century Jews it was not difficult to find fault with these Christians. They were the fanatics who claimed the Messiah had come in the person of Jesus, and awaited his imminent return. For traditional Jews this claim was a scandal. For them, Jesus was no triumphant leader, no messianic king come to usher in a new age. He had been crucified in disgrace. He was no more than an upstart preacher from the provinces who had got into serious trouble earlier in the century. His followers had set themselves up against the authorities of both temple and synagogue and now they were attracting the wrath of God onto all Jewish people. According to many stories in the Hebrew Scriptures, when the children of Israel were unfaithful, their God became angry and turned away, abandoning them to different forms of destruction or exile. The destruction of the temple in Jerusalem seemed to fit this pattern. Someone must have been unfaithful. The different sectarian divisions within Judaism certainly mistrusted each other, but they all mistrusted the Christians. So in the aftermath of the destruction of the temple, Christians and Jews became more and more bitterly divided. All of this lies beneath the surface of Mark's story.

After the opening section, the story continues with a quick scene change. Suddenly Jesus is sitting with his friends Peter, James, John and Andrew. They are on the hill called the Mount of Olives looking across to the temple, and one of them refers back to Jesus's words about the temple and asks "Tell us, when is this going to happen, and what sign will there be that it is all about to take place?".

Jesus then begins a long speech in which he warns his followers not to be deceived by others who will come claiming to be him. He says there will be wars and rumours of war, but that these do not mean the end has come. Worse will follow, for there will be earthquakes and famines. And Jesus's speech continues with this:

> 'Be on your guard: you will be handed over to sanhedrins; you will be beaten in synagogues; and you will be brought before governors and kings for my sake . . .
>
> Brother will betray brother to death, and a father his child; children will come forward against their parents and have them put to death. You will be universally hated on account of my name; but anyone who stands firm to the end will be saved.'
>
> MK.13.9-13

Here Mark portrays Jesus on the Mount of Olives, looking at the temple and talking quietly to four of his friends warning them about hard times to come. And such hard times did indeed come. Following the siege and destruction of Jerusalem many groups of Christians underwent great suffering. Mark's story can be read as evidence that they were beaten; that they were accused before governors and kings; that family members did betray each other, and that they were hated by their neighbours.

Mark's story carries on, even more pertinently. Jesus, still with his friends on the Mount of Olives, continues to speak:

> 'When you see *the appalling abomination* set up where it ought not to be (let the reader understand), then those in Judaea must escape to the mountains . . .'
>
> MK.13.14

Another English translation phrases it slightly differently:

> 'But when you see the desolating sacrilege set up where it ought not to be (let the reader understand), then those in Judea must flee to the mountains . . .'
>
> MK.13.14 (NRSV)

Mark's gospel, like all other writings in the Bible, was designed to be read aloud to the people. In early churches this meant people who were in the process of separating from or being separated from their parent synagogues. These people would share a knowledge both of recent events and of the Hebrew Scriptures, which were also read aloud regularly. Anyone hearing Mark's gospel would certainly have understood the implications of the phrase "the desolating sacrilege set up where it ought not to be".

The expression "desolating sacrilege", also translated as "appalling abomination" is originally used at the end of the book of Daniel. The story in which it is found tells of "a man dressed in linen" appearing to the young Hebrew sage Daniel in a complex, almost hallucinatory vision of strange things to come. This culminates with Daniel asking "My lord, what is to be the outcome?". The reply is:

> 'Go,Daniel,' he said. 'These words are to remain secret and sealed until the time of the End. Many will be cleansed, made white and purged; the wicked will persist in doing wrong; the wicked will never understand; those who are wise will understand. From the moment that the perpetual sacrifice is abolished and the appalling abomination set up: a thousand two hundred and ninety days. Blessed is he who perseveres and attains a thousand three hundred and thirty-five days. But you, go away and rest; and you will rise for your reward at the end of time.'
>
> DN.12.9-13

It can be hard for twentieth century minds to appreciate the ominous force of references to "abominations" and "sacrileges". A helpful source to turn to for more detail is the Jewish historian Flavius Josephus who was born in 37 CE, within few years of the time when Jesus is thought to have been killed. Josephus vividly describes other "desolating sacrileges" in telling how the Holy of Holies, the inner sanctuary of the temple, was either destroyed or desecrated on more than one occasion.

The first of these was only a threat. It took place about 40CE, soon after the Roman emperor Caligula, also known as Gaius Caesar, came to power:

> Gaius Caesar's accession to power so completely turned his head that he wished to be thought of and addressed as a god, . . and proceeded to lay sacrilegious hands on Judaea. He ordered Petronius to march with an army to Jerusalem and erect his statues in the Temple: if the Jews refused them, he was to execute the objectors and enslave all the rest of the population . . .[2]

Josephus goes on to describe how quickly Caligula's general, Petronius, got his army to Palestine, and how the terrified Jews reacted. Petronius left his army and the statues at a place called Ptolemais and went on ahead to Jerusalem, to be greeted by a large crowd. His reaction was surprisingly humane:

> The Jews with their wives and children massed on the plain near the city, and appealed to Petronius first for their ancestral laws and then for themselves. He yielded to the demands of such a formidable crowd, and left the army and the statues in Ptolemai.[3]

In the subsequent negotiations Petronius was so impressed by the courage and devotion of ordinary Jews that he decided at great personal risk to send a recommendation to the emperor that the idea of putting the statues in the temple should be dropped. This is just what happened, chiefly because Caligula was assassinated before the threat could be carried any further.

This threatened desecration of the Holy of Holies was never any more than a threat. But in another account of another

2 Josephus, Flavius, *The Jewish War*; tr. G.A.Williamson, 1959; Penguin Classics edition, London, New York &c, 1981, p. 139.
3 ibid.p.140.

occasion Josephus describes a real desecration of the sanctuary. This was perpetrated fairly early in what Josephus calls the "The Jewish War", the war that ravaged Jerusalem between the years 67CE and 70CE .

In the year 67 CE the Roman emperor Nero sent a general called Vespasian to Palestine to try to settle a revolt that was threatening to spread. Vespasian arrived in Galilee in June and gradually pacified all the towns in the area. He had trouble with one town called Gischala, and he dealt with it last. Here the leader was a man called John. It is hard to evaluate John of Gischala because he and Josephus thoroughly hated each other, so John always gets a bad press, the surviving record being written by Josephus.

John led the resistance in Gischala until the last moment when he ran out and escaped to Jerusalem with the best of his soldiers. There he joined wholeheartedly with the in-fighting between several Jewish factions who were fighting each other harder than they were fighting the Romans. One of the main factions was known as the Zealots, a group much despised by Josephus, perhaps because John of Gischala became their leader. Josephus refers to the Zealots as "terrorists", and he is outraged by their every action, particularly when they gained control of the temple and its sanctuary, the Holy of Holies.

In order to make full use of the temple the Zealots needed priests, but few if any of the temple priests were on their side. The Zealot solution to the problem was to appoint their own priests, and in spite of their best efforts to give this sacrilege an appearance of legality, their action outraged many Jews. As Josephus puts it:

> . . . they transferred their insolence to the Deity and entered the Sanctuary with their polluted feet . . . and the Sanctuary became the centre for their illegal operations. Through their atrocities ran a vein of ironic pretence more exasperating than the actions themselves. For to test the submissiveness of the people and prove their own strength, they attempted to appoint the

> high priests by lot, though . . . the succession was by birth . . . the office fell to one Phanias, son of Samuel, of the village of Aphtha, a man not only not descended from high priests, but too boorish to have any notion of what the high priesthood might be. Anyway they dragged him willy-nilly from his holding and disguised him from head to foot like an actor on the stage, robing him in some sacred vestments and teaching him his cues. To the perpetrators this shocking sacrilege was the occasion for ribald mirth, but the other priests, watching from a distance this mockery of their law, burst into tears, cut to the heart by this travesty of the sacred rites.[4]

Such mockery and sacrilege had known a long history. Two hundred years before the time of Josephus, the Jews in Jerusalem were subject to the Greek emperor known as Antiochus Epiphanes. He was a successor to the Greek conqueror Alexander the Great. Alexander had died very young and left his new empire to be divided up by his generals. The one who gained control of Palestine and Syria founded a dynasty that continued for several generations. When Antiochus came to power he decided it was time to turn the Jews into proper Greek subjects by forcing Greek culture on them and destroying their own. He went so far as to instal an altar to the Greek god Zeus on top of the Jewish altar in the Holy of Holies, then he started enforcing Greek religious rites throughout Palestine. This provoked a revolt.

A priest called Mattathias was so upset by the "desolating sacrilege" which had been erected in the Holy of Holies that he left Jerusalem and settled in a village called Modein. But the desolating sacrilege followed him there, and a sacrifice to Zeus was arranged to take place in Modein. All the leading Jews were forced to appear including Mattathias and his grown sons. The king's officers were determined to make an example of

4 ibid. p.245.

Mattathias, so he and his sons were told to be the first to sacrifice at the new altar. This was too much. The old man refused with a rousing speech about remaining true to the covenant of his ancestors.

The officers of Antiochus pushed Mattathias and his sons aside and they had to watch while another Jew volunteered to do the sacrifice. When Mattathias had watched this for a while he could bear it no longer. He suddenly attacked and killed the apostate Jew. Then he killed the chief officer and pulled down the altar, and with his sons and anyone else who would follow he retreated into the hills. This started one of the best known campaigns of guerrilla warfare in history. Josephus mentions it briefly, but the best account is in the book called First Maccabees. This is one of the collection of books called Apocrypha which is included in some modern Bibles.[5]

There are still more stories of desolating sacrilege to come, taking us even further back in Jewish history. Three centuries before the traumatic events set in motion by Antiochus Epiphanes there were repeated desolations of Jerusalem and its temple. It all started with the death of the revered king Josiah who during a long reign had restored some of the glory to Jerusalem's original temple, the temple built by King Solomon. In 609 BCE Josiah was killed in a battle with Necho, king of Egypt. Necho took control of Jerusalem, but this did not last very long. He was ousted by the upstart Nebuchadnezzar, who became king of Babylon. Nebuchadnezzar expected Jerusalem to acknowledge him, and when the city failed to do so he sent a small army to force the city to submit. The city eventually capitulated and Nebuchadnezzar removed much of the treasure of the temple. He returned to Babylon with this treasure and a number of Jewish hostages, having installed his own puppet king in Jerusalem. The year was 598 BCE.

This sorted out the troublesome state of Judaea for a while but after ten years the puppet king rebelled, and joined forces with the Egyptians in a revolt against Nebuchadnezzar. This

5 for the full story see 1M.2.15-28.

was disastrous. Nebuchadnezzar's wrath was aroused, the revolt was put down and Jerusalem was devastated. With a large army Nebuchadnezzar besieged the place, took it, and desecrated the temple by looting and destroying it along with most of the city. This time when he returned to his own country he took many more hostages. An unknown number of Jews, the elite of Jerusalem, were taken into this well-known captivity in Babylon. This was a desolating sacrilege indeed. All of these powerful stories of destruction and loss are recalled in the term "desolating sacrilege" that Mark attributes to Jesus while he is talking to his friends on the Mount of Olives.

After the reference to "desolating sacrilege", the speech of Jesus in Mark Chapter 13 carries on. First there is a warning of an emergency evacuation that can be taken as a description of the conditions under which some members of the Christian community had to leave Jerusalem about 67-68 CE, when they became refugees. Then comes a section about impending natural disasters that will lead up to the sudden appearance or reappearance of the "Son of Man", an ancient Jewish designation that comes out of the Hebrew Scriptures.[6] The use of this title here expresses the expectation that Jesus will come again to save the world. The final two sections of the speech develop and strengthen this expectation of a "second coming" with warnings about the Son of Man coming suddenly and the need to be ready when he arrives.

Mark's chief interest here is to deal with the immediate expectations and concerns of his own church members. He was writing some thirty-five years after the crucifixion, and his church was still buoyed up by the hopes Jesus had aroused. But at the same time these early Christians were having to cope with the immediate and pressing problems of their everyday lives. They were increasingly alienated from the Jewish synagogues that had originally tolerated them but were now proving hostile. This was wreaking havoc with their social and religious life, putting them sometimes bitterly at odds with the Jews around

6 see below pp.152-154 for more on the Son of Man.

them. Yet in common with these Jews, Christians were suffering as a result of the terrible war that was destroying Jerusalem and its temple, and sharing in the full horror of that war.

When Mark portrays Jesus talking to his friends about a desolating sacrilege the reference is fraught with all that is most terrible in the collective memory of the Jews. He couches the speech in language that conjures up all the violence done against the Jews through the centuries. This was violence and suffering on a grand scale, and the new Christian sect not only saw this being repeated, but saw themselves as the sufferers and the victims of the violence. They clung to their great hope that all this would soon end and they would be vindicated. Knowing these expectations, Mark gives to Jesus highly charged language, full of allusions to the expected end of the world, the "end times" and the "second coming".

This language is directly related to the apocalyptic language that had been slowly developing out of the Hebrew Scriptures to express expectations about the end of the world. For early Christians this apocalyptic language voiced their most fervent hopes, and more. For them the whole process of the end times, the whole process of "apocalypse" was happening then and there. It could be perceived in their sufferings, and in the sufferings of all oppressed Jews. Although the times were terrible, this was what they had been waiting for. They believed the Messiah had come once, in the person of Jesus, and that he was about to come again. Everything they were undergoing was a positive sign of the times.

Exactly the same belief is still held by many Christians today. The end is believed to be nigh, and the signs are perceived all around. Every war, every natural disaster, every man-made disaster is examined as a terrible and a wonderful sign of the end times. Although the wait has been longer than expected, the apocalypse is still believed to be here and now. This belief may seem extreme and foreign to many of us, but it has been sustained for nearly 2000 years.

The story of Jesus sitting with his close friends looking at the view of the temple is pivotal in Mark's gospel. It provides an important vantage point. Mark was writing for an audience that expected the end of the world to come very soon. They expected at any time to be saved from their sufferings and proven right in their beliefs. This brief scene on the Mount of Olives and Jesus's speech would have been welcomed by early Christians who believed passionately that the end was in sight. Stories supporting such a belief would have fuelled dearly held expectations. Mark and the other writers who tell of the life and death of Jesus knew this well. They did not disappoint their audiences.

CHAPTER TWO

Letterwriter

Five men are credited with writing the New Testament accounts of the death of Jesus and its aftermath. Four of these are widely known as the gospel writers, Mark and Matthew, Luke and John. The other is the letterwriter, Paul. In the four books named after the gospel writers all of the stories appear about the final days, the arrest, the trial, the execution and the resurrection of Jesus. Some of these are very long and detailed, some are terse and abrupt, some are told merely as asides. In Paul's letters none of these stories appear, but Paul does allude to the circumstances of Jesus's death and he refers repeatedly to the resurrection.

Whatever we may choose to think or believe about the Christian religion that is rooted in the writings of these five men, one thing is abundantly clear. For better or worse, the gospels of Mark, Matthew, Luke and John and the letters of Paul are amongst the most influential documents in the world. And what they have to say about the events surrounding the death of Jesus is arguably the most influential material within these influential documents. It lies at the very heart of the Christian religion.

So who were these five men who wrote this material? What do we know about them? These simple questions have simple answers; "We are not sure", and "Not very much." Each of these men has been canonized by the Christian church. Their images have been painted and carved; they have been represented on stage, in movies, in novels. For centuries their supposed identities and activities have caused speculation and argument amongst scholars, but despite all this we do not really know much about them. Most of what we do know is deduced from their own writings. To learn about the writers, to learn when their accounts were written and where, we have to look very closely at what they wrote.

Mark and Matthew, Luke and John all tell specific and detailed stories about Jesus in their four gospels. By contrast, Paul says very little about the life, the teachings, or the death of Jesus. He is a preacher and a missionary, a man committed to travelling all over the known world to spread the word about Christianity. He is a letterwriter, not a storyteller. His letters, the opinionated and didactic "epistles of Paul", are addressed to the new Christian congregations springing up all over the territory in which he travelled in the middle of the first century.

The gospel writers and Paul clearly feel no need to provide meticulous historical data. Their concerns are not those of modern biographers or archivists. Their purpose is to pass on a religious message about Jesus rather than to provide historically accurate documents detailing his life and death. This is why their writings do not clearly tell "what really happened". The modern desire for historical accuracy was not their chief concern or motivation, and modern methods of recording history were unknown. Their writings contain no explanatory footnotes, no lists of sources, and certainly they make no pretense at providing reliable dates.

The sweated labour of many scholars over many centuries has attempted to fill in some of the gaps, concluding for one thing that Jesus must have died in the spring sometime between the years 30 and 32 CE. But the question of when the New Testament writers were writing their accounts is more difficult. No original manuscript copies of their works exist to be submitted to carbon dating techniques, and centuries of learned and obscure debate amongst scholars has failed to come up with conclusive dates. But all the same, there is a reasonably general consensus of opinion about the order in which these books were written.

Paul was the earliest writer. His letters were probably written between the years 50 – 63 CE. Next came Mark, the first gospel writer, about the year 70, followed by Matthew somewhere around 75–80, and then Luke, five to ten years later. Last of all was John, writing around 95 – 100 CE.[1]

In the last half of the first century, these five writers appear to have been scattered all over the face of the map, working with new Christian groups in places as far apart as Ephesus, Corinth, and Rome. The precise location of their communities causes even more debate than the question of dates, particularly with Mark and Matthew and Luke. Probably the single most important point emerging from all such debate is that these writers were far apart from each other, writing at different times for different groups of people with different needs.

Of all five writers, Paul is the only one who stands out as a distinct individual. He is the only traceable historical figure, he is the earliest contributor to the writings of the New Testament, and he is certainly the most prolific writer of them all. His letters, and letters attributed to him, make up roughly a quarter of the volume of the New Testament.

Throughout these letters, Paul's voice comes across as an extraordinary combination of crusty intellectual, pulpit-pounding preacher, and dogmatic churchman. As we shall see in later chapters, when it comes to the death and resurrection of Jesus, Paul has very little to say compared to the gospel writers, and no detailed stories to tell. When he wrote his letters Paul either did not know these stories or he did not consider it necessary to tell them. Yet in any discussion of the stories of Jesus's death and resurrection, Paul cannot be overlooked. In one of his letters to the Christians at Corinth he provides the earliest known account of Jesus appearing after his death before a large number of witnesses. There and else-

1 Theories vary about the dates of the gospels. In *Beyond Bethlehem*, we set the date of Mark at 64 CE. Recent research has convinced us that the date should be several years later.
For more see Mack, Burton L., *A Myth of Innocence, Fortress Press, Philadelphia 1988*; pp.315f. Also see below p.32.

where he assumes that his readers know about the death and resurrection of Jesus. [2]

This makes Paul a very important mid-century source of information. He was writing approximately a generation after the death of Jesus, and almost a generation before the first gospel writer, Mark. Paul not only assumes knowledge of the resurrection, he expresses the expectations that were being built around the resurrection. The expectations of first century Christians were highly developed and complex, and Paul makes this very clear. For him the end times are in sight, and the end of the world is imminent:

> We want you to be quite certain, brothers, about those who have fallen asleep, to make sure that you do not grieve for them, as others do who have no hope. We believe that Jesus died and rose again, and that in the same way God will bring with him those who have fallen asleep in Jesus.
>
> We can tell you this from the Lord's own teaching, that we who are still alive for the Lord's coming will not have any advantage over those who have fallen asleep. At the signal given by the voice of the Archangel and the trumpet of God, the Lord himself will come down from heaven; those who have died in Christ will be the first to rise, and only after that shall we who remain alive be taken up in the clouds, together with them, to meet the Lord in the air. This is the way we shall be with the Lord for ever.
>
> 1TH.4.13-17

This comes from one of Paul's earlier letters written to the church in Thessalonika about the year 50 CE, some twenty years

2 for examples of how Paul writes about the death of Jesus see 1CO.15.1-11; RM.6.1-11; & GA.1.1-4. cp. PH.2.7-8 which Paul quotes from an earlier source, and COL.2.11-12 which may not be by Paul. Also see below p.170, footnote #6.

before Mark tells his story of Jesus speaking of the end times on the Mount of Olives. Early Christians believed that Jesus would return soon, very soon, and in glory, to reward the virtuous and to establish a new order, both in heaven and on earth. In his later letters, Paul tends to drop the subject, but thirty years after Paul's death, the gospel writers were still finding occasion to assert this belief in an imminent end.

Paul travelled extensively, from Jerusalem to Rome, by land and by water to the point that his travels are a study in themselves. These travels are reflected in his letters, and they are also vividly described in the book called the Acts of the Apostles. This was written by Luke, the same Luke of the gospel. The book of Acts, probably written some twenty years after Paul's death, is a collection of colourful stories about the beginnings of Christianity. It tells of the activities of early Christian teachers as they worked and travelled, spreading the Christian message. Although it provides valuable insights into the patterns and preoccupations and personalities of early Christianity, it is not a strictly reliable source of information about Paul.[3]

It is in the book of Acts we hear the story of Paul, then called Saul, when he came to Jerusalem shortly after Jesus had been crucified.[4] Saul had been born in a city called Tarsus, near the present day border of Turkey and Lebanon, and he was a proud member of the strict Jewish sect called the Pharisees. As he writes of himself:

> Circumcised on the eighth day of my life, I was born of the race of Israel, of the tribe of Benjamin, a Hebrew born of Hebrew parents. In the matter of the Law, I was a Pharisee; as for religious fervour, I

3 for further discussion of the historical reliability of Acts see: Bruce, F.F., *The Acts of the Apostles: Greek Text with Introduction and Commentary, William B. Eerdmans Publishing Company, Grand Rapids, Michigan (Apollos, Leicester, England) first published 1951*, third edition 1990, see Introduction, section IV a., "Luke as a Historian" pps.21-24.

4 but see Ga.1.22 where Paul himself contradicts this.

> was a persecutor of the Church; as for the uprightness embodied in the Law, I was faultless.
>
> PH.3.5-6 [5]

Not long before the time of Paul's first appearance in Jerusalem the priests who operated the temple in Jerusalem had decided it was time to get rid of the Christians who were starting to appear in the temple courtyards in some numbers. The temple was really very big business. It was the focal point for massive Jewish celebrations every Passover, when tens of thousands of pilgrims would crowd into the city, at least doubling the population. The temple priests were important figures, holding both religious and secular power. According to a story told in the book of Acts, when the new sect of Christians started to become troublesome it was the priests who decided to take action to suppress them.

Young Saul of Tarsus was one of the Pharisees who joined with the priests to harass the Christians, and in the book of Acts we are told that he held the coats of other Jews while they stoned a Christian to death outside Jerusalem. The name of the man being stoned was Stephen, and he is presented as the sacrificial hero of the scene. Saul the Pharisee is treated like the priests and the rest of the Jews. With great resentment they listen to Stephen preaching, and he accuses them of betraying and murdering one he calls the "Upright One."[6]

> They were infuriated when they heard this, and ground their teeth at him. But Stephen, filled with the Holy Spirit, gazed into heaven and saw the glory of God, and Jesus standing at God's right hand. 'Look! I can see heaven thrown open,' he said, 'and the Son of man standing at the right hand of God.'

5 see also AC.26.4-8.

6 "Upright One" is the NJB translation. In other translations, this appears as the "Righteous One" (NIV, NRSV, NEB), or "righteous Servant" (Good News Bible), or "Just One" (AV).

> All the members of the council shouted out and stopped their ears with their hands; then they made a concerted rush at him, thrust him out of the city and stoned him. The witnesses put down their clothes at the feet of a young man called Saul . . . Saul approved of the killing.
>
> AC.7.54-8.1

This stoning seems to have had the effect of scattering many of the Christians who were in Jerusalem. Luke's story in the book of Acts goes on to tell how Saul hears that some Christians have gone to Damascus where they are showing up in the synagogues. It would be natural for them to show up in the synagogues because they regarded themselves as good Jews. We refer to them as Christians, but at this point the term was not used.[7] According to Luke, Saul decides to take action against the Christians in Damascus. This proves to be his undoing:

> Meanwhile Saul was still breathing threats to slaughter the Lord's disciples. He went to the high priest and asked for letters addressed to the synagogues in Damascus, that would authorise him to arrest and take to Jerusalem any followers of the Way, men or women, that he might find.
>
> It happened that while he was travelling to Damascus and approaching the city, suddenly a light from heaven shone all round him. He fell to the ground, and then he heard a voice saying, 'Saul, Saul, why are you persecuting me?' 'Who are you, Lord?' he asked, and the answer came, 'I am Jesus, whom you are persecuting. Get up and go into the city, and you will be told what you are to do.' The men travelling with Saul stood there speechless, for though they heard the voice they could see no one.

7 for the earliest use of the term "Christian" see AC.11.26.

> Saul got up from the ground, but when he opened his eyes he could see nothing at all, and they had to lead him into Damascus by the hand.
>
> AC.9.1-8

The book of Acts then goes on to relate many stories of Paul's travels around the Mediterranean world of his day. Paul is such an important figure in any understanding of the early years of Christianity that it is helpful to try to know what kind of person he was. Two stories about him are particularly telling.

The first shows Paul as the great Christian preacher. It appears in Acts Chapter 20 where we are told of Paul going to a place called Troas which was a port and a considerable Roman administrative centre. Paul is well known here because of a former visit. He stays a week and the night before he is due to leave is a Saturday night, although it is called Sunday in Acts because the Jewish calendar changed days at sundown rather than at midnight. The local Christians gather for a meal to commemorate the last supper of Jesus and his disciples. The meeting room is upstairs and well lit, and the windows or shutters are open.

At this gathering, Paul is the speaker and he goes on and on, "and continued his speech until midnight", as the King James Bible says. This proves too much for one young man called Eutychus who is sitting in a window embrasure. He falls into a deep sleep and sleeps so soundly that he falls out of the third storey window, and "was taken up dead". Not much is said about the ensuing confusion except that Paul goes down to Eutychus and embraces him and tells the people he is alive and well. He then returns to the meeting room, continues with the breaking of bread, and carries on with his interrupted speech until daybreak. In this story Paul is a notable preacher, not easily distracted.

A second vivid story about Paul is told in Acts Chapter 16. This time Paul is in Greece in the Macedonian town of Philippi. This town was a Roman colony, made up largely of veterans from the army. There was no Jewish synagogue so Paul and his companions join some women who meet for prayer on the banks of a nearby river. One of the women called Lydia is converted and they baptise her in the river. This woman is a dye merchant who deals in the expensive purple dye derived from a local shellfish. She invites Paul and his party to stay with her, which they do.

When they return to the river bank they are followed by a clairvoyant girl who bothers them by calling after them. This goes on for days and Paul becomes annoyed. He turns on the girl and says in the manner of an exorcist to her clairvoyant spirit, "I order you in the name of Jesus Christ to leave that woman."

The exorcism works so well that the girl completely loses her clairvoyant powers. This spells trouble. She is a slave and her owners have been making a lot of money from her clairvoyant earnings. They seize Paul, together with Silas one of his companions, and take them to the magistrates who have them publicly beaten and put them in prison for the night. They are put in an inner cell and their feet are chained.

During the night there is an earthquake severe enough to wreck the gaol. This wakes the gaoler who is so sure he has lost all his prisoners that he wants to kill himself. Somehow in the confusion Paul sees this and shouts that they are all there and so there is no need for suicide. The gaoler calls for lights and finds Paul and Silas. According to the story he is so grateful that he converts to Christianity on the spot. He treats their wounds, takes them into his house and is baptised.

In the morning the magistrates send an order to the gaoler to release Paul and Silas:

> 'What!' Paul replied. 'Without trial they gave us a public flogging, though we are Roman citizens, and threw us into prison, and now they want to send us away on the quiet! Oh no! They must come and escort us out themselves.'
>
> AC.16.37

This frightens the magistrates. Paul was indeed a Roman citizen and the maltreatment of a Roman citizen carried severe penalties. So the closing scene of the story has the magistrates coming to the wrecked gaol and begging Paul to come out. They also ask that he leave the city, presumably for his own safety. Paul and Silas consent to leave after they have gone back to the house of Lydia and spoken to all the Christians there. In this story, Paul's confidence in himself, his civil rights, and his religious beliefs is not easily shaken.

Even more revealing and probably far more reliable than these stories from the book of Acts, are Paul's own letters. Written to Christian communities as far apart as Colossae, Rome and Corinth these "epistles of Paul" are more like sermons than letters. Paul speaks as the self-styled apostle, passionately committed to his mission. He is the earliest known arbiter of Christian practice and behavior; a man possessed of high ideals but little patience. His letters reflect all of this. They are authoritarian and judgmental; they contain everything from testy dictates concerning the behavior of women to abstruse theological argument. But although Paul can be provoking and difficult to follow, he does provide a clear indication of the influence and spread of the early Christian churches. The communities he was writing to had heard about Jesus, and were struggling to understand the significance of his life and teachings. Time and again, Paul tries to answer questions, quell doubts, and solve problems for early Christians.

> . . . Wake up from your stupor as you should and leave sin alone; some of you have no understanding of God; I tell you this to instil some shame in you.
>
> Someone may ask: How are dead people raised, and what sort of body do they have when they come? How foolish! . . .
>
> . . . Now I am going to tell you a mystery: we are not all going to fall asleep, but we are all going to be changed, instantly, in the twinkling of an eye, when

> the last trumpet sounds. The trumpet is going to sound, and then the dead will be raised imperishable, and we shall be changed, because this perishable nature of ours must put on imperishability, this mortal nature must put on immortality.
>
> 1CO.15.34-36, 51-53 [8]

Repeatedly in his letters Paul attempts to clarify Christian beliefs for the early churches he has helped establish. This is far from easy. In everything that he does and says, Paul is breaking new ground. He has assigned to himself a hard job, organising new groups of Christians, and expounding Christian ideas for them. His writings show a theology in the making. The members of the new churches are trying to assimilate and put into practise what they know and believe about Jesus. Not surprisingly, problems arise for them, and equally unsurprisingly, Paul has no simple answers for them. His advice and his explanations are frequently expressed in complex ways and couched in complex language.

But when Paul breaks out of his web of difficult explanations he can express his religious ideas in clear and beautiful language that is unmatched anywhere else in the New Testament. The most famous of these passages is his praise of love, or charity as it is called in the King James Bible:

> Though I speak with the tongues of men and of angels, and have not charity, I am become as sounding brass, or a tinkling cymbal . . .
>
> . . . Charity suffereth long, and is kind; charity envieth not; charity vaunteth not itself, is not puffed up,
>
> Doth not behave itself unseemly, seeketh not her own, is not easily provoked, thinketh no evil;
>
> Rejoiceth not in iniquity, but rejoiceth in the truth;

8 for more on 1CO.15 see below, pp.227-228, 267-268.

Beareth all things, believeth all things, hopeth all things, endureth all things.

Charity never faileth . . .

1CO.13.1-8 (AV)

The man who can express religious principles in such a way can be expected to have devoted followers. But over the centuries Paul's followers have placed enormous weight on all his writings, regardless of their clarity or practicality. His advice to new churches is still doggedly followed by churches that are far from new. His instructions about proper Christian behaviour, complete with his limited view of the role of women, still have the power to cause turmoil, even if they make no sense in a modern context. His complicated explanations of Christian belief, including his comments on the resurrection of Jesus, are held to be above argument and question, even though their meaning can be very unclear.

Important as they are, no part of the writings of Paul can be considered above argument or question. This is true of any form of writing. It is certainly true when we turn to look at the stories told in the four gospels.

CHAPTER THREE

Storytellers

All of the stories about the life and death of Jesus in the gospels of the New Testament are recorded in the names of Mark and Matthew and Luke and John. Unlike Paul, almost nothing is known of these four men as individuals. It is uncertain even if they existed as historical figures. Behind each writing of Mark, Matthew, Luke and John there was certainly an early church, and probably some kind of literary collective at work. The gospels should be read as collaborative efforts, rather than as the work of one person writing all alone. It is only for the sake of clarity that these writers are usually referred to in the singular.

The internal evidence of their own writings provides the only real source of information about these writers, or sets of writers. From this, the circumstances and preoccupations of the writers emerge, an approximation of the dates and places of the writing can be reached, and a picture takes shape, albeit imperfect and partial, of these men and their worlds. There are a few scraps of information about the gospel writers available from outside sources, but such information is generally both scant and unreliable.

These four gospel writers or sets of writers speak with distinct voices. They certainly do not tell one "Bible story" about the death of Jesus and its aftermath; they tell four separate sets of stories. These are sometimes startlingly different sets of stories, each told in a characteristic style. Mark is abrupt,

Matthew can be extremely didactic, Luke is usually kind and gentle, John speaks as a visionary and a prophet.

Lines of relationship can be drawn amongst these writers. There are particularly strong links between Luke and Matthew and Mark. These three are known as "synoptic" gospels. Broadly speaking, they tell expanded or contracted versions of the same stories, although sometimes in different settings or with different characters. Matthew and Luke almost certainly knew the gospel of Mark and were drawing on it as they wrote. Amongst the gospel writers John is the odd man out, his gospel is structured very differently from the others. To some degree he must have used the writings of Luke and Matthew and Mark, but the links are not straightforward.

The Writings of Mark

The earliest detailed stories about the life and death of Jesus are told in Mark's gospel. Increasingly, this gospel has come to be accepted as the "control" text for the other gospels, for it is the earliest and arguably the most authoritative source of information about the life and death of Jesus. Yet Mark cannot be considered a reliable "biographer" of Jesus in the modern sense of the word. He was writing his stories over thirty years after the death of Jesus. Some scholars argue that he was working from an authoritative oral tradition of stories about Jesus. Some argue for the existence of a lost source or sources of written information. Some dismiss such theories entirely and suggest that Mark simply made up most or even all of the stories he tells about Jesus. Mark himself does not reveal his sources.

What Mark does reveal very tellingly in his gospel is the extent and nature of the political and religious tensions in first century Palestine. He reiterates constantly that Jesus's teachings give rise to political and religious debate, either amongst the disciples, or between Jesus and the religious authorities of synagogue and temple. The tensions Mark describes reflect those surrounding him at the time he was writing. In other words, he tells us as much if not more about the problems of his own era in the later part of the first century as he does about the earlier part of the century when Jesus was alive.

Little is known or even conjectured about Mark himself. Perhaps this is not surprising. Compared to the other gospels, Mark's stories are austere and brief and his gospel is short, with the result that there are few apocryphal tales about who Mark might have been. One, and perhaps the only engaging theory on the subject, is that Mark might have been the young man who lost his clothes.

Mark reports that there were a number of people present at the arrest of Jesus at the place called Gethsemane. The disciples of Jesus were there and also a squad of soldiers sent by the chief priests to carry out the arrest. It is clear that Mark also envisages at least a few other followers of Jesus in this crowd, among them Judas who betrayed Jesus. After Jesus is arrested, Mark describes how all Jesus's friends run away, but then he adds these two sentences:

> A young man followed with nothing on but a linen cloth. They caught hold of him, but he left the cloth in their hands and ran away naked.
>
> MK.14.51-52

These sentences are not repeated by any other writer anywhere in the New Testament. Over the centuries there has been some speculation that the young man might have been Mark, the writer of the gospel himself, although few scholars take this seriously today. [1]

The name Mark appears quite often in the New Testament and in other early Christian literature. There is John Mark, the son of a woman called Mary who, according to the book of Acts, lived in Jerusalem not long after the death of Jesus. This Mark together with another man called Barnabas did some travelling with Paul, who left them in Cyprus because they would not go any further. In some of his letters Paul speaks of a Mark who

1 for more naked young men see GN.39.12 and possibly AM.2.16.

was a cousin of Barnabas and could well be the same man. Paul, as portrayed in Acts, speaks well of this Mark, as if he could and did count on him for a great deal of help in his work for the church.[2]

The name makes another appearance near the end of the first letter of Peter where Mark is called "son."[3] This is not necessarily the same Mark, but this mention gives some slight credence to another theory about the writer of Mark's gospel being an associate of Peter, the disciple of Jesus.

The earliest mention of Mark outside the New Testament does not appear until the fourth century CE. Typically of anything to do with Mark, this reference is brief and unelaborate. It is found in the writings of an early Christian bishop called Eusebius, who quotes another even earlier Christian bishop called Papias who quotes a yet earlier source called John the Presbyter who refers very vaguely to someone called Mark:

> In his own book Papias gives us accounts of the Lord's sayings obtained from . . . the presbyter John . . . I must now follow up . . . with a piece of information which he sets out regarding Mark, the writer of the gospel: "This, too, the presbyter used to say. 'Mark, who had been Peter's interpreter, wrote down carefully, but not in order, all that he remembered of the Lord's sayings and doings. For he had not heard the Lord or been one of his followers, but later, as I said, one of Peter's. Peter used to adapt his teachings to the occasion, without making a systematic arrangement of the Lord's sayings, so that Mark was quite justified in writing down some things just as he remembered them. For he had one purpose only—to leave out nothing that he had heard, and to make no misstatement about it.'" Such is Papias' account of Mark.[4]

2 see AC.12.12; AC.12.25 and AC.15.39.

3 see 1P.5.13.

4 *Eusebius: The History of the Church from Christ to Constantine*, trans. G.A Williamson, revised and edited by Andrew Louth, Penguin Classics edition 1989, pp.103f.

From this slender reference, critics ancient and modern have built up the hopeful notion that Mark was a sort of secretary to Peter around the year sixty CE when Peter was preaching in Rome. Peter is thought to have been crucified in the year 64 CE, and Mark's gospel could have been assembled around that time. But this theory linking Mark to Peter in Rome gives rise to a problem. It seems to contradict what the gospel itself indicates.

Judging from how he writes of the temple in Jerusalem, it seems more likely that Mark's gospel was assembled somewhere near or just inside the borders of Galilee around the year 70 CE. This would place him on the edge of a storm of political activity.

70 CE is a pivotal date in ancient history. It was the year of the end of the cataclysmic war between the occupying Roman forces and the rebel Jewish forces in Judaea and Galilee. This war ended in the complete destruction of Jerusalem and its temple.

By any standard the political scene of this period was appalling. For Jewish people it was particularly bitter, because their promised land was under siege. This was the land of Israel, the land believed to be that promised to the Hebrew people centuries ago in the time of Abraham. This was Israel, that had been such a proud and powerful nation. By the middle of the first century CE Israel was nothing of the kind. For over a century it had been under the power of Rome. The whole region, more broadly known as Palestine, had been splintered into different provinces and territories that fell under the shifting jurisdictions of various Roman governors and their puppet rulers. Judaea, including Jerusalem, was in the southern part of this region; Galilee was in the north. At the time Mark was writing, these adjacent territories were in different jurisdictions.

For generations, futile rebellion had followed futile rebellion. This culminated in the crushing defeat of the Jewish rebels in 70 CE, and the total destruction of the temple in Jerusalem. This was a brutal and deliberate act on the part of the Romans. To this day, the temple has still not been rebuilt.

It is not definitely known if Mark was Jewish or if he was from the non-Jewish population that had been long established in Galilee, but it is clear in his representation of Jesus, who lived and died many years earlier, that Mark is strongly influenced by the events going on around him at the time he was writing:

> As he was leaving the Temple one of his disciples said to him, 'Master, look at the size of those stones! Look at the size of those buildings!' And Jesus said to him, 'You see these great buildings? Not a single stone will be left on another; everything will be pulled down.'
>
> MK.13.1-2

Mark's gospel emphasises that Jesus is seen as a threat to the temple, both to the jurisdiction of its priests and to the buildings themselves. This is apparent in Mark's story of Jesus on trial before the Sanhedrin when false witnesses accuse him of threatening to destroy the temple:

> . . . Several, indeed, brought false witness against him, but their evidence was conflicting. Some stood up and submitted this false evidence against him, 'We heard him say, "I am going to destroy this Temple made by human hands, and in three days build another, not made by human hands."'
>
> MK.14.56-58

In or around 70 CE comments like these would be of consuming interest to a community near Jerusalem made up of people belonging to the new Christian church. From the very beginning, this Christian sect of Judaism had been preoccupied with the awkward process of defining itself as something distinct from other strains of Judaism. This was part of a process that saw Christian groups gradually pulling away from increasingly hostile synagogues. Exactly how this occurred and over what period remains unclear, but this process of redefinition meant that Christians slowly achieved, or were forced to achieve, autonomy and independence. Mark's gospel reflects this process. When he portrays Jesus as a threat to the temple a very serious point is being made. This temple, the nerve centre of Judaism, was being destroyed as Mark wrote, and Christians had to come to some understanding of what this meant to them. As a sect rooted in Judaism they were deeply affected, but as the new Christian church they could understand the destruction as the necessary death of an old order. Their Christian perspective therefore liberated them from adherence to the temple traditions. In the eyes of temple adherents, this was outrageous. All of this is reflected in how Mark writes.

The Writings of Matthew

If little information has come down to us about Mark less still has reached us about Matthew. His name is mentioned in his own gospel and also in Mark and Luke and in the book of Acts. But there is a muddle of names. Here is how Jesus meets a man called Matthew in the gospel that carries his name:

> As Jesus was walking on from there he saw a man named Matthew sitting at the tax office, and he said to him, 'Follow me.' And he got up and followed him.
>
> Now while he was at table in the house it happened that a number of tax collectors and sinners came to sit at the table with Jesus and his disciples. When the Pharisees saw this, they said to his disciples, 'Why does your master eat with tax collectors and sinners?' When he heard this he replied, 'It is not the healthy who need the doctor, but the sick. Go and learn the meaning of the words: *Mercy is what pleases me, not sacrifice.* And indeed I came to call not the upright, but sinners.'
>
> MT.9.9-13

Mark tells this story differently:

> As he was walking along he saw Levi the son of Alphaeus sitting at the tax office, and he said to him, 'Follow me.' And he got up and followed him.
>
> When Jesus was at dinner in his house, a number of tax collectors and sinners were also sitting at table with Jesus and his disciples; for there were many of them among his followers. When the scribes of the Pharisee party saw him eating with sinners and tax collectors, they said to his disciples, 'Why does he eat with tax collectors and sinners?' When Jesus heard this he said to them,'It is not the healthy who need the doctor, but the sick. I came to call not the upright, but sinners.'
>
> MK.2.14-17

These passages establish the identity of the publican, or tax collector who is called both Matthew and Levi. They do nothing to establish that this Matthew alias Levi was Matthew the writer of the gospel. Two or three generations after the writing of the gospels a tradition became established asserting that Matthew was indeed this tax collector, but as in the case of the naked young man being Mark, there is no supporting evidence.[5] These are just colourful and not particularly helpful theories.

No one knows where Matthew wrote his gospel, but he appears to be writing from a place influenced by the teachings of the Jewish school which had been established in the town of Jamnia near Jerusalem, shortly after the terrible war that had destroyed the temple. In comparison with Mark, Matthew's writings show a far more distinct split between Christians and the synagogue authorities. This split certainly had become more and more bitter in the years following the destruction of the temple. In the mid-eighties CE, shortly after Matthew was writing his gospel, the increasing tension between Christians

5 for more on the identification of Matthew see NJB p. 1599.

and the Jewish authorities is evident in a fierce denunciation that was issued against Christians. Called the "Birkhath-ha-Minim," this was a Jewish prayer that was rewritten to become a curse against all Christians and "minim", or heretics.[6]

The harassment of and hostility towards Christians probably varied from synagogue to synagogue. Matthew's writing can be understood to indicate that in his area some kind of formal split had occurred and Christians had been expelled from the synagogue and forced to set up their own meeting places. The Judaic laws and traditions are much debated, sometimes very bitterly, and Jesus and his followers are often accused of being at fault, as in the story of Jesus speaking and eating with a tax collector.

None of this determines just who wrote the gospel we call Matthew. It does, however, provide an idea of the kind of political and religious tensions which were almost certainly at work behind the writing of this gospel. For any understanding of Matthew, this can be very helpful.

The Writings of Luke

For the identity of Luke there is more evidence, although it remains thin. He is a more prolific writer than either Matthew or Mark, usually credited with having written the book of Acts as well as the gospel of Luke. He is also mentioned more than once in Paul's letters.

Luke's name appears in the letter known as "Colossians" written to the church at Colossae, a town near Hierapolis in what is now Turkey. This letter was written about the year 62 CE.

6 i for more on the place of Matthew's church see Senior, Donald, C.P.; *The Passion of Jesus in the Gospel of Matthew*; (vol.1 of *The Passion Series)* Michael Glazier, Wilmington, Delaware; 1985; 2nd. printing 1989; pp.12-13. See also Ellis, Peter F.; *Matthew: His Mind and Message*; The Liturgical Press, Collegeville, Minnesota, 1974, pp.5-6.

ii for more on the Birkhath-ha-Minim and Matthew's church, see *Beyond Bethlehem*, pp 42ff.

It closes with greetings from a list of mutual friends who are said to be with Paul in prison, possibly in Rome.

> Aristarchus, who is here in prison with me, sends his greetings, and so does Mark, the cousin of Barnabas . . . Greetings from my dear friend Luke, the doctor, and also from Demas . . .
>
> COL.4.10-14

This is the only evidence for the very strong tradition of Luke being a physician. Paul's other reference to him carries no such information. This appears in a letter to a man named Philemon:

> Epaphras, a prisoner with me in Christ Jesus, sends his greetings; so do my fellow-workers Mark, Aristarchus, Demas and Luke.
>
> PHM.23-24

The evidence about Luke within the book of Acts is more direct. It probably comes from Luke himself, describing his activities as one of a group of missionaries inspired by Paul.

> One night Paul had a vision: a Macedonian appeared and kept urging him in these words, 'Come across to Macedonia and help us.' Once he had seen this vision we lost no time in arranging a passage to Macedonia, convinced that God had called us to bring them the good news.
>
> AC.16.8-10

On other occasions in the book of Acts, Luke writes of "us" or "we", an unspecified group travelling around to tell the world about Jesus's life and teachings.[7] All of this seems to

7 for the "we" passages see: AC.16.12-17; AC.20.5-21; AC.27.1 to 28.16; and in some versions AC.11.28.

indicate that Luke, like Paul, travelled widely to spread the new Christian religion.

All this evidence about Luke is external to his gospel, but like Matthew and Mark, his gospel also provides indirect, internal evidence about himself and his circumstances. Whether or not Luke can be satisfactorily identified as an early missionary or a physician, his gospel certainly indicates that he was writing at some distance, both in time and place, from Jerusalem. One possible location for the writing of his gospel is Corinth, where the state of the church was of such concern to Paul in his letters. Writing from Corinth, or somewhere like Corinth, Luke is not so preoccupied as Mark and Matthew with the political and religious troubles of Jerusalem. His gospel is far less defensive about the hostility of the Jews. His outlook is more generous and his style more sophisticated.

From the very beginning, Luke adopts a more elevated tone than either Matthew or Mark:

> Seeing that many others have undertaken to draw up accounts of the events that have reached their fulfilment among us, as these were handed down to us by those who from the outset were eyewitnesses and ministers of the word, I in my turn, after carefully going over the whole story from the beginning, have decided to write an ordered account for you, Theophilus, so that your Excellency may learn how well founded the teaching is that you have received.
>
> LK.1.1-4

This opening classifies Luke as someone trained to write in the style of a Greek historian, confidently addressing his narrative to the unidentified "Theophilus", who was probably a distinguished Greek official, perhaps even Luke's patron. Greek was the common language of educated people of the Mediterranean world in the first century. All of the gospel writers knew Greek and wrote their gospels in Greek, but of all of them Luke writes in the most elegant and polished style. He could quite possibly have been a slave or a recently freed slave, because highly educated slaves were in demand as tutors as well as physicians.

Judging by the content of his stories Luke was a gentler man than the others. His stories are consistently more detailed, more colourful, more human than either Mark or Matthew. This becomes clear in how he tells the story of the lost sheep, for instance, or in how he describes Jesus during the vigil leading up to his arrest, or in how he reports Jesus's words from the cross.[8]

The Writings of John

John's gospel quite evidently stands apart from the others. The stories he tells about Jesus are usually far more elaborate than those of Mark or Matthew or Luke. He tells stories they do not mention, he takes some of their stories and retells them very differently. He often drifts away from stories altogether into abstract passages that seem very like sermons.

There is some outside evidence about a writer called John, but it is confused. The trouble starts with one look at the table of contents of almost any Bible. There are no fewer than four books called "John", and a fifth called "Revelation" that is sometimes called "The Revelation of St.John the Divine". This does nothing to help clarify what is known about John the writer of John's gospel.

Attempting to identify John often leads to arguments about a "Johannine style" that may or may not relate the various "John" books one to another, and may or may not indicate that one man wrote them all. There are also arguments as to whether the John of the gospel is the "beloved disciple", the best-loved follower of Jesus who is unnamed in the gospel of John. There

8 for the lost sheep see LK.15.4-7 (cp. MT.18.12-14)
for Jesus in Gethsemane see LK.22.39- 46 (see below pp.125-126).
for the words from the cross see LK.23.34-46 (see below pp. 195-196).

is support for this idea in the writings of Irenaeus, a second century leader of the Christian church.

> ...John, the disciple of the Lord, who also had leaned upon his breast, did himself publish a Gospel during his residence at Ephesus in Asia.[9]

There is no further support for this identification of John with the beloved disciple. The notion is no more conclusive than the Matthew-tax-collector, Luke-physician, and Mark-naked-young-man identifications. In the face of such unsatisfactory theories and arguments, it remains worthwhile to look at the evidence about John and his community that can be found within his gospel. There is a great deal.

John, or the body of writers responsible for his gospel, was almost certainly leading a group of Christians in a community in the eastern Mediterranean region towards the end of the first century. The exact location of his community is unknown. Suggestions include Alexandria, Antioch, and Ephesus. Of all these, Ephesus is the most favoured location, probably because of Irenaeus's early assertion that this was where John wrote the gospel. This town was a large port and trading centre in the Greek-speaking half of the Roman Empire. As the leader of a minority group of Christians who were an offshoot of a minority group of Jews in the larger population of Greeks, the writer of John's gospel provides a document that does more than tell

9 i quoted in Morris, Leon; *The Gospel According to John*, in the series *The New International Commentary on the New Testament*, William B. Eerdmans Publishing Company, Grand Rapids, Michigan, 1971, p.58. Taken from the *Ante-Nicene Fathers*, (American Reprint of the Edinburgh Edition, Grand Rapids Michigan) Vol. 1, p.414, Avd. Haer., III, 1.1

ii for more on the authorship of John see Temple, William; *Readings in John's Gospel (First and Second Series)*; MacMillan & Co; London; 1947 pp x- xi

iii for the beloved disciple see JN.13.23 & JN.20.7; in JN.21.19-24 the author of the epilogue seems to say he is the beloved disciple.

stories. It is also a subtle and complex book of teachings and spiritual guidance.

The gospel starts with a flourish in the lengthy prologue, a much quoted if little understood passage that is best known in English in the mellifluous words of the King James Bible:

> In the beginning was the Word, and the Word was with God, and the Word was God.
> The same was in the beginning with God . . .
>
> JN.1.1-2 (AV)

The language and style of John's gospel is often obscure and difficult to follow, yet there are passages where his concerns and preoccupations become very clear. This occurs particularly when he speaks of commonplace but very real fears experienced regularly by his Christian community:

> His parents spoke like this out of fear of the Jews, who had already agreed to ban from the synagogue anyone who should acknowledge Jesus as the Christ.
>
> JN.9.22

> And yet there were many who did believe in him, even among the leading men, but they did not admit it, because of the Pharisees and for fear of being banned from the synagogue: they put human glory before God's glory.
>
> JN.12.42-43

> They will expel you from the synagogues, and indeed the time is coming when anyone who kills you will think he is doing a holy service to God.
>
> JN.16.2

John's gospel is not long. That there are three such passages, none of them necessary to the story being told, indicates deeply held fears of hostile action by the synagogue. These passages seem to affirm that even at some distance from the heart of the Jewish world in Palestine, tensions between Jews, in this case Greek Jews, and the offspring Christian church were increasing rapidly. They were bad enough a generation earlier when Mark was writing in Galilee. They had spread far and become much worse by John's time. Christians were more clearly asserting their identity as a group set apart, and mainstream Jews more clearly wanted to be rid of them

In the following chapters we will see how, as decades passed during the first century, the stories told by the four gospel writers about Jesus changed and developed and grew. This is only to be expected. All stories are told in a particular way, at a particular time, and for a particular reason. All stories reflect the storytellers and the interests of the storytellers. All storytellers are human beings; fallible in judgement, selective in memory. They have prejudices and weaknesses, they have political and religious viewpoints, they are naturally affected by the forces of the society around them.

As we will see, the stories and the ideas that take shape in the gospels are rooted in a network of earlier stories and earlier ideas, and those in turn are rooted in yet earlier ones. This is a very ancient process. The writings of Mark and Matthew, Luke and John are all part of this. They reflect the process and they contribute to it.

CHAPTER FOUR

Entry

When they were approaching Jerusalem . . . many people spread their cloaks on the road, and others greenery which they had cut in the fields. And those who went in front and those who followed were all shouting, '*Hosanna! Blessed is he who is coming in the name of the Lord!* Blessed is the coming kingdom of David our father! *Hosanna* in the highest heavens!'

MK.11.1-10

The way the gospels tell their stories, this episode is the beginning of the end. When Jesus arrives in Jerusalem he seems set on the path that leads to his death. This part of the story is popular and colourful, beloved of Sunday School books, filmmakers and theatre directors alike. Clad in white, looking humble and heroic, Jesus enters Jerusalem riding a well-behaved donkey, while enthusiastic crowds fill the air with hosannas and throw down their palm fronds in front of him, declaring he is the son of David, the chosen leader from God. This is how the story is told in Christian churches on Palm Sunday, the Sunday before Easter, when lopsided little crosses made of palm leaves are distributed. This is the opening scene of the famous passion play at Oberammergau in Germany where the entry into Jerusalem provides the first big crowd scene of the seven-hour long production enacting the stories of Jesus's death and resurrection.

The popular appeal of the story of Jesus's entry into Jerusalem is easy to understand. It seems a happy account, triumphant and cheerful and not very complicated. But as with all stories of the events leading up to Jesus's death, behind this description of the entry into Jerusalem lie layer upon layer of other stories.

Mark and Matthew, Luke and John all tell of Jesus coming into Jerusalem, and they all tell of the crowd crying out "Hosanna". They all also use the phrase "Blessed is he who is coming in the name of the Lord". Almost verbatim, this phrase is a repetition of earlier triumphant cries. "Blessed in the name of Yahweh is he who is coming!" says Psalm 118, an ancient festival hymn, "We bless you from the house of Yahweh". [1]

The echoes from the past do not stop here. These positive and happy gospel accounts of the entry into Jerusalem recall many other positive and happy passages in the Hebrew Scriptures that announce the coming of a new leader for Israel and the coming of a new age. By the time of Jesus this was felt to be long overdue. Reduced to being a powerless colony of Rome, Israel had reached a state of political ignominy and shame, the victim of many centuries of oppression.

The nation had fallen from great glory. Nearly a thousand years earlier in the distant time of King David and his son Solomon, the combined kingdoms of Israel and Judah had been among the great powers of the world, honoured by all known nations, kings and potentates. By slow and painful degrees, chronicled in detail in the Hebrew Scriptures, the glory had departed out of Israel, but the hope for its return had never died:

> Arise, shine out, for your light has come,
> and the glory of Yahweh has risen on you.
> Look! though night still covers the earth
> and darkness the peoples,
> on you Yahweh is rising

1 Ps.118.26. Yahweh is one of the names in the Hebrew Scriptures for God. In Hebrew it is JHWH, the name too holy to be spoken.

and over you his glory can be seen.
The nations will come to your light
and kings to your dawning brightness.
Lift up your eyes and look around:
all are assembling and coming towards you,
your sons coming from far away
and your daughters being carried on the hip . . .

Instead of your being forsaken and hated,
avoided by everyone,
I will make you an object of eternal pride,
a source of joy from age to age.

IS.60.1-4,15

This, from the near the end of the book of Isaiah, is one of many optimistic passages in scripture whose influence can be glimpsed in the accounts of the entry into Jerusalem. This section of the book of Isaiah was written in a time of new hope for Israel, following the catastrophic sixth century BCE when the powers of Babylon had destroyed Jerusalem and taken the elite of Israel captive. In this passage new hope and confidence are ringingly declared for the shattered nation after the long years of exile in Babylon.

The effect of Isaiah and other great visionaries of the scriptures on the gospel writers is incalculable. They were more, infinitely more, than a direct and powerful influence. They were a source. Their writings and proclamations were, for the gospel writers, the great source of all prophecy and all truth; they provided indisputable, God-given information about all that affected Israel and its people. As the gospel writers compiled their accounts of the life of Jesus they were trying to show that the fulfilment of Israel's hopes and the hopes of the entire world had been realized. If proof was needed in the stories that were told to express this, the place to look was the writings of the scriptures. The gospel writers consistently and repeatedly turn to the scriptures for support, for details and for ideas to help them tell their stories about Jesus.

Sometimes this habit of turning to the scriptures leads to memorable confusions in the gospels. A renowned example of this comes in the story of the entry to Jerusalem, in the shape of the donkey. Mark goes into considerable detail about this donkey:

> When they were approaching Jerusalem, at Bethphage and Bethany, close by the Mount of Olives, he sent two of his disciples and said to them, 'Go to the village facing you, and as you enter it you will at once find a tethered colt that no one has yet ridden. Untie it and bring it here. If anyone says to you, "What are you doing?" say, "The Master needs it and will send it back here at once."' They went off and found a colt tethered near a door in the open street. As they untied it, some men standing there said, 'What are you doing, untying that colt?' They gave the answer Jesus had told them, and the men let them go. Then they took the colt to Jesus and threw their cloaks on its back, and he mounted it.
>
> MK.11.1-7

In retelling Mark's story in his gospel, Matthew muddles it up. He introduces a second donkey:

> . . . then Jesus sent two disciples, saying to them, 'Go to the village facing you, and you will at once find a tethered donkey and a colt with her. Untie them and bring them to me . . .'
>
> MT.21.1B-2

then a little later we hear:

> So the disciples went and did as Jesus had told them. They brought the donkey and the colt, then they laid their cloaks on their backs and he took his seat on them.
>
> MT.21.6-7

So here are the two donkeys. And in the middle of his story, Matthew quotes from the Hebrew Scriptures:

> This was to fulfil what was spoken by the prophet:
> *Say to the daughter of Zion:*
> *Look, your king is approaching,*
> *humble and riding on a donkey*
> *and on a colt, the foal of a beast of burden.*
>
> MT.21.4-5

What Matthew is really doing here is combining passages from two of the prophets. The first line "Say to the daughter of Zion" comes from the book of Isaiah:

> Say to the daughter of Zion, 'Look, your salvation is coming;
> with him comes his reward, his achievement precedes him!'
>
> IS.62.11

The last three lines cited by Matthew, where he mentions the two donkeys, come from the book of Zechariah. This passage was written several centuries before Matthew, just after the long exile of the Israelites in Babylon had ended. When King Nebuchadnezzar of Babylon occupied the land of Israel he completely destroyed the temple in Jerusalem in the year 587 BCE. Forced into exile, the elite of the Israelite people lived for seventy years "by the rivers of Babylon", trying to "sing the Lord's song in a strange land".[2] When Zechariah was writing the exiles had returned, and the temple in Jerusalem was being rebuilt.

The book of Zechariah is divided into two parts; the first eight chapters being written by the vehement prophet Zechariah, and the following six by an unnamed writer who

2 i for more on Nebuchadnezzar's conquest of Jerusalem see above, pp.12-13.
ii see PS.137 (AV) for these quotations.

lived over a century later, whose writings have been added to those of Zechariah. These two writers share a passionate hope for the future and an anger for past injustices. They both look for the restoration of Israel:

> Yahweh Sabaoth says this:
> I have been burning with jealousy for Zion.
> with furious jealousy for her sake.
>
> Yahweh says this:
> I am coming back to Zion
> and shall live in the heart of Jerusalem.
> Jerusalem will be called Faithful City
> and the mountain of Yahweh Sabaoth, the Holy
> Mountain.
>
> ZC.8:2-3[3]

That is from Zechariah himself. Very shortly afterwards in the text, his anonymous fellow writer launches into the passage that caught Matthew's eye:

> '. . . Rejoice heart and soul, daughter of Zion!
> Shout for joy, daughter of Jerusalem!
> Look, your king is approaching,
> he is vindicated and victorious,
> humble and riding on a donkey,
> on a colt, the foal of a donkey.
> He will banish chariots from Ephraim
> and horses from Jerusalem;
> the bow of war will be banished.'
> He will proclaim peace to the nations,
> his empire will stretch from sea to sea,
> from the River to the limits of the earth.
>
> ZC.9.9-10

3 "Sabaoth" is a word that implies "armies". "Yahweh Sabaoth" means God of the armies, translated in the AV as "Lord of Hosts".

In the book of Zechariah there is great passion, great vision, and great hope for Israel, but there are not two donkeys. Matthew's quotation is misleading. This is made clear by looking at a more literal translation of the Hebrew in the passage Matthew quotes:

> ... behold, thy king cometh unto thee: he is just, and having salvation; lowly, and riding upon an ass, even upon a colt the foal of an ass.
>
> ZC.9.9B (RV)

What is happening here is the normal poetic practice in Hebrew of repeating a phrase for emphasis, but in slightly different words. So the word "donkey" or in this case "ass" is simply being emphasised as a form of humble transport; it is not being multiplied into two donkeys. But Matthew does just that, producing two donkeys in his gospel. The problem arises because Matthew is quoting a Greek translation of the Hebrew Scriptures instead of the original Hebrew. The Greek version available to Matthew reads:

> ... behold, the King is coming to thee, just, and a saviour; he is meek and riding on an ass, and a young foal.
>
> ZC.9.9B[4]

This clearly means two donkeys, and that is what Matthew understands it to mean. In his gospel he often quotes from the Greek translation of the Hebrew Scriptures, a practice that

4 from *The Septuagint with Apocrypha*, translated by Sir Lancelot C.L.Brenton, Samuel Bagster & Sons, London, 1851; reprinted 1986 and 1987 by Hendrickson Publishers, Peabody, Ma., U.S.A. The Septuagint is a Greek version of the Hebrew Scriptures. It was commissioned by Ptolemy Philadelphus ruler of Egypt 285-247 BCE, and named after the seventy translators. See *Beyond Bethlehem* pp.49ff.

sometimes leads to complicated linguistic and even theological problems.[5]

The gospel accounts of the entry into Jerusalem all echo an earlier story from one of the books of the Maccabees. These books tell of the heroic resistance movement in the second century BCE when large and well organized groups of Jewish guerilla fighters were battling the Greek overlords in their land. The wars were bitter and bloody and long, and for the gospel writers they were fairly recent history. The rebellious Mattathias started off the resistance movement, and his son Simon Maccabeus "eminent high priest, commander-in-chief and ethnarch of the Jews" as he is declared to be, leads his army to take the Greek occupied citadel at Jerusalem.[6] A triumphal entry to the city ensues:

> The occupants of the Citadel in Jerusalem . . . begged Simon to make peace with them, and he granted this, though he expelled them and purified the Citadel from its pollutions. The Jews made their entry on the twenty-third day of the second month in the year 171, with acclamations and carrying palms, to the sound of lyres, cymbals and harps, chanting hymns and canticles, since a great enemy had been crushed and thrown out of Israel. Simon made it a day of annual rejoicing.
>
> 1M.13:49-51

In Luke's account, there are two incidents added to the story of Jesus's entry into Jerusalem. Each of these reflects the contemporary political tensions of the late first century, and conjures up stories of former political tensions in Israel. In the first of these, as Jesus is proceeding on the donkey, some

5 for example MT.1.23 and the use of the word "virgin" taken from a mistranslation of IS.7.14. See *Beyond Bethlehem*, pp.47-55.
6 quoted from 1M.13.42. See above pp.11-12 for more on this story.

Pharisees who are in the crowd ask him to tone down the politically dangerous exuberance of his followers. Jesus is quoted replying:

> 'I tell you, if these keep silence, the stones will cry out.'
>
> LK.19.40

The second incident is also recorded as part of the ride. While Jesus is still on the back of the donkey his first sight of the city brings this reaction:

> As he drew near and came in sight of the city he shed tears over it and said, 'If you too had only recognised on this day the way to peace! But in fact it is hidden from your eyes! Yes, a time is coming when your enemies will raise fortifications all round you, when they will encircle you and hem you in on every side; they will dash you and the children inside your walls to the ground; they will leave not one stone standing on another within you, because you did not recognise the moment of your visitation.'
>
> LK.19.41-44

This is remarkably similar in tone to the speech from Chapter 13 of Mark's gospel in which Mark records what Jesus is reported to have said on the Mount of Olives as he looks over Jerusalem. Yet Luke was writing later than Mark, and much further away from Jerusalem.

The words Luke attributes to Jesus also bear a strong resemblance to the description Josephus gives of the destruction of Jerusalem and its temple. Josephus was writing a little earlier than Luke, in about 75 CE, and his account of the fall of the temple is memorable:

> Next (the Romans) came to the last surviving colonnade of the outer court. On this the women and children and a mixed crowd of citizens had found a refuge—6000 in all. Before Caesar could reach a decision about them or instruct his officers, the soldiers, carried away by their fury, fired the colonnade from below; as a result some flung themselves out of the flames to their death, others perished in the blaze: of that vast number there escaped not one.[7]

And later:

> There was no one left for the soldiers to kill or to plunder, not a soul on which to vent their fury . . . So Caesar now ordered them to raze the whole City and Sanctuary to the ground, leaving the towers that overtopped the others . . . and the stretch of wall enclosing the City on the west—the wall to serve as protection for the garrison that was to be left, . . . All the rest of the fortifications encircling the City were so completely levelled with the ground that no one visiting the spot would believe that it had once been inhabited.[8]

These accounts of destruction by Josephus seem like the retelling of another similar story. In the Hebrew Scriptures, Nebuchadnezzar's previous destruction of Jerusalem and the temple, nearly six hundred years earlier, is described in comparable terms:

> In the fifth month, on the seventh day of the month—it was in the nineteenth year of Nebuchadnezzar king of Babylon—Nebuzaradan commander of the guard, a member of the king of Babylon's staff, entered Jerusalem. He burned down the Temple of

7 Josephus, *The Jewish War*, p. 360.
8 ibid. p.374.

Yahweh, the royal palace and all the houses in Jerusalem. The Chaldaean troops who accompanied the commander of the guard demolished the walls surrounding Jerusalem. Nebuzaradan commander of the guard deported the remainder of the population left in the city, the deserters who had gone over to the king of Babylon, and the rest of the common people.

2K.25.8-11 [9]

Luke was writing his gospel for Christians who were not Jews, but Gentiles. They were already independent of the Jewish synagogues and authorities. But because Christian thought and belief remained firmly rooted in Judaism, the recent history of the war in Jerusalem had a profound and far reaching influence. For Luke's congregation in distant Corinth, or somewhere near Corinth, it would have been impressive to hear the speech of Jesus predicting terrible things to come in Jerusalem. To hear such a speech knowing of the war and the destruction of the temple, and at the same time knowing the stories of the ancient destruction of Jerusalem by Nebuchadnezzar, and at the same time knowing of the contemporary difficulties faced by Christians, would bring past and present together. The knowledge of each event would reinforce the authority and the impact of the others, and all would be understood to be either foreshadowed or echoed in the words Luke attributes to Jesus.

In John's gospel the story of the entry into Jerusalem is shorter than the others:

The next day the great crowd of people who had come up for the festival heard that Jesus was on his way to Jerusalem. They took branches of palm and went out to receive him, shouting:

'*Hosanna!*
Blessed is he who is coming in the name of the Lord,

9 for more see 2K.24.18-25.30; or JR.52.

the king of Israel.'
Jesus found a young donkey and mounted it—as scripture says:
Do not be afraid, daughter of Zion;
look, your king is approaching,
riding on the foal of a donkey.
At first his disciples did not understand this, but later, after Jesus had been glorified, they remembered that this had been written about him and that this was what had happened to him.

JN.12.12-16

John was writing considerably later than the other gospel writers, near the turn of the first century, and for a congregation with even less direct contact with the concerns of Jerusalem. By then, Jerusalem had long since been destroyed, and the memory of that war and all that it signified was fading. The way John tells it, the disciples did not at the time understand the nature of Jesus's entry to Jerusalem, but later, thinking of it, they remembered "that this had been written about him". For John, what has been written, the allusions and stories and voices from the Hebrew Scriptures, are very important despite his distance in time and place from Jerusalem. His congregation is, after all, made up of predominantly Jewish Christians for whom these scriptural references are vital in understanding the role of Jesus.

The story of the entry into Jerusalem provides a convenient dividing point in the narratives of all the gospels. Up until now, Jesus has been an itinerant preacher and healer and miracle worker, moving from place to place in the countryside of Galilee and of Judaea. Now he is in Jerusalem and official attention becomes more keenly focused on him. In the narratives of Mark and Matthew and Luke this is the point at which Jesus directly challenges the Jewish authorities in Jerusalem and attracts the hostile attention that will soon lead to his arrest and execution. In John's gospel the story of the entry to Jerusalem is substantially the same, but he states more definitely that Jesus is already in trouble well before this time. [10] According to John, this comes to a head immediately before Jesus comes to Jerusalem, when the Jewish authorities convene and decide to kill him. This is largely because of Lazarus.

10 see JN.7.1; JN.7.25-31; cp. MK.3.6; MT.12.14; LK.6.11.

CHAPTER FIVE

Lazarus

In John's gospel, before Jesus arrives in Jerusalem he is in a town called Ephraim. The way John tells it, he is there because he is in danger from the Jewish authorities:

> . . . they were determined to kill him. So Jesus no longer went about openly among the Jews, but left the district for a town called Ephraim, in the country bordering on the desert, and stayed there with his disciples.
>
> JN.11.53-54

This place was about fifteen miles north of Jerusalem. In the first century it was in a different political jurisdiction from that of the immediate area surrounding Jerusalem. The other gospels do not mention Jesus going to Ephraim, nor do they tell John's story that leads up to the departure for Ephraim. The story is of the raising of a dead man called Lazarus in a town called Bethany. John devotes an entire chapter of his gospel to this story.

Being much closer to Jerusalem than Ephraim, the town of Bethany was well within the reach of the temple authorities. According to John's gospel Jesus had been in trouble with these authorities in Jerusalem for some time. John's chronology maintains that three months earlier Jesus had visited Jerusalem and there had been an attempt to stone him and a further attempt to arrest him.[1] Both times he had escaped, then he travelled down to the banks of the Jordan to the place where he had been baptised by John the Baptist some two years or so earlier. Like Ephraim, this was also outside the jurisdiction of those who were trying to kill him. While he was there Jesus received a message from some friends, two sisters called Martha and Mary and their brother Lazarus who lived in Bethany. Lazarus was ill and could Jesus come at once to be with him? Jesus is reported to have considered the matter for two days, and then he says, "Let us go back to Judaea."

The disciples argue that it is too dangerous to go to Bethany but Jesus says "Our friend Lazarus is at rest; I am going to wake him." The disciples point out that if he is resting he is sure to get better, and then Jesus puts it more plainly, telling them that Lazarus is dead, and they must go to him. Thomas, one of the disciples says, "Let us also go to die with him".

When Jesus reaches Bethany Lazarus is indeed dead and his body has been buried four days already. He is met by Martha who says that if Jesus had been there Lazarus would not have died. Then she adds that she knows if Jesus asks something of God it will be granted.

> Jesus said to her, 'Your brother will rise again.'
> Martha said, 'I know he will rise again at the resurrection on the last day.' Jesus said:
> I am the resurrection.
> Anyone who believes in me, even though that person dies, will live,
> and whoever lives and believes in me
> will never die.
> Do you believe this?
> 'Yes, Lord,' she said, 'I believe that you are the Christ, the Son of God, the one who was to come into this world.'
>
> JN.11.23-27

1 see JN.10.22ff.

After this exchange Martha goes to get her sister Mary. Mary comes to greet Jesus with some friends who are grieving with her and she says the same as her sister, that if Jesus had been there Lazarus would not have died. Jesus, after joining in the grief then asks where Lazarus is buried, and he weeps as they all go towards the tomb which is a cave covered with a large stone. He asks for the stone to be removed, and Martha the practical sister says, "Lord, by now he will smell; this is the fourth day since he died.", or as the King James Bible more pithily states: "Lord, by this time he stinketh: for he hath been dead four days." Jesus replies that if she believes she will see the glory of God. So the stone is removed and Jesus prays aloud:

> Father, I thank you for hearing my prayer.
> I myself knew that you hear me always,
> but I speak
> for the sake of all these who are standing
> around me,
> so that they may believe it was you who sent me.

> When he had said this, he cried in a loud voice, 'Lazarus, come out!' The dead man came out, his feet and hands bound with strips of material, and a cloth over his face. Jesus said to them, 'Unbind him, let him go free.'
>
> JN.11.41B-44[2]

John goes on to describe how the chief priests and the Pharisees get wind of this story and call a meeting to decide what to do about Jesus. The Pharisees were a distinct religious sect usually at odds with the temple priests. The priests were of the sect or party known as Sadducees. These two groups generally loathed each other but at this point they need each other's support. They are all afraid that the raising of Lazarus will attract an even bigger following to Jesus. They fear this will

2 cp. JN.20.4-10.

antagonise their Roman overlords who have no desire to see large popular movements arising in this troublesome part of the empire. The whole nation would be endangered if the anger of the Romans were aroused, and the position of the temple authorities would become untenable. Their exercise of secular power was considerable, but it was entirely subject to the pleasure of the Romans. If those in charge of the temple wanted to retain their power, they had to remain in the good books of their political masters, and to avoid confrontation they would be ruthless with troublemakers.[3]

The head of the priestly authorities in Jerusalem was one Caiaphas. He was high priest, a position he held with considerable political adroitness for over seventeen years. In John's gospel Caiaphas is given a memorable speech when the authorities gather to decide what to do about Jesus. He says that Jesus must die for the sake of them all:

> 'You do not seem to have grasped the situation at all; you fail to see that it is to your advantage that one man should die for the people, rather than that the whole nation should perish.' He did not speak in his own person, but as high priest of that year he was prophesying that Jesus was to die for the nation—and not for the nation only, but also to gather together into one the scattered children of God. From that day onwards they were determined to kill him.
>
> JN.11.49B-53

So the story of the raising of Lazarus leads to a meeting of chief priests and Pharisees and to their decision that Jesus must die. This is the point in John's gospel when Jesus prudently leaves the district, "for a town called Ephraim, in the country bordering on the desert."

3 for more on the power of the temple authorities under the Romans, see below p.147.

The story of Lazarus is the most elaborate miracle story of John's gospel. In the following chapter of his gospel John refers to Lazarus twice:

> . . . a large number of Jews heard that he was there and came not only on account of Jesus but also to see Lazarus whom he had raised from the dead. Then the chief priests decided to kill Lazarus as well, since it was on his account that many of the Jews were leaving them and believing in Jesus.
>
> JN.12.9-11

The other mention comes in John's account of Jesus's entry to Jerusalem:

> The crowd who had been with him when he called Lazarus out of the tomb and raised him from the dead kept bearing witness to it; this was another reason why the crowd came out to receive him: they had heard that he had given this sign. Then the Pharisees said to one another, 'You see, you are making no progress; look, the whole world has gone after him!'
>
> JN.12.17-19

In the other gospels there is no mention of Lazarus at all, either in the crowd scene when Jesus comes into Jerusalem, or in any of the earlier stories.

The other gospels do tell stories of people being raised from the dead, but these stories are more muted than the story of Lazarus. As time passed in the first century the descriptions of Jesus raising dead people became more complex and colourful. John, writing last, offers the most dramatic and detailed story of all in his account of Lazarus. Luke, with his comparatively tame story of Jesus reviving a young man, comes a pale second. He tells how, in a town called Nain, a widow's son has died and Jesus stops the funeral procession and touches the bier:

> 'Young man I tell you: get up.' And the dead man sat up and began to talk, and Jesus *gave him to his mother*. Everyone was filled with awe and glorified God saying, 'A great prophet has risen up among us; God has visited his people.' And this view of him spread throughout Judaea and all over the countryside.
>
> LK.7.14-17

This story is unique to Luke's gospel, just as Lazarus is to John's. The only story of this nature that is common to more than one gospel is of Jesus reviving a young girl believed to be dead. In Mark, before arousing the girl Jesus says to her grieving parents "The child is not dead, but asleep."[4] The same words are echoed by Matthew and Luke in their stories of the girl. Although others in the story say the girl is dead, Jesus speaks of her as being asleep.

By contrast, in the story of Lazarus the word "dead" is used by Jesus. "Our friend Lazarus is at rest;" says Jesus to his disciples, "I am going to wake him". But John soon resolves the ambivalence of the words "at rest", or in some English translations "asleep". When the disciples do not understand what Jesus means, he says plainly that Lazarus is dead. The story of Lazarus asserts more strongly than anything in the other gospels that Jesus recalls a truly dead person to life.

For this story, as for the other gospel stories of Jesus reviving apparently dead people, there are few obvious and direct models in the Hebrew Scriptures. Specific stories of the raising of the dead are few and far between. Probably the best known of these tells of the prophet Elijah. In the minds of the Jewish people, Elijah was amongst the greatest of the prophets. He lived around 875-850 BCE, and his history is recorded in the first book of Kings in the Hebrew Scriptures. According to one story, Elijah resuscitates a dead child.

The story starts with Elijah predicting a severe drought, and

4 see MK.5.21-43; MT.9.18- 26 and LK.8.40-56.

then sheltering near a wadi or creek that is tributary to the Jordan. There he is miraculously fed by ravens. When the creek dries out Elijah goes to a place near Sidon where he meets a widow gathering sticks. He asks her to fetch him a drink of water which she does, and then he asks for food. She says she is nearly out of food and that after she has baked the last of her grain with the last of her oil she expects that she and her son will starve to death. Elijah says:

> 'Do not be afraid, go and do as you have said; but first make a little scone of it for me and bring it to me, and then make some for yourself and for your son. For Yahweh, God of Israel, says this:
>
> Jar of meal shall not be spent,
> jug of oil shall not be emptied,
> before the day when Yahweh sends
> rain on the face of the earth.'
>
> 1K.17.13-14

So the widow goes and does what Elijah says and she and her son and Elijah are able to live off that barrel of meal and that jug of oil till the end of the famine.

But after the famine there is more trouble. The son falls sick, and "in the end he expired." The widow is desperate:

> 'Give me your son,' (Elijah) said and, taking him from her lap, he carried him to the upper room where he was staying and laid him on his bed. He cried out to Yahweh, 'Yahweh my God, do you mean to bring grief even to the widow who is looking after me by killing her son?' He stretched himself on the child three times and cried out to Yahweh, 'Yahweh my God, may the soul of this child, I beg you, come into him again!' Yahweh heard Elijah's prayer and the child's soul came back into his body and he revived. Elijah took the child, brought him

> down from the upper room into the house, and gave him to his mother. 'Look', Elijah said, 'your son is alive.' And the woman replied, 'Now I know you are a man of God and the word of Yahweh in your mouth is truth itself.'
>
> 1K.17.19-24 [5]

In this story Elijah affirms his identity as a "man of God" by raising the widow's son. So it is with Jesus in John's story of Lazarus. Through his words and actions, Jesus is affirmed as the embodiment of the resurrection of the dead.

In John's gospel, the recognition Jesus receives following the raising of Lazarus proves dangerous. As the Pharisees point out to each other disapprovingly, "the whole world" comes running after Jesus because of the fame of this miracle. The increased public attention places Jesus under the fierce scrutiny of the Jewish authorities who decide they must get rid of him. The Lazarus miracle provides background for John's account of the death and resurrection of Jesus and leads directly to it.

Many similar details appear in the two sets of stories. Jesus, like Lazarus, is in the grave for three days.[6] He too is buried in a tomb that has a stone rolled across the entrance. His grave cloths and the cloth covering his face are described by John in the same way as the grave cloths of Lazarus. Mary of Magdala asks the same question about Jesus as he asks about Lazarus, "Where have you put him?", and she weeps outside the tomb just as the sisters of Lazarus weep outside his tomb.

Even more significant than the shared similarity of detail in these two sets of stories is the shared theme of resurrection. According to John, when Jesus arrives in Bethany he becomes involved in a discussion about resurrection with Martha, the sister of Lazarus. After she asserts her belief that Lazarus will rise again on the final day, Jesus declares that he is, in the words

5 see 2K.4.18-37 for a similar story about Elijah's successor, Elisha. for more on Elijah see below pp.191-194; 253-255; 273-274.

6 for more on the three days see below pp.221-224.

of the King James Bible "the resurrection and the life". This identification of Jesus with resurrection ends with the requirement that people believe in him. Shortly after, when he is praying for Lazarus, Jesus says he is doing so in order that people will believe. Later, John states that because of the Lazarus miracle people do believe in Jesus and flock around him. The whole story of Lazarus being brought to life is an invitation to believe in the much debated concept of resurrection; that of Lazarus, that of Jesus, that of all believers.

In the words John attributes to Martha when she says that she believes Lazarus will "rise again at the resurrection on the last day", she gives voice to a belief of many Jews in the first century . This "last day" will mark the triumph of the great leader coming to save Israel. At the time of this triumph all faithful Jews who have died will come to life again and share in the final glory of the end of the world. Not all Jews shared this belief, but at the time John was writing, belief in resurrection had gained considerable strength amongst certain Jews, and it was widely accepted in Christian communities. Christianity was spreading and the new churches maintained not only that Jesus had risen bodily from the dead, but that all the righteous would similarly be resurrected to an everlasting life.

This Christian attitude towards resurrection developed directly from the teachings of the Pharisees on resurrection. The Pharisees were one of the most powerful of Jewish groups, and for many generations their influence had been increasing. They had become political and religious rivals of the priestly caste of the Sadducees, centred in Jerusalem, a caste that could trace its origins all the way back to Zadok the priest in the time of King David. The Sadducees did not hold with what were to them far-fetched notions about resurrection developed by the Pharisees. [7] This is evident not only in the gospels; it is abundantly

7 i for more on Sadducees see NJB, p.1613n.
ii for more on Zadok the priest see 2S.8.17; 2S.15.29; 2S.15.35; 2S.20.25; 1K.1.8. Also see 1K.1.45 and 1K.2.35.
iii for the Sadducee's attitude to resurrection see MK.12.18- 27; MT.22.23-33; LK.20.27- 38.

clear in one of the more lively stories told about Paul in the book of Acts.

In this story Paul has been preaching in Jerusalem, telling of his conversion to Christianity on the road to Damascus, and confessing his earlier persecution of Christians. His Jewish audience is not at all friendly, and they become so incensed with Paul's preaching that a noisy demonstration ensues. This brings down the wrath of the Roman tribune, who has Paul seized and then orders that he be flogged. Paul is taken to the Roman fortress and put in chains, but just as the flogging is about to begin Paul, who appears to be completely undaunted by all of this, produces his trump card. He points out that such treatment is not legal because he is a Roman citizen by birth. The tribune becomes alarmed at this and arranges a hearing in front of the Jewish court of Jerusalem, the Sanhedrin.

Paul is equally undaunted by the Sanhedrin and he announces to all who are there that he has a clear conscience. Unfortunately Paul fails to recognize the high priest and becomes involved in an altercation with him that succeeds in inflaming the whole assembly. When he finds out his mistake Paul calmly apologises but it does no good. Realizing his only hope lies in diversionary tactics, Paul then sets out to stir up dissent amongst his opponents. Given his background as a Pharisee, he knows just how to do this. All he has to do is mention "resurrection".

> Now Paul was well aware that one party was made up of Sadducees and the other of Pharisees, so he called out in the Sanhedrin, 'Brothers, I am a Pharisee and the son of Pharisees. It is for our hope in the resurrection of the dead that I am on trial.' As soon as he said this, a dispute broke out between the Pharisees and Sadducees, and the assembly was split between the two parties. For the Sadducees say there is neither resurrection, nor angel, nor spirit, while the Pharisees accept all three. The shouting grew louder, and some of the scribes from the Pharisees' party

> stood up and protested strongly, 'We find nothing wrong with this man. Suppose a spirit has spoken to him, or an angel?' Feeling was running high, and the tribune, afraid that they would tear Paul to pieces, ordered his troops to go down and haul him out and bring him into the fortress.
>
> AC.23.6-10

This story continues very dramatically. A Jewish plot to kill Paul comes to the attention of the Roman tribune, and he decides to send Paul away for his own safety. Paul travels under armed guard to Caesarea, and from there he appeals to Caesar and is sent on to Rome, surviving shipwreck on the way.

Paul knew that the very mention of resurrection would spark disagreement amongst the Jewish authorities in Jerusalem. Like most religions at most times, the Jewish religion was in a state of evolution in the first century. Many different ideas were abroad, many different debates were current, many different controversies preoccupied the minds of the authorities.

After the year 70 CE when the temple was destroyed, the Sadducees were also destroyed; their power base was gone. It was left to the Pharisees to provide the solid core of leadership and teaching needed by the synagogues in such troubled times. In this way the ideas of the Pharisees gained authority during the latter part of the first century, including their ideas about the resurrection of the dead. At the same time the Christian sect took these already existing ideas about resurrection and developed them in their own way.

The concept of resurrection finds little expression in the Hebrew Scriptures. References to it are scattered and idiosyncratic, and they do not add up to anything approaching a clear set of beliefs. However by the first century CE discussion on the subject of resurrection had been around for some time. One of the earliest references comes in the book of the prophet Ezekiel, probably written during the time of the Babylonian exile.

In looking forward to the re-establishment of the nation of Israel, Ezekiel was seized with strange, macabre visions of a glory yet to come. One of the strangest of his visions is of a whole valley of dry bones coming to life and being transformed into an immense army. As Ezekiel watches this, his God speaks to him and explains:

> 'Son of man, these bones are the whole House of Israel. They keep saying, "Our bones are dry, our hope has gone; we are done for." So, prophesy. Say to them, "The Lord Yahweh says this: I am now going to open your graves; I shall raise you from your graves, my people, and lead you back to the soil of Israel. And you will know that I am Yahweh, when I open your graves and raise you from your graves, my people . . ."'
>
> EZK.37.11-14

In a section of the book of Isaiah that could have been written as late as the third century BCE, there is another declaration about the dead arising. This comes as part of a hopeful cry to the God of Israel, a declaration that oppression is past and that the nation will now once again be enlarged and know glory. When this glory is regained, the very dead will rejoice.

> Your dead will come back to life, your corpses will rise again.
> Wake up and sing, you dwellers in the dust,
> for your dew will be a radiant dew,
> but the earth will give birth to the shades.
>
> IS.26.19

In the later writings of scripture, references to the resurrection of the dead became more frequent. These references go hand in hand with an increasing emphasis on the coming end of the world. This is described in apocalyptic language telling of the horrors of the end times, and of the terrible final battles that will be fought. Those who are known to be righteous will be spared, and the dead who were righteous will be raised to glory. The book of Daniel, written in the second century BCE, describes some of this in detail:

> . . . That will be a time of great distress, unparalleled since nations first came into existence. When that time comes, your own people will be spared—all those whose names are found written in the Book. 'Of those who are sleeping in the Land of Dust, many will awaken, some to everlasting life, some to shame and everlasting disgrace . . .'
>
> DN.12.1-2

Some of the apocryphal writings also assume a belief in the resurrection of the dead. In the second book of Maccabees, seven Jewish brothers and their mother face a horrible death at the hands of the Greek oppressors of the second century BCE. For having refused to eat pork they are all tortured at great length by the Greeks, but they are sustained by the hope of a new life:

> When the first had left the world in this way, they brought the second forward to be tortured. After stripping the skin from his head, hair and all, they asked him, 'Will you eat some pork, before your body is tortured limb by limb?' Replying in his ancestral tongue, he said, 'No!' So he too was put to the torture in his turn. With his last breath he exclaimed, 'Cruel brute, you may discharge us from this present life, but the King of the world will raise us up, since we die for his laws, to live again for ever.'
>
> 2M.7.7-9

Another brother cries out in a similar fashion when his turn comes:

> 'Ours is the better choice, to meet death at men's hands, yet relying on God's promise that we shall be raised up by him; whereas for you there can be no resurrection to new life.'.
>
> 2M.7.14

All of these scattered references to the resurrection of the dead, from the prophets through to the books of the Maccabees, make assertions about the dead rising, but they are short on specific details about just what this means. At times a bodily resurrection seems to be implied; at times it is spiritual. At times all of the righteous seem to be promised such a resurrection; at other times only a select few.

Although they had been developing within the Hebrew Scriptures over a long period, and although by the first century they were becoming more widespread, Jewish ideas and beliefs about the resurrection of the dead were far from clear. In turn, Christian ideas about Jesus's resurrection and about the hoped for resurrection of all Christians at the time of the second coming are far from clear in the gospels. It could hardly be otherwise, for these ideas were developing from a very hazy background.

CHAPTER SIX

Temple

Mark is very clear in his story about the sequence of events when he tells of Jesus going into Jerusalem. First of all Jesus goes to Bethany, the village just east of Jerusalem by the Mount of Olives where Lazarus and his sisters lived, and there he arranges for the donkey on which he enters the city. Once in Jerusalem he visits the temple briefly and then goes back to Bethany for the night.

On the next day Jesus returns to the city, and on the way there he feels hungry:

> Seeing a fig tree in leaf some distance away, he went to see if he could find any fruit on it, but when he came up to it he found nothing but leaves; for it was not the season for figs. And he addressed the fig tree, 'May no one ever eat fruit from you again.' And his disciples heard him say this.
>
> MK.11.12-14

This strange little incident is dropped into the narrative at that point with no explanation, though Mark returns to it in short order. This has come to be known as Jesus "cursing" the fig tree. In Mark's story Jesus then carries on into the city and to the temple where a more momentous event takes place:

> . . . and he went into the Temple and began driving out the men selling and buying there; he upset the tables of the money changers and the seats of the dove sellers . . . And he taught them and said, 'Does not scripture say: *My house will be called a house of prayer for all peoples?* But you have turned it into a *bandits' den.*' This came to the ears of the chief priests and the scribes, and they tried to find some way of doing away with him; they were afraid of him because the people were carried away by his teaching.
>
> MK.11.15B-18

The first impression from these two stories, temple and tree alike, is quite contrary to the image of Jesus built up by Mark in the earlier chapters of his gospel. Unreasonable annoyance with a harmless tree, and violent aggression within the temple precinct do not seem to tie in with the reports of Jesus the sympathetic healer and preacher.

All four gospels include stories of Jesus taking angry action in the temple. Three gospels relate parables concerning fig trees, and Mark and Matthew also tell stories of the "cursing" of a fig tree.[1] Only Mark interweaves the action against the fig tree with the action against the temple. According to Mark, after Jesus has upset the tables of the moneychangers he again notices the tree:

> Next morning, as they passed by, they saw the fig tree withered to the roots. Peter remembered. 'Look, Rabbi,' he said to Jesus, 'the fig tree that you cursed has withered away.' Jesus answered, 'Have faith in God. In truth I tell you, if anyone says to this mountain, "Be pulled up and thrown into the sea," with no

1 for another story see MT.21.18-22; for the parables see MK.13.28f, MT.24.32f, and LK.21.29-31.

doubt in his heart, but believing that what he says will happen, it will be done for him.'

MK.11.20-23

This story makes Jesus seem testy and irritable and quite unreasonable. Given that the scene is set by Mark at the time of Passover, which is a springtime festival, the best Jesus could hope for from a fig tree would be small immature green fruit. These small early figs are edible, but most of them fall from the trees and a second fruiting leads to the real fig crop later in the season. In horticultural terms it is perfectly natural to find a fig tree with no fruit on it in the springtime. It is even perfectly natural to find wild self-sown fig trees that are male trees, and always barren. Anyone born and raised in a country where fig trees are native would know all this. So it is not very helpful to look at this story strictly in horticultural terms, for in that way it makes no sense at all. It is more useful to ask what lies behind the story.

There are a number of references to fig trees in the Hebrew Scriptures that provide a different way of looking at this story. Two of these references occur in the book of the prophet Jeremiah who lived in Jerusalem before and during its conquest by King Nebuchadnezzar of Babylon. This came to a head first in 597 BCE, when Nebuchadnezzar besieged Jerusalem and took it as part of his empire, installing a puppet king. This king later rebelled and put himself and his territory under the protection of the Pharaoh of Egypt. This was a poor scheme, for in the year 586 BCE Nebuchadnezzar again took Jerusalem, and this time he completely devastated the city and destroyed the temple.

Before all this happens Jeremiah gives a series of ominous prophecies warning of troubles to come. Always outspoken and usually gloomy, Jeremiah declares that the bad behaviour of the Jewish people will have dire consequences. The way Jeremiah understands his role, the God of Israel is using him to forewarn the people of troubles to come:

'. . . Now I shall bring on you
a nation from afar, House of Israel,
Yahweh declares,
an enduring nation,
an ancient nation,
a nation whose language you do not know,
nor can you grasp what they say.
Their quiver a gaping tomb,
they are all of them fighters.
They will devour your harvest and your food,
devour your sons and daughters,
devour your flocks and herds,
devour your vines and fig trees,
and demolish your fortified towns
in which you trust—with the sword!'

JR.5.15-17

Here Jeremiah includes figs as a valued crop that will share the destruction of the nation. The threat to this crop is part of the larger, more ominous threat to the entire nation.

Later, Jeremiah again refers to figs:

> Yahweh gave me a vision: set out in front of the Temple of Yahweh were two baskets of figs. This was after Nebuchadnezzar king of Babylon had led away Jeconiah son of Jehoiakim, king of Judah, away into exile from Jerusalem, with the chief men of Judah, the blacksmiths and metalworkers, and had taken them to Babylon. One basket contained excellent figs, like those that ripen first; the other contained very bad figs, so bad they were uneatable. Yahweh said to me, 'What do you see, Jeremiah?' 'Figs', I answered . . .

JR.24.1-3

Jeremiah's God goes on to explain that the good figs are like the elite of Jerusalem who have been taken into exile in Babylon, and he says that he will look after these good people and bring them back to the land of Israel. The bad figs are like the unworthy remnant of Jerusalem who remained in the country and looked for protection from Egypt. To Jeremiah this was tantamount to unfaithfulness to God, and it is the unfaithful who will be cursed and destroyed.

In another passage, Jeremiah speaks more generally about how people flourish or fail like trees, depending on their allegiance to the God of Israel:

> Yahweh says this,
> 'Accursed be anyone who trusts in human beings,
> who relies on human strength
> and whose heart turns from Yahweh.
> He is like scrub in the wastelands:
> when good comes, it does not affect him
> since he lives in the parched places of the desert,
> uninhabited, salt land.
>
> Blessed is anyone who trusts in Yahweh,
> with Yahweh for his reliance.
> He is like a tree by the waterside
> that thrusts its roots to the stream:
> when the heat comes it has nothing to fear,
> its foliage stays green;
> untroubled in a year of drought,
> it never stops bearing fruit.'
>
> JR.17.5-8

Jeremiah was working within a well-established tradition of what could be termed agricultural imagery. Consistently throughoought the scriptures the fruitfulness of vine, or fig tree, or corn, or grain is praised and cherished. Life depends on such crops, and in a country surrounded by desert they are very hard won. It is small wonder that the fate of the people of Israel, their virtues and their vices, their successes and their failures are so often described in terms related to the crops they grew.

Further examples of this are many and varied. The prophet Habakkuk, known as one of the "minor" prophets, was writing at roughly the same time as Jeremiah. The book of Habakkuk is short. It is a poetic book, made up of prayers and oracles and a dialogue between Habakkuk and his God. He is preoccupied with a continuing political crisis because Judah was being invaded by the Chaldaeans. Among his writings is a lament for the produce of the land:

> . . . the fig tree is not to blossom,
> nor will the vines bear fruit,
> the olive crop will disappoint
> and the fields will yield no food;
> the sheep will vanish from the fold,
> no cattle in the stalls.
>
> HAB.3.17

A century before this, another minor prophet called Micah also identified Israel's troubles with those of tree and field:

> How wretched I am,
> a harvester in summer time,
> like a gleaner at the vintage:
> not a single cluster to eat,
> none of those early figs I love!
> The faithful have vanished from the land:
> there is no one honest left.
> All of them are on the alert for blood,
> every man hunting his brother with a net.
> Their hands are adept at wrong-doing:
> the official makes his demands,
> the judge gives judgement for a bribe,
> the man in power pronounces as he pleases.
>
> MI.7.1-3

At approximately the same time as Micah, the prophet Hosea was also raising his voice in despair at what he considered the faithless carryings-on of the people of Israel. He too uses agricultural imagery to show how some Israelites turned from their own God and began worshipping the god Baal:

> It was like finding grapes in the desert when I found Israel,
> like seeing early fruit on a fig tree when I saw your ancestors;
> but when they reached Baal-Peor they devoted themselves to Shame
> and became as loathsome as the thing they loved . . .
>
> . . . Their wickedness appeared in full at Gilgal,
> there I came to hate them.
> Because of the wickedness of their deeds
> I shall drive them from my home,
> I shall love them no longer;
> all their princes are rebels.
> Ephraim is blasted,
> their root has dried out,
> they will bear no more fruit.
>
> HO.9.10,15-16

When Mark tells his strange story of a fig tree bearing no fruit he is writing within this tradition of fruitfulness as the reward for the faithfulness and virtue of the people of Israel. By the same token, unfruitfuless is the result of unfaithfulness and wrongdoing.

As we have seen, Mark tells of the fig tree in almost the same breath as he describes Jesus's anger in the temple. Both of these stories seem to point to events at the time of the writing of the gospel, a time that very probably coincided with the destruction of the temple. Mark and his community were doubtless horrified by the devastation in Jerusalem, yet paradoxically convinced that much of this was well deserved. The temple authorities are described by Mark in entirely negative terms. They are portrayed as the unfaithful, the unfruitful; argumentative and unproductive and corrupt, an old regime that is rejected by the newly formed Christian sect of Judaism. Jesus takes violent action against the unfaithful temple just as he does against the unfruitful tree. In each case these stories can be understood as parables about the doomed temple and all it stood for.

In the early part of the first century the temple was a huge administrative complex, ruled by a jealous priestly elite and complete with its own policing force of temple guards. It could contain tens of thousands of people in its various enclosures. This was the very heart of Jewish political and religious life; the centre for pilgrimage and for Passover sacrifices. It stood on a site chosen a thousand years earlier by King David. The first temple had been built by his son Solomon when Israel was truly a great power. This temple was destroyed by Nebuchadnezzar in the year 586BCE, and a new temple took its place with the rebuilding that started later in the same century. The second temple lasted until about fifteen years before Jesus's birth, when it was pulled down to be replaced by a temple of a magnificence exceeding even that of Solomon. The building of this third and final temple was begun by Herod the Great, the puppet king of Judaea.

Building temples was a slow business, and the building of the third temple carried on from about 20BCE until 60CE. Only ten years after completion, this entire temple complex was devastated by the Romans. At the time described by Mark, during the lifetime of Jesus, the temple was at the centre of a massive construction industry and it was becoming bigger and more elaborate year by year.

At the time of Passover, when Jesus is reported by Mark to have entered Jerusalem and to have angrily attacked some merchants in the temple, the place would have been packed with people. What with tens of thousands of pilgrims, as well as priests, guards, and merchants selling animals for the sacrifices, it was bustling with social and commercial activity. Animals for the sacrifices had to be without blemish and a priest had to certify that they were acceptable, so the merchants needed the good will and co-operation of the priests. Temple transactions amounted to very big business. In Mark's version of the story, Jesus steps seriously out of line in protesting against these practices. Such a gesture in such a setting was a futile and rash act, not expected from a little-known preacher from out of town.[2] But this gesture and protest ring true, given the scriptural background.

Jesus's actions as described by Mark are part of a long tradition. He was one of a line of troublesome preachers and prophets speaking out to maintain the purity of the temple, and so to defend its sanctity. "My house will be called a house of prayer for all peoples" declares the book of Isaiah,[3] and whenever the temple authorities appear to be stepping out of line, voices of protest are raised in the scriptures.

Most notable of all is the voice of Jeremiah. From the book of Jeremiah comes the outcry "Do you look on this Temple that bears my name as a den of bandits?", the very phrase Mark puts into the mouth of Jesus. Jeremiah rails against the practices tolerated by the temple authorities:

> '. . . Steal, would you, murder, commit adultery, perjure yourselves, burn incense to Baal, follow other gods of whom you know nothing? — and then come and stand before me in this Temple that bears my name, saying: Now we are safe to go on doing all these loathsome things! Do you look on this Temple that bears my name as a den of bandits? . . .'
>
> JR.7.9-11

2 i for more on Herod's temple see Josephus, Flavius: *Antiquities of the Jews*, translated by William Whiston, Edinburgh, William P. Nimmo, no date; book 15, chapter 11.
ii for more on Jesus's action in the temple see Sanders, E.P., *Jesus and Judaism*, Fortress Press, Philadelphia, 1985, pp.69ff. See also Douglass, James W.; *The Nonviolent Coming of God*; Orbis Books; Maryknoll, New York; 1991; pp.91ff.
iii for more on the Passover sacrifice see below, pp.98-100, 106.
3 IS.56.7.

Jeremiah then goes on to describe what God has declared he will do to punish the wrongdoers of the temple. He recalls that in another time the shrine at Shiloh was destroyed by the wrath of God. Shiloh lay to the north, within twenty miles of Jerusalem, and before the time of King David it was a major shrine of the Israelites. But this shrine met a sad fate, and the same fate is dolefully pronounced by Jeremiah for the temple of Jerusalem. According to Jeremiah, Yahweh has declared:

> ". . . I shall treat this Temple that bears my name,
> and in which you put your heart, the place that I
> gave you and your ancestors, just as I treated Shiloh,
> and I shall drive you out of my sight, as I did all your
> kinsfolk, the whole race of Ephraim."
>
> JR.7.14-15[4]

Recalling the destruction of Shiloh is a powerful emotional ploy on Jeremiah's part. The famous priest Eli lived at Shiloh, along with the child Samuel who became the great prophet who chose and anointed the first kings of Israel.[5] The ark of the covenant, believed to contain the tablets on which Moses inscribed the ten commandments, was kept at the shrine of Shiloh. When the Israelites and the Philistines were engaged in a long and bloody war, the Israelites sent for the ark of the covenant to be brought to their camp. At first the Philistines were duly intimidated, but they took heart and carried on with the fighting. In the process they slaughtered some thirty thousand Israelites, defeating the army completely. For good measure, the Philistines then took possession of the ark of the covenant. Back in Shiloh, when Eli the priest heard this terrible news he promptly fell over and died. From then on nothing more is heard of Shiloh as a shrine.[6]

In his long and doom-laden oracles about the fate awaiting

4 for more on Jeremiah and temple see below pp.149-150.
5 for more on Samuel see below pp.84- 86.
6 for the rest of this story see 1s.4.1- 18.

Israel, Jeremiah leaves little room for hope. He believes his God to be angry, despairing and vengeful and he recites the wrongdoings of the nation like a litany, often using familiar images to make his point:

> I shall put an end to them, Yahweh declares,
> no more grapes on the vine,
> no more figs on the fig tree
> only withered leaves . . .
>
> JR.8:13

And later:

> Who is there to pity you, Jerusalem,
> who to grieve for you,
> who to go out of his way
> and ask how you are?
> 'You yourself have rejected me, Yahweh declares,
> you have turned your back on me;
> so I have stretched my hand over you and destroyed you.
>
> JR.15.5-6

Jeremiah is only one of many powerful and familiar voices from the Hebrew Scriptures that echoed across time to Mark as he was writing his gospel. It is a particularly significant voice carrying a very appropriate message, because as Mark wrote Jerusalem was again in deep trouble. The people had tried to rebel against their Roman oppressors, but rebellion was failing, and the city and temple were facing destruction.

In Mark's gospel, the story of Jesus in the temple and the story of the fig tree together imply that the temple was a place of the unfaithful and of the corrupt. Mark's idea here is to show where the responsibility lies for bringing down the wrath of God on the temple and on Jerusalem; to show that the wrongdoings of the Jewish establishment were deeply rooted, and that the temple had sown the seeds of its own destruction.

Mark's gospel tells of Jesus trying, like Jeremiah, to protest against wrongdoing in the temple. But like the fig tree that would bear no fruit, the temple was doomed. And according to Mark, in taking his action against the temple, Jesus himself is doomed. From this point on, the authorities in Jerusalem can tolerate him no longer. They must now be rid of him:

> And he taught them and said, 'Does not scripture say: *My house will be called a house of prayer for all peoples?* But you have turned it into a *bandits' den.*' This came to the ears of the chief priests and the scribes, and they tried to find some way of doing away with him; they were afraid of him because the people were carried away by his teaching.
>
> MK.11.17-18

CHAPTER SEVEN

Anointings

From the very beginnings of their gospels, Mark and Matthew, Luke and John all try to make it very clear who Jesus is. When Jesus is introduced in the first verse of the first chapter of the gospel of Mark he is called "Jesus Christ", and without further preamble Mark launches into his stories. His first appearance in Matthew's gospel is also in Chapter one verse one, and also as "Jesus Christ". Matthew then follows this with a long and complicated genealogy giving an account of Jesus's ancestors, tracing his forebears from Abraham and including the great king David among others. At the end of this genealogy Matthew begins to tell his stories by announcing the birth of Jesus "who is called Christ".[1]

Luke has detailed and engaging stories to tell when he introduces Jesus. In Chapter one verse thirty-two the angel Gabriel says to the astonished Mary, "You are to conceive in your womb and bear a son, and you must name him Jesus", and continues by explaining that this Jesus is descended from David and will be the inheritor of an eternal kingdom. In Chapter two when Jesus is born, Luke tells of another angel appearing to the terrified shepherds at the time of Jesus's birth " . . . Today in the town of David a Saviour has been born to you; he is Christ the Lord."

1 for more on Matthew's genealogy see *Beyond Bethlehem*, Chapters 2 and 3.

John is more circuitous. In his prologue he says that Jesus is the mysterious "word made flesh", then Jesus is variously described by John the Baptist as "the Son of God", "the Chosen One of God" and "the lamb of God". Later the disciple Andrew says "We have found the Messiah", at which point the gospel writer adds ". . . which means the Christ."[2]

All these declarations come to the conclusion that he is "Jesus the Christ". Jesus is simply a given name. To this day there are many babies born who are named Jesus. Christ, on the other hand, is a title. The root of the word is Greek and its Hebrew equivalent is the word "Messiah". There are strong links between the concepts of "christ" or "messiah", and the concept of "king". Specifically, this is because the word christ or messiah means one who has been anointed, and in the Hebrew world kings were anointed.

In all four of the gospels, stories are told of Jesus being anointed. The stories of the anointings typically occur at small gatherings, or at mealtimes, and the act of anointing usually gives rise to some kind of debate or discussion amongst those present. To be anointed with oil or precious ointment was an act with many meanings. For those who could afford it, anointing was a luxury that was part of a normal toilet. For others, it was an occasional and very special honour, a sign of blessing and gladness. Then there was the anointing of a dead body, part of the normal preparation for burial. And finally, there were sacred anointings. These were bestowed on great men, singling them out for a special purpose.

Christians who gathered in first century congregations were familiar with Jewish traditions, and knew the stories of sacred anointings from the Hebrew Scriptures. These usually show that a leader has been dedicated to God. The book of Leviticus tells of Moses anointing Aaron and his sons when

2 i for more on the "word" see NJB, p.1745, n.
ii for "son of God" and "chosen one of God" see JN.1.29 (NRSV and NJB translations); and for "lamb of God" see JN.1.34.
iii for Messiah/Christ see JN.1.41.

they become priests. The prophet Elijah anoints Elisha as his successor. The book of Isaiah speaks of the prophet as one anointed by God.[3]

The anointing of Jesus carries with it a wealth of different implications. On the face of it, this act is no more than a special luxury bestowed on him while he is amongst friends. And as Jesus says in Mark's gospel, this also shows that his body has been anointed beforehand for burial.[4] Then there are other, unspoken levels of significance in this anointing. These are messianic and kingly and sacred. For not only does the term "Messiah" mean the anointed one, but the title "King of the Jews" carries with it stories of past anointings. In all of the gospels Jesus is referred to as "King of the Jews" or "King of Israel", and in the Hebrew Scriptures to be a king of the Jews was to be anointed.

The first king of the Jews to be anointed was Saul, who lived more than a thousand years before Jesus. This was when Israel was approaching its great and golden days and was on course to become, albeit briefly, an influential and powerful kingdom in the ancient world. Saul was the first king of Israel, and he was anointed by the leading religious prophet, or seer, of the time, the man called Samuel.

The story of Saul's anointing is told in the first book of Samuel. It begins with a wealthy man who lives a few miles from Jerusalem who has lost his donkeys. He has a handsome son called Saul. He sends Saul with a servant to search for the valuable animals. After a day or so Saul says that maybe they should turn back before his father starts to worry, but the servant knows about Samuel the seer and suggests that they first consult him. There is a problem because it is customary to have a present for the seer and Saul has nothing to give. But the servant says he has a little silver, so they go in search of Samuel instead of going home. On the way they meet some girls at the

3 see LV.8, all; EX.29.7FF; NB.3.3; 1K.19.6; IS.61.1.
4 see MK.14.8.

well outside Shiloh and ask where Samuel is to be found. The girls give them directions and tell them to hurry because Samuel is about to start a sacrifice. They soon meet Samuel on the way to the shrine. He is expecting them because his God has told him not only that Saul is coming, but that he is to be the first king for Israel. He invites Saul to the feast following the sacrifice, seats him in the place of honour and gives him the best cut of the meat. And on the next day:

> Saul got up, and Samuel and he went outside together. They had walked as far as the end of the town when Samuel said to Saul, 'Tell the servant to go on ahead of us, but you stand still for a moment, so that I can make known to you the word of God.' Samuel took a phial of oil and poured it on Saul's head; he then kissed him and said, 'Has not Yahweh anointed you as leader of his people Israel? You are the man who is to govern Yahweh's people and save them from the power of the enemies surrounding them . . .'
>
> 1s.9.26-10.1

Samuel goes on to tell Saul of many things that will happen in the next few days as he walks home to his father. This all is to culminate in a great sacrifice and feast at Gilgal when Samuel will announce what he has done.

All these things happen as Samuel says and Saul becomes the first king of Israel. Unluckily he is a disastrously bad king. After trying unsuccessfully to make him see the error of his ways, Samuel follows the instructions of his God and declares David to be the next king. He is anointed in a manner similar to Saul, this time with better luck for Israel.[5]

David goes on to become the greatest king in the history of Israel. He was the founder of a powerful kingdom, the leader

5 for the story of Samuel anointing David see 1s.16.1-13.

who established the glory of Israel. Many great songs of praise and lament and blessing in the scriptures are credited to David.[6] These are the psalms. Probably the best known of them all is Psalm 23, which in the King James Bible begins with the words "The Lord is my Shepherd". At the end of this psalm, the act of anointing is celebrated in its broadest sense, as a symbol of blessing and abundance and gladness:

> Thou preparest a table before me
> in the presence of mine enemies:
> thou anointest my head with oil;
> my cup runneth over.
>
> Surely goodness and mercy shall follow me
> all the days of my life:
> and I will dwell in the house of the Lord for ever.
>
> PS.23.5-6 (AV)

For more than four centuries, in spite of division and decline, the kings of Israel and later of Judaea continued in the tradition of David and Saul. Shortly after the year 600 BCE the last of the kings was dethroned and the elite of the Jews were deported to Babylon by Nebuchadnezzar. All through the Babylonian exile the hope stayed alive that one day the kingdom would be restored. Even when the captivity ended and the kingdom was not restored, the hope endured. When in 167 BCE the priest Mattathias staged his personal rebellion against the colonising Greek forces in Israel, the subsequent guerrilla war led by his sons was highly successful. This gave new life to the hope for a renewed kingdom of Israel, but during the century that followed this hope slowly died. Israel could not retain its independence, and once again the land was conquered and colonised, this time by Rome.[7]

6 The psalms come from many sources. Although they are often ascribed to him, it is doubtful that David wrote any of them.

7 for more about Mattathias see above pp.11-12.

As these devastating events unfolded during the second and first centuries BCE, new beliefs and expectations were developing within Judaism. These were redefining the hope that had sustained the Jewish people for so long, the hope that in God's good time he would restore the kingdom and raise up a great leader for the faithful people of Israel. As time passed, this concrete political desire for delivery from the Gentiles and for the return of the kingdom of Israel took on a new dimension. In some circles it was increasingly expected that under the long-awaited leader there would be a shattering war to mark the end times when the wicked would be punished and the faithful rewarded. Even the dead were expected to rise and join in this final battle. The title of the leader who would be chosen by God to rule was the "anointed one", the messiah. Such expectations were expressed in a variety of ways during the second and first centuries BCE and around the time of Jesus. Different groups within Judaism developed their own different versions of these expectations. The awaited leader was variously expected to be kingly, or priestly; a great prophet, a great warrior, a great teacher. The literature of the Dead Sea Scrolls even indicates that more than one leader may have been expected.[8] Inevitably these expectations produced many would-be messiahs; visionaries and rebels, prophets and soldiers alike. This led to the confusion of claims that lies behind a story Luke tells in the book of Acts. He records a cautionary speech on the subject of messiahs, and credits the speech to the eminent Pharisee called Gamaliel.

The story leading up to the speech is this. A few months after the crucifixion of Jesus, Peter and some of the apostles are

8 i for detailed discussion of these different expectations see Horsley, Richard A., and Hanson, John S., *Bandits, Prophets, and Messiahs: Popular Movements in the Time of Jesus*, Seabury, Minneapolis, Chicago, New York, 1985, pp.88-134.
ii for more on messianic expectations in the Dead Sea Scrolls see Vermes, G., *The Dead Sea Scrolls in English*, Penguin, London, 1962, pp. 47-51.
iii for more on apocalyptic expectations see above pp.14-15.

arrested in Jerusalem by the high priest and some of the Sadducees. Overnight "an angel of the Lord" opens the prison and they get away. The next day they go back into the temple and continue to preach about Jesus until they are arrested again and brought before the Sanhedrin. There they are accused of disobeying an order to stop such preaching, and of trying to fix the guilt for the death of Jesus on the priests and the Sanhedrin. Peter and the apostles reply that for them obedience to God comes before obedience to men and that they have every intention of continuing in the footsteps of Jesus. At this the members of the council are enraged and want the Christians put to death. This is when Gamaliel, a revered member of the Sanhedrin, intervenes:

> 'Men of Israel, be careful how you deal with these people. Some time ago there arose Theudas. He claimed to be someone important, and collected about four hundred followers; but when he was killed, all his followers scattered and that was the end of them. And there was Judas the Galilean, at the time of the census, who attracted crowds of supporters; but he was killed too, and all his followers dispersed. What I suggest, therefore, is that you leave these men alone and let them go. If this enterprise, this movement of theirs, is of human origin it will break up of its own accord; but if it does in fact come from God you will be unable to destroy them. Take care not to find yourselves fighting against God.'
>
> AC.5.36-39

It is not surprising that revolutionary leaders like Theudas and Judas the Galilean were able to gather followers around them. Given the political tensions of first century Palestine under the Romans, and the expectations for a leader to arise within Israel, this was almost inevitable. The political and religious idealogies of the Jews blended together in a way that was highly charged and, for a colonised people, very dangerous. It was in precisely this atmosphere that Jesus lived and died.

By the time Mark was writing his gospel Jesus had been dead for over thirty years and the political and religious tensions in Palestine were, if anything, worse. Any claim to be a messiah of the Jewish people was potentially inflammatory. Yet Mark, along with all the other gospels, repeatedly asserts that Jesus is Christ, and Christ, as we said at the beginning of the chapter, is the Greek equivalent of the word "messiah", and "messiah" means the anointed one. What is happening here is that as Christianity spread in the first century, a broader definition of the idea of a messiah was developing in the understanding of this new movement. This stressed that Jesus's role was to save not only the faithful people of Israel, but all mankind. Yet for Mark's congregation of Christians whose expectations were informed by Jewish traditions and scripture, the idea of the messiah as the anointed one was deeply rooted. To be the messiah Jesus should be seen to have been anointed during his lifetime. But the way Mark tells the stories of the trial of Jesus, his execution and burial, leaves no time for an anointing during Jesus's final days and hours. Even his dead body was not anointed in the usual manner of a Jewish burial because he was so hurriedly laid in the tomb. There had to be an earlier story of anointing in Jesus's lifetime.

Just how Mark came by his story of the anointing is not known. There may have been such stories about Jesus in circulation that Mark used in his own way for his own storytelling purposes. There may have been no such stories, and Mark may simply have created one to fill a need.[9] Mark provides no footnotes and his sources are unknown. But what the gospel does have is an anointing story that fills the perceived need very well.

The way Mark tells it, a few days after Jesus is reported to have entered Jerusalem, the following scene takes place. It is two

9 for more on the anointing story see Mack, Burton L., *A Myth of Innocence*, p.209. Mack says, "It was most probably composed by Mark or a colleague in his community."

days before Passover, and Jesus is at Bethany visiting the house of Simon the leper:

> . . . he was at table when a woman came in with an alabaster jar of very costly ointment, pure nard. She broke the jar and poured the ointment on his head. Some who were there said to one another indignantly, 'Why this waste of ointment? Ointment like this could have been sold for over three hundred denarii and the money given to the poor'; and they were angry with her. But Jesus said, 'Leave her alone. Why are you upsetting her? What she has done for me is a good work. You have the poor with you always, and you can be kind to them whenever you wish, but you will not always have me. She has done what she could: she has anointed my body beforehand for its burial. In truth I tell you, wherever throughout all the world the gospel is proclaimed, what she has done will be told as well, in remembrance of her.'
>
> MK.14.3-9

Matthew introduces a few changes to this story, but basically his version agrees that Jesus is anointed with expensive oil at Bethany in the house of Simon the leper by an unnamed woman.[10] Matthew specifies that it is the disciples who discuss the action with disapproval, unlike Mark who says only that "some" were indignant and murmured amongst themselves.

In Luke's gospel the story moves to an earlier period of Jesus's life and the story itself has altered. Jesus is not at Bethany but somewhere in Galilee where he has been travelling around different towns and villages. One day a Pharisee asks him in to a meal and during the meal they are interrupted:

10 see MT.26.6-13; JN.12.1-8 has a different version of the story.

> ... suddenly a woman came in, who had a bad name in the town. She had heard he was dining with the Pharisee and had brought with her an alabaster jar of ointment. She waited behind him at his feet, weeping, and her tears fell on his feet, and she wiped them away with her hair; then she covered his feet with kisses and anointed them with the ointment. When the Pharisee who had invited him saw this, he said to himself, 'If this man were a prophet, he would know who this woman is and what sort of person it is who is touching him and what a bad name she has.' Then Jesus took him up and said, 'Simon, I have something to say to you.'
>
> LK.7.37-40

When Jesus gets the Pharisee's attention he tells a short parable about two debtors. One of them owes a small sum, the other a large and when they cannot pay the lender forgives the debts. Then Jesus asks the question, "Which of them will love him more?", and the Pharisee, whose name appears to be Simon, makes the obvious answer. Then Jesus goes on to suggest that as the woman who had anointed him thought she was forgiven the most, she had made him, Jesus, the most welcome:

> 'You see this woman? I came into your house, and you poured no water over my feet, but she has poured out her tears over my feet and wiped them away with her hair. You gave me no kiss, but she has been covering my feet with kisses ever since I came in. You did not anoint my head with oil, but she has anointed my feet with ointment. For this reason I tell you that her sins, many as they are, have been forgiven her, because she has shown such great love. It is someone who is forgiven little who shows little love.'
>
> LK.7.44-47

In changing the location and the details of the story a decade or so after Mark wrote it down, Luke creates no real problem for most readers. Such stories were part of a floating tradition that shifted and changed over time. But in what immediately follows this story, Luke does create a problem. The scene changes as Jesus's walking tour continues, and Luke describes some of the people who went along:

> Now it happened that after this he made his way through towns and villages preaching and proclaiming the good news of the kingdom of God. With him went the Twelve, as well as certain women who had been cured of evil spirits and ailments: Mary surnamed the Magdalene, from whom seven demons had gone out, Joanna the wife of Herod's steward Chuza, Susanna, and many others . . .
>
> LK.8.1-3

This description of individual followers of Jesus is so near Luke's anointing story that the two are often assumed to be very closely linked, and in a very specific way. This assumed link is almost entirely spurious, but it is very colourful. It has led to many tall tales about one particular character in the story; "Mary surnamed the Magdalene".

The dubious logic goes something like this. In Luke's gospel the woman who does the anointing is described as a sinner, and Mary Magdalene is shortly thereafter described as having had seven devils within her. Tainted as they both are by sin and the devil, these women are assumed to be one and the same. In this way, the nameless, sinful woman with her pot of ointment becomes identified in popular legend as Mary Magdalene herself. Then, because sinfulness in women is so often assumed to be sexual in nature, the nameless woman described as a sinner is assumed to be a prostitute; therefore Mary Magdalene with her seven devils also becomes a prostitute.

Because of how Luke tells of the sinful woman abasing

herself, and weeping, and touching Jesus, his version of the anointing story has undeniably erotic overtones. Given that Luke then goes on to describe Mary Magdalene as a close follower of Jesus, and because she is so often identified as a reformed prostitute, there have been countless tales told of a close relationship between Jesus and Mary Magdalene. These stories combine eroticism, romance and religiosity, to produce fanciful notions about a love affair between Mary and Jesus. She becomes a reformed prostitute exuding sexual attraction and piety, and Jesus an agonized celibate who manages, usually, to resist sexual temptation. Such stories often dwell on the prolonged repentance of Mary Magdalene, and portray her as one of Jesus's most passionate followers. There are many versions of these tales; in fiction, in film, and in paintings. Male writers, producers, or artists are usually responsible, revealing in the end more about themselves and their preoccupations than about either Mary Magdalene or Jesus.

Fantasies about the relationship between Mary Magdalene and Jesus are no more than that. The perceived link between two passages in Luke's gospel that leads to the weaving of such fantasies is fragile. It receives no support either from biblical scholars or, more importantly, from the other gospels. Although Mary Magdalene appears in all four gospels, nowhere else is there the slightest indication either that she may have been a prostitute, or even that she is the character who anoints Jesus. Mark and Matthew provide no hint whatsoever as to who this woman is, and John identifies her as another person altogether.

In John's version of this story we return to Bethany, to the revivified Lazarus and his sisters.

> Six days before the Passover, Jesus went to Bethany, where Lazarus was, whom he had raised from the dead. They gave a dinner for him there; Martha waited on them and Lazarus was among those at table. Mary brought in a pound of very costly oint-

> ment, pure nard, and with it anointed the feet of Jesus, wiping them with her hair; the house was filled with the scent of the ointment. Then Judas Iscariot—one of his disciples, the man who was to betray him—said, 'Why was this ointment not sold for three hundred denarii and the money given to the poor?' He said this, not because he cared about the poor, but because he was a thief; he was in charge of the common fund and used to help himself to the contents. So Jesus said, 'Leave her alone; let her keep it for the day of my burial. You have the poor with you always, you will not always have me.'
>
> JN.12.1-8

This story is set six days before the Passover instead of Mark's two days, it is in the house of Lazarus and his sisters instead of the house of Simon the leper, and the anointing is done by Mary, the sister of Martha and Lazarus, instead of by an anonymous woman. But as in Mark and Matthew's version of the story the supper is in Bethany, Jesus is lavishly anointed, and the story concludes with the complaint about the expense of the ointment and the saying of Jesus about the needs of the poor. In John's story, there is a similarly sensual tone to that in the story told by Luke. The very odour of the ointment can be sensed, hanging heavy in the air.

It can be hard for a twentieth century western mind to credit the details of these stories; the use of such costly ointment, the lavish anointing of head and feet, the combination of sensuality and religious experience. Such things seem foreign, slightly bizarre, very strange. But it would not have seemed so to the first century audiences of the gospels. The imagery, the eroticism, the use of precious ointment would have been perfectly familiar to anyone who knew the Hebrew Scriptures, especially the Song of Songs. Originating many centuries earlier, perhaps as far back as the time of Solomon, son of the great king David, this is a poem of erotic love, an exchange between the beloved and the lover. The Song is full of opulent, sensual imagery. In the Jewish world of the first century this poem was hailed as one of the holiest parts of scripture.[11]

While the king rests in his own room
my nard yields its perfume.
My love is a sachet of myrrh
lying between my breasts.

SG.1.12-13

What is this coming up from the desert
like a column of smoke,
breathing of myrrh and frankincense
and every exotic perfume?

SG.3.6

Before the day-breeze rises,
before the shadows flee,
I shall go to the mountain of myrrh,
to the hill of frankincense.

You are wholly beautiful, my beloved . . .

SG.4.6-7

The lover in the Song of Songs is seeking the beloved; awaiting, recognising, recalling the beloved in joyous detail. Over many centuries, the Song has been variously understood as the highest form of religious devotion, as pure eroticism, as Israel awaiting a king, as the Christian church awaiting Jesus. The influence of the Song reverberates through the Hebrew Scriptures. When a king is honoured or recognised, when the hope for fulfilment for Israel is expressed, when great wealth or

11 for how the famous Rabbi Akiba praised the Song of Songs see Hastings, James(ed.); *A Dictionary of the Bible*; Charles Scribner's Sons; New York; 1902; vol.4; p.589.

honour is heaped on a leader, the rich language and images of the Song are echoed.[12]

This influence of the Song within the scriptures is indirect. It is impossible to prove in any categoric fashion. No clear line of straightforward literary dependence can be solemnly traced from book to book, from story to story, leading back to the Song. This is impossible, given that the date of composition of the Song is unknown. Many scholars and other readers of the Bible may disagree with the very idea that the Song can be heard, however faintly, in other writings. This highlights the point we raised in our introduction, that the perception of links amongst different biblical writings is not a precise art, with clearcut rights and wrongs governing procedure. There is room for poetic interpretation and for personal preferences, just as there is room for discussion and for disagreement.

For us, echoes of the Song can be heard, sometimes very faintly and briefly, not only within the Hebrew Scriptures, but also in the New Testament. For example in Matthew's gospel, when the child Jesus is sought by the three sages bearing costly gifts, words and images of the Song of Songs are distantly recalled. In John's gospel, after the death of Jesus, Mary of Magdala comes to the tomb where he is buried and she laments because she does not find him, just as in the Song the lover finds herself alone, calling out: "I sought but could not find him."[13] In all the gospels, the very mention of costly ointment being used to anoint Jesus recalls the exotic ointments and riches so lavishly described in the Song, and this becomes even clearer in Luke and John when the story is more sensual in tone and language.

This sensuality is part of the language in the anointing stories. It is part of the process of declaration and recognition implicit in the anointings. It is part of how the gospels reveal,

12 for example see EX.30.22- 32; PS.45.7-8 & 14-15 or EZK.16.10-14. for the influence of the Song in the gospels see MT.26.6-12; MK.14.3-9; LK.7.37-40 or JN.12.1-6; cp.MT.2.11; MK.16.1; LK.23 56 or JN.19.39-40.

13 see SG.5.6; CP JN.20.13; also see below pp.258-259.

directly and indirectly, their beliefs about Jesus. They declare he is the "anointed one" which means the Christ, the leader who is to come and rescue mankind, the one they have been desiring and awaiting so long. They declare this in a way that is rich and strange; in language that calls to mind earlier recognitions, earlier desires, earlier anointings. They declare this in a way that is utterly appropriate to their own time, and to their own frame of reference.

CHAPTER EIGHT

Supper

In Mark's gospel the story of the anointing of Jesus during a meal at Bethany is followed very shortly by the description of another meal, this time in Jerusalem. This is one of the best known suppers ever described in any literature. According to Mark, it takes place at the time of the feast of the Passover, the time of the eating of unleavened bread.

> On the first day of Unleavened Bread, when the Passover lamb was sacrificed, his disciples said to him, 'Where do you want us to go and make the preparations for you to eat the Passover?'
>
> MK.14.12

Jesus sends his followers into the city where they "prepared the Passover". This was a procedure that followed ancient precedents.

The Passover meal is a Jewish tradition that can be traced back to the book of Exodus. This is one of the books of the Torah, which means the Law, in the Hebrew Scriptures. It is a record of stories from the hazy beginnings of the history of the Jewish people. Exodus tells of the sojourn of the Israelites in Egypt, and how Moses leads them back to the promised land of Canaan. "Let my people go" is the cry of Moses to the Pharaoh of Egypt, and when the Pharaoh does not agree, the God of Moses strikes Egypt with nine plagues. Still the Pharaoh does not agree to free the children of Israel, so the God of Israel arranges for one final disaster, that the first-born of Egypt shall all die. On a specified night the angel of death will pass through Egypt. In order that the Israelites be spared, God instructs Moses to tell them all to slaughter a special animal and to follow these detailed instructions:

> '. . . Some of the blood must then be taken and put on both door-posts and the lintel of the houses where it is eaten. That night, the flesh must be eaten, roasted over the fire; it must be eaten with unleavened bread and bitter herbs. . . . . That night, I shall go through Egypt and strike down all the first-born in Egypt, man and beast alike. . . . The blood will be a sign for you on the houses where you are. When I see the blood I shall pass over you, and you will escape the destructive plague when I strike Egypt. This day must be commemorated by you, and you must keep it as a feast in Yahweh's honour. You must keep it as a feast-day for all generations; this is a decree for all time.
>
> EX.12.7-14

So the avenging angel passes over their houses and the blood of the sacrificed animals saves the Israelites, but as for the rest "there was great wailing in Egypt, for there was not a house without its dead". And so the Pharaoh asks Moses to take the Israelites away to their own land. They go, leaving in such a hurry that their bread had no time to rise. This part of the story of the exodus from Egypt has shaped the Passover sacrifice and celebration ever since.

The animals sacrificed at Passover were lambs, and by the time of Jesus these "paschal lambs" were slain in their thousands at the temple in Jerusalem. They were then eaten with unleavened bread and bitter herbs at the evening meal. After the temple was destroyed in 70 CE the massive annual slaughter of the lambs was discontinued, but to this day a symbolic shank of lamb appears on the table at Passover meals in Jewish homes, along with the unleavened bread and the bitter herbs.

When Jesus and his disciples gather for their Passover supper this is the annual commemoration of the liberation of the Jewish people from Egypt. It is a time of celebration, with pilgrims crowding into Jerusalem for the temple sacrifices and subsequent feasting. But according to Mark, when the disciples all gather with Jesus for their meal, he strikes a cautionary note right away:

> When evening came he arrived with the Twelve. And while they were at table eating, Jesus said, 'In truth I tell you, one of you is about to betray me, one of you *eating with me*'. They were distressed and said to him, one after another, 'Not me, surely?' He said to them, 'It is one of the Twelve, one who is dipping into the same dish with me . . .'
>
> MK.14.17-20

In all four gospels Jesus is reported saying words to the effect that the person who will betray him is there with him at the same table, and that all the others will desert him. The gospels insist on this. It must be so, the story of Jesus as Messiah is bound to be told in such terms, because these patterns of treachery and cowardice are very strong within the scriptures. The gospel writers are showing Jesus as the continuation and the culmination of a rich tradition of scriptural stories and themes. In doing this they emphasise his status and his identity, particularly in relation to the great king David, for one of the expectations about the coming Messiah was that he would be the kingly successor of David.

In many different texts David grieves over the treatment he has received at the hands of cowardly and treacherous friends. Several well known laments attributed to David in the psalms are reflected in the accounts of Jesus's betrayal at the final supper:

Even my trusted friend on whom I relied,
who shared my table, takes advantage of me.

PS.41.9[1]

I have no more place in their hearts than a corpse,
or something lost.
All I hear is slander
—terror wherever I turn—
as they plot together against me,
scheming to take my life.

PS.31.12-13

Were it an enemy who insulted me,
that I could bear;
if an opponent pitted himself against me,
I could turn away from him.

But you, a person of my own rank,
a comrade and dear friend,
to whom I was bound by intimate friendship
in the house of God!

PS.55.12-14

Although the connection between King David and these psalms is far from clear, some of them do seem to relate to experiences of his that are chronicled in other places in the scriptures. It is doubtful that he composed the psalms himself. The authorship of all the psalms is a matter of debate amongst scholars. Although many of them are headed "of David", and some copies of the psalter have been entitled in an all-embracing fashion "The Psalms of David", many of them were probably written by David's court poets and musicians after his death. Some may even have been written centuries later, and some may be compilations created from fragments of earlier lyrics. The

1 for more on Psalm 41 see below, pp.129, 140.

psalms therefore represent the voices of many unknown writers over a long period of time.[2] They alternately celebrate and lament the fate of Israel, and the fate of Israel's leaders.

In Mark's gospel, after Jesus's words about betrayal, the supper continues:

> And as they were eating he took bread, and when he had said the blessing he broke it and gave it to them. 'Take it,' he said, 'this is my body.' Then he took a cup, and when he had given thanks he handed it to them, and all drank from it, and he said to them, 'This is my blood, the blood of the covenant, poured out for many . . .'
>
> MK.14.22-24 [3]

Matthew's description of this supper is essentially the same as Mark's, but in Luke's report Jesus passes the wine twice:

> Then, taking a cup, he gave thanks and said, 'Take this and share it among you, because from now on, I tell you, I shall never again drink wine until the kingdom of God comes.' Then he took bread, and when he had given thanks, he broke it and gave it to them, saying, 'This is my body given for you; do this in remembrance of me.' He did the same with the cup after supper, and said, 'This cup is the new covenant in my blood poured out for you.'
>
> LK.22.17-20

In Luke and in Matthew and Mark, Jesus is consistently quoted referring to "the covenant" or "blood of the covenant". This looks back to the book Exodus, to an agreement between

2 for more on David and the psalms see above pp.85-86, also below, pp.140-141, 200-201.
3 see also MT.26.26-28.

Moses and his people and their God. Moses is the intermediary between God and the Israelites, and it is to Moses that the details of the covenant are revealed.

> Moses then went up to God, and Yahweh called to him from the mountain, saying, 'Say this to the House of Jacob! Tell the Israelites, "You have seen for yourselves what I did with the Egyptians and how I carried you away on eagle's wings and brought you to me. So now, if you are really prepared to obey me and keep my covenant, you, out of all peoples, shall be my personal possession, for the whole world is mine. For me you shall be a kingdom of priests, a holy nation." Those are the words you are to say to the Israelites.' So Moses went and summoned the people's elders and acquainted them with everything that Yahweh had bidden him, and the people all replied with one accord, 'Whatever Yahweh has said, we will do.' Moses then reported to Yahweh what the people had said.
>
> EX.19.3-8

This covenant is revealed to Moses on Mount Sinai in a dense cloud of smoke, with the God of Israel speaking in or through peals of thunder. The ten commandments are part of this covenant, and they are passed on by Moses to the people standing at the base of the mountain:

> Seeing the thunder pealing, the lightning flashing, the trumpet blasting and the mountain smoking, the people were all terrified and kept their distance. 'Speak to us yourself,' they said to Moses, 'and we will obey; but do not let God speak to us, or we shall die.' Moses said to the people, 'Do not be afraid; God has come to test you, so that your fear of him, being always in your mind, may keep you from

> sinning'. So the people kept their distance while
> Moses approached the dark cloud where God was.
>
> EX.20.18-21[4]

The covenant between God and the Israelites then has to be ratified:

> Moses put all Yahweh's words into writing, and early next morning he built an altar at the foot of the mountain, with twelve standing-stones for the twelve tribes of Israel. Then he sent certain young Israelites to offer burnt offerings and sacrifice bullocks to Yahweh as communion sacrifices. Moses then took half the blood and put it into basins, and the other half he sprinkled on the altar. Then, taking the Book of the Covenant, he read it to the listening people, who then said 'We shall do everything that Yahweh has said; we shall obey.' Moses then took the blood and sprinkled it over the people, saying, 'This is the blood of the covenant which Yahweh has made with you, entailing all these stipulations.'
>
> EX.24.4-8

In this way the people of Israel are marked with sacrificial blood as they enter into an agreement with their God, an agreement sealed with this blood.

When they were writing their accounts of the last supper, the gospel writers knew what had happened to Jesus. They knew that his blood had been shed when he was crucified. They did not believe that this had happened randomly, or in vain. They believed that Jesus's blood was shed as the culmination of a long tradition of sacrificial blood, that it was shed to save his followers and to mark them as a preferred people who would be spared and exalted when Jesus returned in glory. His blood was to them the symbol of a "new covenant", a new agreement

4 for more on this cloud see pp.255-256, 256 footnote #13.

between God and humanity that would usher in a new age. As with the covenant when Moses negotiated directly with God,[5] so too there was an intermediary between God and his people for this new covenant. According to the gospels, this was Jesus, at once mediator and victim.

Stories of blood sacrifices go back much further in the scriptures than the story of the covenant ratified on Mount Sinai. Long before the time of Moses, at the very limits of what could be called recorded history, are the stories of Abraham. He is the mythic founder of the dynasty that became the twelve tribes of Israel. One of the most famous stories about Abraham tells how he believes his God requires him to sacrifice Isaac, his only son. With heavy heart he sets out to do so::

> Isaac spoke to his father Abraham. 'Father?', he said. 'Yes, my son,' he replied. 'Look,' he said 'here are the fire and the wood, but where is the lamb for the burnt offering?' Abraham replied, 'My son, God himself will provide the lamb for the burnt offering.' And the two of them went on together. When they arrived at the place which God had indicated to him, Abraham built an altar there, and arranged the wood. Then he bound his son and put him on the altar on top of the wood. Abraham stretched out his hand and took the knife to kill his son.
>
> GN.22.7-10

At that point, the angel of the Lord calls out to Abraham telling him to spare the boy and to sacrifice instead a ram that is caught by its horns in a nearby bush. This is the point in the Hebrew Scriptures where it is made clear that animal sacrifice is sufficient, and that human sacrifice is not acceptable to the God of Israel. Over the centuries this set the Hebrew people apart from their neighbours who regularly persisted in human sacrifice.

5 for the prior covenant with Abraham see GN.15.18 & GN.17.2-21.

The destruction of the temple in 70 CE led to a different, and far more abrupt change of religious practice. Until then, daily animal sacrifice at the temple had been an integral part of the Jewish religion. At the time of festivals, especially at Passover, the number of animals slaughtered almost defies belief. While the temple was crammed with pilgrims, hundreds of thousands of lambs were killed, and the scene was transformed into something like an abbatoir. The courtyards of the temple ran with the blood of the lambs.[6] About the time Mark was writing his gospel this practice ceased. The temple was completely destroyed and the Jewish practice of animal sacrifice was destroyed with it, never to be resumed.

Christians were affected by this change. They were, after all, an offspring sect of the Jewish religion. The way the gospel writers describe Jesus at the last supper he appears as a kind of sacrificial alternative. All four gospel writers show a Jesus who is aware of his coming death and who comments on his role as a sacrificial victim whose blood will be shed for the good of all. This is the familiar language of animal sacrifices atoning for the sins of the people of Israel, although here it is used in a different way.

Mark and Matthew and Luke all show Jesus establishing a ritual in which wine and bread are shared, and through this ritual he explains his role. He presents the wine and bread at a Passover meal as if they are his own blood and body, a sacrifice representing a new religious covenant between God and humanity, a covenant sealed with blood and sacrifice just as the old one was. This explanation was already familiar in Christian circles by the time Mark was writing. Much earlier in the first century, Paul was using similar sacrificial language[7] and was referring to the blood of Jesus as the blood of "the new covenant".

In the New Testament there are six accounts of a last supper of Jesus and his followers. Four of these appear in the four

6 Leading up to 70 CE, Josephus tells of three million Passover pilgrims in one year, and in another year he extrapolates 255,600 sacrificial animals into 2,700,200 pilgrims. See Josephus, *The Jewish War*, p.150 and p.372.

7 see 1CO.11.25; RM.3.21-26.

gospels, with John telling a very different story from the others. Paul refers to the last supper twice. These are the earliest accounts of the Christian ritual that is now variously termed the communion, the mass, the eucharist, or the Lord's supper. Many tortuous complexities have grown up around this Christian practice, but at its simplest this is a symbolic meal recalling Jesus's last supper with his followers.

The practice goes back to the very beginnings of Christianity. The book of Acts reports that shortly after the death of Jesus, his followers went regularly to the temple and "met in their houses for the breaking of bread"[8], which seems to mean sharing meals. Some years later when the disciples were known as Christians they continued to share meals when they met.

In Paul's first letter to Corinth, written about the year 56 CE, two chapters are given over to the behaviour of the church at its regular communal meals. Such meals were normal social gatherings, and Paul is concerned that at them the assembly should "eat the Lord's supper"[9] with propriety. Twice he refers specifically to the practice of breaking bread and sharing the cup of wine. Each of these passages resembles the descriptions of the last supper in the gospels. The first is brief:

> The blessing-cup, which we bless, is it not a sharing in the blood of Christ; and the loaf of bread which we break,is it not a sharing in the body of Christ?
>
> 1CO.10.16

The second gives more detail:

> For the tradition I received from the Lord and also handed on to you is that on the night he was betrayed, the Lord Jesus took some bread, and after he had given thanks, he broke it, and he said, 'This is my

8 see AC.5.46; cp. AC.4.42.
9 see 1CO.11.20 (AV)

> body, which is for you; do this in remembrance of me.' And in the same way, with the cup after supper, saying, 'This cup is the new covenant in my blood. Whenever you drink it, do this as a memorial of me. Whenever you eat this bread, then, and drink this cup, you are proclaiming the Lord's death until he comes . . .'
>
> 1CO.11.23-26

Forty years or so after Paul was writing about the last supper, John wrote his gospel account of the final meal. It is very different from anything found in the other gospels or in Paul's writings.

> They were at supper, and the devil had already put it into the mind of Judas Iscariot son of Simon, to betray him. Jesus . . . got up from table, removed his outer garments and, taking a towel, wrapped it round his waist; he then poured water into a basin and began to wash the disciples' feet and to wipe them with the towel he was wearing.
>
> He came to Simon Peter, who said to him, 'Lord, are you going to wash my feet?' Jesus answered, 'At the moment you do not know what I am doing, but later you will understand.' 'Never!' said Peter, 'You shall never wash my feet.' Jesus replied, 'If I do not wash you, you can have no share with me.' Simon Peter said, 'Well then, Lord, not only my feet, but my hands and my head as well.' Jesus said, 'No one who has had a bath needs washing, such a person is clean all over. You too are clean . . .'
>
> JN.13.2-10

John's story of the washing of feet calls to mind earlier footwashing stories from the Hebrew Scriptures. Probably the best known example is in the book of Genesis, when the patriarch Abraham is visited by his God, who appears to him in the guise of three strangers:

> Yahweh appeared to him at the Oak of Mamre while he was sitting by the entrance of the tent during the hottest part of the day. He looked up, and there he saw three men standing near him. As soon as he saw them he ran from the entrance of the tent to greet them, and bowed to the ground. 'My lord,' he said 'if I find favour with you, please do not pass your servant by. Let me have a little water brought, and you can wash your feet and have a rest under the tree. Let me fetch a little bread and you can refresh yourselves before going further, now that you have come in your servant's direction.'
>
> GN.18.1-5 [10]

Footwashing is consistently described in the scriptures as an act of hospitality and humility. In John's gospel Peter is appalled when Jesus offers to humble himself by washing Peter's feet, and he protests vehemently. Jesus then explains to Peter what this footwashing means and why it is necessary.

> '. . . you do not know what I am doing, but later you will understand . . .'
> 'If I do not wash you, you can have no share with me.' . . .
> 'No one who has had a bath needs washing, such a person is clean all over. You too are clean . . .'
>
> JN.13.7-11

John's story continues with Jesus returning to the table and going on with his teaching. There is a break for the story of

10 i for more on GN.18.1-5 see below p.243.
ii for more footwashing stories see GN.19.2; GN.24.32; and 1S.25.41.

Judas's betrayal, and this is followed by nearly forty biblical verses of what is essentially a long sermon attributed to Jesus. It takes up all of Chapter 14 of John's gospel and closes with Jesus saying "Come now, let us go".

In this section of John's gospel another reality may lie behind the narrative. This is the early church practice of baptism. The word baptism, taken from the Greek, means "to dip" or "to wash", and baptism was practised by early Christians as an initiation into the church. There is no happy consensus amongst scholars or commentators about this, but there is a tradition supporting the idea that John's description of the footwashing is an oblique account of initiation into the church through a ritual ceremony of washing. If this is so, Jesus's words to Peter and his subsequent sermon could reflect the words of early church leaders at such baptisms.[11]

After the footwashing and the sermon in Chapter 14, Jesus continues to speak to his disciples at even greater length, though on different themes throughout Chapters 15 and 16 of the gospel. Then John moves directly into the story of the arrest of Jesus. Nowhere does he tell of the "eucharistic" supper with its sacrifical overtones and its references to the covenant. Yet in a different manner, John's gospel strongly emphasises Jesus's role as an innocent sacrificial victim.

At the beginning of the gospel as soon as the the prologue is finished there is a short section about John the Baptist who is there specifically to recognise and introduce Jesus. This is done in the words "Look, there is the lamb of God that takes away the sin of the world . . . ," a phrase still repeated in Christian songs and prayers.[12] Later in his gospel John emphasises the sacrificial role of Jesus even further:

11 for a discussion of this possibility see: Brown, Raymond E.; *The Gospel According to John*, Vol.2, (xiii–xxi), in the series *The Anchor Bible*; Doubleday; New York.; 1970, see pages 564 – 568.

12 see JN.1.29

'. . . I am the living bread which has come down from heaven.
Anyone who eats this bread will live for ever;
and the bread that I shall give
is my flesh, for the life of the world.'

JN.6.51

This passage calls to mind not only the sharing of the bread at the last supper, but another story from the book of Exodus. This is a story of miraculous food. The children of Israel are starving as they make their way out of Egypt. The God of Moses sees their suffering and says: "I shall rain down bread for you from the heavens". And so it is:

"... next morning there was a layer of dew all round the camp. When the layer of dew lifted, there on the surface of the desert was something fine and granular, as fine as hoarfrost on the ground. As soon as the Israelites saw this, they said to one another, 'What is that?' not knowing what it was. 'That,' Moses told them, 'is the food which Yahweh has given you to eat . . .'

The House of Israel named it 'manna'. It was like coriander seed; it was white and its taste was like that of wafers made with honey.

EX.16.13-15,31

For forty years, according to the book of Exodus, this manna from heaven feeds the children of Israel, sustaining them until they reach the promised land.

In John's gospel Jesus is identified as the food that will sustain life, as well as the sacrifice made "for the life of the world". This is implied in the other gospels, and also in the writings of Paul. The definition of Jesus as sustenance and sacrifice is expressed most vividly in the descriptions of the last supper. The roots of this definition lie deep within the Hebrew Scriptures.

CHAPTER NINE

Gethsemane

According to both Mark and Matthew, after the final supper Jesus and his followers leave for the Mount of Olives and they find themselves at a place called Gethsemane:

> They came to a plot of land called Gethsemane, and he said to his disciples, 'Stay here while I pray.' Then he took Peter and James and John with him. And he began to feel terror and anguish. And he said to them, 'My soul is sorrowful to the point of death. Wait here, and stay awake.' And going on a little further he threw himself on the ground and prayed that, if it were possible, this hour might pass him by.
>
> MK.14:32-35

The way the story is told by Mark it is now late evening, and it is clear that a crisis is pending. Jesus has predicted that his hour has come and that he will shortly be betrayed. Matthew follows Mark's story very closely, but Luke is somewhat different. He does not name a place called Gethsemane, saying only that Jesus and his followers go "as usual" to a place on the Mount of Olives. Luke then goes into far more detail in his description of Jesus's agony that night:

> When they reached the place he said to them, 'Pray not to be put to the test'. Then he withdrew

> from them, about a stone's throw away, and knelt down and prayed. 'Father,' he said, 'if you are willing, take this cup away from me. Nevertheless, let your will be done, not mine.' Then an angel appeared to him, coming from heaven to give him strength. In his anguish he prayed even more earnestly, and his sweat fell to the ground like great drops of blood.
>
> LK.22.40-44

John tells a very different story. He mentions nothing of Jesus being in agony as he prays, but moves swiftly ahead with the story of the arrest of Jesus. More or less in passing, he mentions the location:

> . . . Jesus left with his disciples and crossed the Kidron valley where there was a garden into which he went with his disciples. Judas the traitor knew the place also, since Jesus had often met his disciples there, so Judas brought the cohort to this place together with guards sent by the chief priests and the Pharisees, all with lanterns and torches and weapons.
>
> JN.18.1-3

What all the gospel writers have in common here is that after the final meal, they move Jesus to a place outside Jerusalem. Mark, Matthew and Luke agree this is near or on the Mount of Olives. John places it across the Kidron valley, and he specifies that it is a "garden". The idea of a garden clearly exerts strong appeal because the place very quickly became known in Christian circles as the "garden of Gethsemane". The garden has strong precedents, going back to the very beginning:

> Yahweh God planted a garden in Eden, which is in the east, and there he put the man he had fashioned. From the soil, Yahweh God caused to grow every kind of tree, enticing to look at and good to eat, with the tree of life in the middle of the garden,

> and the tree of the knowledge of good and evil . . .
> Yahweh God took the man and settled him in the garden of Eden to cultivate and take care of it.
>
> GN.2.8-9,15

This was the original garden that has come to be known as the paradise of Adam and Eve. The word "paradise" is from the Persian and means "enclosed garden".

The significance of the idea of a garden is easy to understand, particularly in a hot and dry climate where gardens hold a special charm as places of refuge and shelter, with trees and water and shade. In the Hebrew Scriptures gardens are protected places, enclosed, set apart and beautiful. Yet once gardens are attained or reached, they are often lost or threatened. The protected enclosure of the garden of Eden was fated not to last:

> The man and his wife heard the sound of Yahweh God walking in the garden in the cool of the day, and they hid from Yahweh God among the trees of the garden. But Yahweh God called to the man. 'Where are you?' he asked. 'I heard the sound of you in the garden,' he replied. 'I was afraid because I was naked, so I hid.' 'Who told you that you were naked?' he asked. 'Have you been eating from the tree I forbade you to eat?'
>
> GN.3.8-11

Adam and Eve are banished from the garden of Eden and the way back is barred forever, guarded by an angel with a flaming sword. God condemns humanity to a harsh fate outside the garden:

> '. . . Accursed be the soil because of you!
> Painfully will you get your food from it
> as long as you live.

It will yield you brambles and thistles,
as you eat the produce of the land.
By the sweat of your face
will you earn your food,
until you return to the ground,
as you were taken from it.
For dust you are
and to dust you shall return.'

GN.3.17-19

Other gardens are celebrated in the Hebrew Scriptures, notably in the Song of Songs, a poem perhaps as old as the story of the garden of Eden. Whether the Song is taken as a poem of erotic love or as an allegory of the love of God for the people of Israel, the images of the garden in the Song are amongst the most vivid in the poem. When the two lovers find each other in the garden, there is beauty, and there is safety:

She is a garden enclosed,
my sister, my promised bride;
a garden enclosed,
a sealed fountain.
Your shoots form an orchard of pomegranate trees,
bearing most exquisite fruit:
nard and saffron,
calamus and cinnamon,
with all the incense-bearing trees;
myrrh and aloes,
with the subtlest odours.
Fountain of the garden,
well of living water,
streams flowing down from Lebanon!

Awake, north wind,
come, wind of the south!
Breathe over my garden,

to spread its sweet smell around.
Let my love come into his garden.
let him taste its most exquisite fruits.

SG.4.12-16

Later in the Song, this harmony is shattered when the lovers cannot find each other:

I opened to my love,
but he had turned and gone.
My soul failed at his flight,
I sought but could not find him,
I called, but he did not answer.

The watchmen met me,
those who go on their rounds in the city.
They beat me, they wounded me,
they took my cloak away from me:
those guardians of the ramparts!

SG.5.6-7

In a late addition to the book of Daniel, written less than two hundred years before the time of Jesus, there is another enclosed and protected garden.[1] It belongs to the husband of Susanna, and in this garden she comes to grief. She is a virtuous and innocent woman, married to one Joakim, a rich Jew living in Babylon. Every day she walks in the safety of the garden but because she is so beautiful she is spied upon by two elders of the Jewish community. She is unaware of this:

. . . one day Susanna came as usual, accompanied
only by two young maidservants. The day was hot

1 The book of Daniel has two distinct parts. One is part of the Hebrew Scriptures, and the other including the story of Susanna is part of the Apocrypha. For a brief discussion of Daniel see NJB pp.1177-1179.

> and she wanted to bathe in the garden. There was no one about except the two elders, spying on her from their hiding place. She said to the servants, 'Bring me some oil and balsam and shut the garden door while I bathe'.
>
> DN.13.15-17

This proves to be Susanna's undoing. The two elders emerge from hiding and try to rape her. When she resists they say that unless she co-operates they will tell the whole world that they found her making love to a young man. She resists despite this threat, and the two elders tell their false story. A meeting is held to decide what to do and the two elders condemn Susanna as an adulteress, demanding that she be put to death:

> Since they were elders of the people and judges, the assembly accepted their word: Susanna was condemned to death. She cried out as loud as she could, 'Eternal God, you know all secrets and everything before it happens; you know that they have given false evidence against me. And now I must die, innocent as I am of everything their malice has invented against me!'
>
> DN.13.41-43

At this point the young Daniel comes to the rescue and by dint of some fairly straightforward detective work he manages to prove that Susanna is innocent. So the two elders are put to death instead of her. Daniel becomes a hero, and nothing more is heard of Susanna following this story of treachery in a garden.

The theme of innocent suffering dominates the stories of Jesus in the garden. He is facing what the gospel writers know will be great humiliation and a disgraceful death. They portray him as an innocent man aware of all this in advance. In the stories of the last supper, Jesus is shown to be aware that soon he must suffer for the good of all.

This is an ancient religious concept, that one being should suffer or be made to suffer for all. In the book of Leviticus in the Hebrew Scriptures it finds early expression in the story of the scapegoat. This describes the widespread folk custom of diverting the sins of a community onto an animal and then driving this animal away. The way the story is told in Leviticus, an atoning sacrifice is required of Aaron, the brother of Moses, because his sons have offended God. A number of animals are required:

> '. . . From the community of Israelites he will receive two he-goats for a sacrifice for sin and a ram for a burnt offering. After offering the bull as a sacrifice for his own sin and performing the rite of expiation for himself and his family, he will take the two he-goats and place them before Yahweh at the entrance to the Tent of Meeting. Aaron will then draw lots over the two goats, one lot to be for Yahweh and the other lot for Azazel. Aaron will then take the goat on which the lot "For Yahweh" has fallen, and offer it as a sacrifice for sin. But the goat on which the lot "For Azazel" has fallen, will be placed alive before Yahweh, for the rite of expiation to be performed with it, and for it then to be sent to Azazel in the desert . . .'
>
> LV.16.5-10

In ancient Hebrew belief this Azazel was a demon of the desert. After the goat of Yahweh is killed and its blood scattered on the altar in ceremonial fashion, Azazel's goat is brought out:

> '. . . Aaron will then lay both his hands on its head and over it confess all the guilt of the Israelites, all their acts of rebellion and all their sins. Having thus laid them on the goat's head, he will send it out into the desert under the charge of a man waiting ready,

and the goat will bear all their guilt away into some desolate place . . .'

LV.16.21-22

Humans also could take on this role of the sacrificial creature who takes on the sins of the people. In the Hebrew Scriptures this can be seen in Psalm 88. The history of this psalm is very hazy, so different interpretations and theories flourish accordingly. One of the more colourful theories has been put forward by Professor Michael Goulder. He understands Psalm 88 as the cry of lament of a drowning priest or shaman, or seer.[2]

This theory is based on the idea that some time after the Hebrews conquered the city of Dan near the source of the river Jordan in about the 11th century BCE, there was trouble with the crops. Such difficulties were not uncommon, and at this stage the Hebrews were desert nomads, unaccustomed to farming and its problems. They discovered that the Canaanites they had defeated had a custom to ensure good harvests year after year. It was a ceremony in which the sins of the community were put on the head of a shaman and the shaman was then buried alive, along with all offenses against the gods. The easiest place to bury him was at a point where a creek disappeared into the ground. This would appease the gods, and the crops could be expected to improve.

This custom presented the Hebrews with a problem, for they had a taboo against human sacrifice of any sort. So an ingenious solution was reached. Someone had the bright idea of temporarily burying the shaman in the underground creek and then after a decent interval fishing him out at least half alive.

If this supposition is anywhere near correct Psalm 88 started as the lament of one of the shamans who was pulled out of the water and revived. The lyric is now greatly overlaid from much copying and editing, but enough remains to express the terror of the innocent victim who has done no violence to anyone:

2 for more on PS.88 see Goulder, M.D., *The Psalms of the Sons of Korah*, JSOT Press, Sheffield, 1982; ch.VII; pp.195-210.

Yahweh, God of my salvation,
when I cry out to you in the night,
may my prayer reach your presence,
hear my cry for help.

For I am filled with misery,
my life is on the brink of Sheol;
already numbered among those who sink into oblivion,
I am as one bereft of strength,
left alone among the dead,
like the slaughtered lying in the grave,
whom you remember no more,
cut off as they are from your protection.

You have plunged me to the bottom of the grave,
in the darkness, in the depths;
weighted down by your anger,
kept low by your waves.

PS.88.1-7

In Psalm 69 there is a similar tone of terror, in the darkness and in the depths. According to another theory of Michael Goulder, the scapegoat here is none other than David the king who seems to be drowning in a dark pit: [3]

Save me, God, for the waters
    have closed in on my very being.

I am sinking in the deepest swamp
    and there is no firm ground.

I have stepped into deep water
    and the waves are washing over me.

3 i for more on PS.69 see Goulder, M.D., *The Prayers of David*, JSOT Press, Sheffield, 1990; ch.9; pp.217-229.
ii also see below pp.199-201.

I am exhausted with calling out, my throat is hoarse,
    my eyes are worn out with searching for my God.

. . . .

Rescue me from the mire before I sink in;
    so I shall be saved from those who hate me,
    from the watery depths.
Let not the waves wash over me,
    nor the deep swallow me up,
nor the pit close its mouth on me.

PS.69.1-3, 14-15

Despite any or all theories about their origins, little can be known definitely about the background of either Psalm 69 or Psalm 88. If the plight of the distraught king and the unfortunate shaman lie behind these psalms, this had probably faded from memory long before the gospels were written. These powerful laments were by then incorporated into the larger body of psalms in the Hebrew scriptures. The strength of their outcry of despair long outlived any knowledge of their background.

These laments were well known to the gospel writers, as were all the psalms. They were part of their very thought and language. The psalms are probably the most important influence on the gospel writers in how they describe the arrest, trial and crucifixion of Jesus. Time and again the psalms provide the form and content, detail and tone of the gospel stories. This means that in Gethsemane, the nature of Jesus's outcry to his God is entirely familiar:

Yahweh, hear my prayer,
let my cry for help reach you.
Do not turn away your face from me
when I am in trouble . . .

PS.102.1-2

Take pity on me, God, take pity on me,
for in you I take refuge,
in the shadow of your wings I take refuge,
until the destruction is past.

PS.57.1

From the depths I call to you, Yahweh:
    Lord, hear my cry.
Listen attentively
    to the sound of my pleading! . . .

I rely, my whole being relies,
    Yahweh, on your promise.
My whole being hopes in the Lord,
    more than watchmen for daybreak . . .

PS.130.1-2, 5-6

My God, my God, why have you forsaken me?
The words of my groaning do nothing to save me.
My God, I call by day but you do not answer,
at night, but I find no respite.

PS.22.1-2

The outcry of more than one innocent sufferer can be heard here. The psalms are a collection of lyrics from many sources, written over several centuries. Their influence is extraordinary, and their effect far-reaching.

Within the Hebrew Scriptures, from one book to another, the layers of text reflect each other and seem often to repeat each other, strangely, like a hall of mirrors. Some reflections are clear, others are dim; some are easy to trace to their source, others are confusing. The passage below comes from the book of Job, that archetypal sufferer of the Hebrew Scriptures:

And now the life in me trickles away,
    days of grief have gripped me.

At night-time sickness saps my bones
I am gnawed by wounds that never sleep . . .

. . . He has thrown me into the mud;
I am no more than dust and ashes.

I cry to you, and you give me no answer;
I stand before you, but you take no notice.
You have grown cruel to me,
and your strong hand torments me unmercifully.

JB. 30.16–21

Job's words often seem to reflect those of the psalmists. He is the most outstanding and the most innocent of all sufferers in the Hebrew Scriptures. Although he is a faithful and good servant of God, devastating misfortunes are heaped upon him. When the first round of these has ended Job has lost everything; his family, his possessions, his home, his servants. His reaction to this is acceptance, expressed in a famous blessing. The best known English version of this blessing is in the King James Bible:

Then Job arose, and rent his mantle, and shaved his head, and fell down upon the ground, and worshipped,
And said, Naked came I out of my mother's womb, and naked shall I return thither: the Lord gave, and the Lord hath taken away; blessed be the name of the Lord.

JB.1.20–21 (AV)

These words echo in Gethsemane when Jesus, like Job, falls to the ground to pray. He says "For you everything is possible. Take this cup away from me. But let it be as you, not I, would have it."[4]

The similarities between the story of Gethsemane and the

4 see MK.14.36.

story of Job do not stop there. Job too faces his disasters in the company of friends:

> The news of all the disasters that had fallen on Job came to the ears of three of his friends. Each of them set out from home—Eliphaz of Teman, Bildad of Shuah, and Zophar of Naamath—and by common consent they decided to go and offer him sympathy and consolation. Looking at him from a distance, they could not recognise him; they wept aloud and tore their robes and threw dust over their heads. They sat there on the ground beside him for seven days and seven nights. To Job they spoke never a word, for they saw how much he was suffering.
>
> JB.2.11-13

This silent vigil of Job's three friends is their shining moment. For the next thirty-odd chapters they do nothing but talk, offering Job a great deal of gratuitous and unhelpful advice. But in their long vigil they are true friends, silently sharing his affliction and sorrow.

In Gethsemane, Jesus's friends do not share his vigil. They fall asleep. "My soul is sorrowful to the point of death", says Jesus as he begins his night of prayer in Mark's gospel. "Wait here and stay awake."

> He came back and found them sleeping, and he said to Peter, 'Simon, are you asleep? Had you not the strength to stay awake one hour? Stay awake and pray not to be put to the test. The spirit is willing enough, but human nature is weak.' Again he went away and prayed, saying the same words. And once more he came back and found them sleeping, their eyes were so heavy; and they could find no answer for him. He came back a third time and said to them,

'You can sleep on now and have your rest. It is all over . . .'

MK.14.37-41

In this description of Jesus and his sleeping followers, as in the whole story of Gethsemane, we are being presented with a multi-layered narrative with many possible explanations and interpretations. These need not be mutually exclusive. On one level, this story can be read as a report of the events of the night of Jesus's arrest. Such an interpretation is impossible to prove or disprove. On another level, this story can be understood as an imaginative creation of Mark's based on many different scriptural allusions, including a variation on the well known story of Job's friends keeping vigil with him in his suffering. Another alternative is that we are being presented with a set of words and speeches especially assembled to meet the needs of Mark's church.

This last alternative would suggest that Mark's stories of the last days and hours of Jesus were used as a set of notes, or readings, by the leaders of an early church vigil held in memory of those days and hours. The exhortations about watching and praying and the difficulty of staying awake reflect a problem very familiar to anyone who has tried to meditate through a night-long vigil. No less a person than Paul is reported to have had the same trouble when Eutychus not only fell asleep, but fell out of the window while Paul preached a lengthy night-time sermon.[5]

By the time Luke writes the story of the sleeping disciples some ten or fifteen years after Mark, the details have changed. Not only does an angel appear to Jesus in the garden but:

When he rose from prayer he went to the disciples and found them sleeping for sheer grief. And he said

5 see AC.20.7-12; also see above p.23.

> to them, 'Why are you asleep? Get up and pray not
> to be put to the test.'
>
> LK.22.45-46

Characteristically, Luke is more sympathetic here than either Mark or Matthew. In his story Jesus does not return three times to the disciples, just this once. Their inability to stay awake is emphasised far less, and they sleep for "sheer grief". This could be explained simply by saying Luke is a more kindly writer; it could be explained by saying he had access to different information; or it could be explained by saying his church put less emphasis on the keeping of vigils. None of these possibilities exclude the others.

In the three gospels that tell it, the story of Jesus's despair and prayer in Gethsemane carries great emotional impact. It seems that Jesus knows what is coming and in a very human way wishes he could be spared. But he stays in Gethsemane and prays; and he prays alone. His words to his God place him in the tradition of the innocent sufferer, at once lamenting and accepting his fate. This is a tradition that is remarkable because it celebrates not the victorious oppressor, but the victim. History of almost every kind is usually related from the point of view of the victor, but here we are given the reaction of the victim. Jesus is about to be betrayed by a friend; he will be tried, tortured and killed that very day.

> And going on a little further he threw himself on
> the ground and prayed that, if it were possible, this
> hour might pass him by.
>
> MK.14.35

As the story unfolds in the gospels, this hour does not pass away from Jesus. He neither flees nor fights. He accepts his fate without bitterness and without resistance. According to Mark, when Jesus returns from praying for a third time and still finds his followers asleep he says:

> 'You can sleep on now and have your rest. It is all over. The hour has come. Now the Son of man is to be betrayed into the hands of sinners. Get up! Let us go! My betrayer is not far away.'
>
> MK.14.42

CHAPTER TEN

Betrayal

The way the story goes according to Mark and Matthew and Luke Jesus's fate is sealed well before the vigil in Gethsemane. According to Mark:

> Judas Iscariot, one of the Twelve, approached the chief priests with an offer to hand Jesus over to them. They were delighted to hear it, and promised to give him money; and he began to look for a way of betraying him when the opportunity should occur.
>
> MK.14.10-11

Matthew and Luke tell essentially the same story, but Matthew is more specific about the financial arrangements:

> Then one of the Twelve, the man called Judas Iscariot, went to the chief priests and said, 'What are you prepared to give me if I hand him over to you?' They paid him thirty silver pieces, and from then onwards he began to look for an opportunity to betray him.
>
> MT.26.14-16

This story of Judas and his thirty pieces of silver has become synonymous with the theme of betrayal by a friend. The theme is very ancient. In their accounts of Judas, the gospel writers were building on an already rich tradition of stories of betrayal, often betrayal by a friend, and at a meal.

"Even my trusted friend on whom I relied, who shared my table, takes advantage of me." declares Psalm 41. Psalm 55 cries out against the treachery of " . . . a person of my own rank, my comrade and dear friend." The same kind of grief and the same sense of outrage are repeated in the book of the prophet Obadiah, some four or five centuries before the time of Jesus:

> Your allies all pursued you right to the frontier,
> your confederates kept you in suspense, then got the better of you,
> your own guests laid a trap for you . . .
>
> OB.1.7

In Mark and Matthew and Luke the conspiracy between Judas and the chief priests takes place before the final meal of Jesus and his disciples. Then during the final meal, Judas's treachery is foretold by Jesus.

> And while they were at table eating, Jesus said, 'In truth I tell you, one of you is about to betray me, one of you *eating with me.*' They were distressed and said to him, one after another, 'Not me, surely?' He said to them, 'It is one of the Twelve, one who is dipping into the same dish with me . . .'
>
> MK.14.18-20

The gospel of John tells much the same story but in greater detail. When asked by his worried disciples who amongst them would betray him Jesus says:

> 'It is the one to whom I give the piece of bread that I dip in the dish.' And when he had dipped the piece of bread he gave it to Judas son of Simon Iscariot. At that instant, after Judas had taken the bread, Satan entered him. Jesus then said, 'What you

> are going to do, do quickly.' . . . As soon as Judas had taken the piece of bread he went out. It was night.
>
> JN.13.26-30

Later that night, which is the night of Passover according to Mark and Matthew and Luke, Jesus and his followers are in Gethsemane, and there, according to all four gospels, Judas finds them:

> Judas, one of the Twelve, came up and with him a number of men armed with swords and clubs, sent by the chief priests and the scribes and the elders. Now the traitor had arranged a signal with them saying, 'The one I kiss, he is the man. Arrest him, and see he is well guarded when you lead him away.' So when the traitor came, he went up to Jesus at once and said, 'Rabbi!' and kissed him. The others seized him and arrested him. Then one of the bystanders drew his sword and struck out at the high priest's servant and cut off his ear.
>
> MK.14.43-47

The gospels vary in the details they provide in this story. John omits the famous kiss of betrayal. Matthew has a short speech about the sword being unnecessary because there are "more than twelve legions of angels" that Jesus can ask for if he wishes for help. Peter is identified as the owner of the sword only in John's gospel. Luke has Jesus heal the ear of the high priest's servant. John provides a name for the high priest's servant. Mark describes a young man who follows Jesus when he is taken away and is seized, but slips out of his clothing and "ran away naked".

These variations are typical of the accounts of Jesus's last days. The gospels tell notably similar stories, but they tell them differently and with different details. Sometimes these details provide the best points of entry to the stories, sometimes it is more helpful to step back to look at the broader patterns of the stories. With the story of Judas's betrayal, both approaches prove helpful. We will start by looking at some of the details.

Perhaps one of the best known incidents of the betrayal of Jesus is Judas's kiss, described by Mark and Matthew and Luke. This kiss has a clear precedent in the story of another betrayal. The story goes back to the political machinations of the great king David, and specifically to an incident related in the second book of Samuel.

A rebellion against David had been led by his son Absalom, and it continued until Absalom was killed in battle. After this David is described entering into a period of exaggerated mourning. When he recovers he seems also to have recovered some of his political skills, but not all at once. The rebellion of Absalom had been very serious, far more than the act of a jealous son who wanted his father's throne. There was deep seated suspicion between the "ten tribes" of Israel who lived to the north of Palestine, and the other two tribes in Jerusalem and the south. Because Absalom had his support from the northern tribes, David must mend his political fences there to hold the kingdom together.

To do this he enlists a nephew, Amasa, who had fought against him under Absalom. Amasa takes charge of the combined armies of the kingdom, replacing a man called Joab, an excellent soldier who had been very loyal to David. Shortly after there is another rebellion in the north led by "a scoundrel called Sheba". David sends Amasa to deal with this, but Amasa delays taking action, and questions are raised about Amasa's loyalty to David. Meanwhile Joab joins in the pursuit of Sheba with a force of his own men. As they set out, they meet Amasa:

> They were near the great stone at Gibeon when Amasa met them, coming the other way. Joab was wearing his uniform, over which he had buckled on a sword hanging from his waist in its scabbard; the sword came out and fell. Joab said to Amasa, 'Are you well, brother?' and, with his right hand, took Amasa by the beard to kiss him. Amasa paid no

> atttention to the sword, which Joab had now picked up, and Joab struck him with it in the belly, spilling his entrails all over the ground. He did not need to strike a second blow; and Amasa died . . .
>
> 2S.20.8-10

By the last verse of the chapter Joab is back in charge of David's armies, declaring "whoever is for David, follow Joab!"

It is easy to see how Joab's kiss of greeting before he kills Amasa can be related to Judas's kiss. Details and incidents like this from the Hebrew Scriptures filter continually into the stories of the gospels. Take, for instance, the way Matthew describes what Judas does after Jesus is arrested:

> When he found that Jesus had been condemned, then Judas, his betrayer, was filled with remorse and took the thirty silver pieces back to the chief priests and elders saying, 'I have sinned. I have betrayed innocent blood.' They replied, 'What is that to us? That is your concern.' And flinging down the silver pieces in the sanctuary he made off, and went and hanged himself. The chief priests picked up the silver pieces and said, 'It is against the Law to put this into the treasury; it is blood-money'. So they discussed the matter and with it bought the potter's field as a graveyard for foreigners, and this is why the field is still called the Field of Blood. The word spoken through the prophet Jeremiah was then fulfilled: '*And they took the thirty silver pieces, the sum at which the precious One was priced by children of Israel, and they gave them for the potter's field, just as the Lord directed me.*'
>
> MT.27.3-10

This story is told only by Matthew. Only Matthew mentions the specific number of thirty pieces of silver, only Matthew has Judas return the money in remorse, only Matthew has

Judas hang himself, only Matthew explains what the priests do with the blood-money and only Matthew cites the prophet Jeremiah.[1] Single-handedly, Matthew creates a complicated story that connects to older, even more complicated stories.

Although Matthew claims to be quoting Jeremiah in this passage he is really combining references from Jeremiah with a quotation from the prophet Zechariah. The potter's field and the idea of a tainted burial ground are the details that come straight from Jeremiah. [2]

Jeremiah was the great prophet of the late seventh, early sixth century BCE. At one point he prophesies doom to the sinful children of Israel because they are carrying out human sacrifices at a place called Topheth.

> 'Yes, the people of Judah have done what displeases me, Yahweh declares. They have set up their Horrors in the Temple that bears my name, to defile it, and have built the high places of Topheth in the Valley of Ben-Hinnom, to burn their sons and their daughters: a thing I never ordered, that had never entered my thoughts. So now the days are coming, Yahweh declares, when the people will no longer say Topheth or Valley of Ben-Hinnom, but Valley of Slaughter. Topheth will become a burial ground, for lack of other space; the corpses of this people will be food for the birds of the sky and the animals of earth, and there will be no one to drive them off . . .'
>
> JR.7.30-33

1 In AC.1.18 Luke does mention the blood money. He says that Judas: '. . . bought a plot of land with the money he was paid for his crime. He fell headlong and burst open, and all his entrails poured out. Everybody in Jerusalem heard about it and the plot came to be called "Bloody Acre".'

2 i for more on Matthew's use of both Jeremiah and Zechariah see NJB p.1657 notes (d) and (e).
ii see also JR.32 and how Jeremiah purchases a field.

In order to bring the Israelites back into line Jeremiah is given special instructions by his God. He is to take an earthenware pot to Topheth, and there he is to break the pot into pieces in front of an assembly of priests and elders. Jeremiah's God tells him what to say, and speaking for his God Jeremiah prophesies disaster to this place where the blood of the innocent has been shed:

> '"Because of this place, I shall empty Judah and Jerusalem of sound advice; I shall make them fall by the sword before their enemies, by the hand of those determined to kill them . . . And I shall make this city an object of horror and derision . . .
>
> You must break this jug in front of the men who are with you, and say to them, "Yahweh Sabaoth says this: I am going to break this people and this city just as one breaks a potter's pot, so that it can never be mended again . . ."'
>
> JR.19.7-8,10-11

Jeremiah is put into the stocks for making this unwelcome speech, but he is proven right. Doom does indeed shortly follow. Nebuchadnezzar attacks, the elite of Israel are taken captive and deported to Babylon, and Jerusalem and the temple are destroyed. Bearing in mind that Matthew was writing a few years after another catastrophic destruction of Jerusalem, his reference to another unclean burial ground, the "Field of Blood", would resonate with the uncomfortable warnings of Jeremiah from the "Valley of Slaughter" at the time of the earlier destruction.

The sum of thirty pieces of silver first is mentioned in the book of Zechariah. This comes as part of a long and confusing parable about the treachery of the rulers of the skittish people of Israel. The time of the writing of this parable dates back to about four hundred years before Matthew, shortly after the conquest of Palestine by Alexander the Great. This conquest left confusion in its wake, with merchants and politicians making fortunes out of the misfortunes of the people. The prophet tells of these carryings-on in a story in which uncaring shepherds get charge over a flock of sheep. The shepherds are equated with politicians or priests who allow merchants to make fortunes buying and selling the sheep for slaughter. The sheep are the children of Israel. As if in a dream the prophet tells of being appointed by the Lord to take the place of both shepherds and merchants and to outdo them in the selling of the sheep. He appears to be almost as critical of the sheep as he is of the shepherds and merchants:

> . . . . I pastured the sheep myself, getting rid of three shepherds in one month. But I lost patience with them, and they equally detested me. I then said, 'I am not going to pasture you any more; the one doomed to die can die; the one doomed to perish can perish; and the rest can devour one another.'
>
> ZC.11.7-9

With that the prophet breaks his staff, signalling that he will no longer take any responsibility for the people of Israel. Yet even though in this dream-parable the prophet has despaired of caring for the sheep, he expects to be paid for his services and he confronts the merchants:

> I then said to them, 'If you see fit, give me my wages; if not, never mind'. So they weighed out my wages: thirty shekels of silver. Yahweh said to me, 'Throw it to the smelter, this princely sum at which they have valued me!' Taking the thirty shekels of silver, I threw them into the Temple of Yahweh, for the smelter.
>
> ZC.11.12-13

This section of text in the book of Zechariah is very confused, but the underlying theme at the end of the story is unmistakable. Both the prophet and his God doubt the value of the payment and view it as an insult to their own worth. The money is returned to the treasury, also translated as "the smelter", of the temple. It is the same in Matthew's story of Judas. The money that was the price placed on the head of Jesus is returned to the treasury of the temple.

Just before the account of Judas's betrayal, Mark makes use of the book of Zechariah in another story. He cites from it directly when Jesus foretells Peter's denial and the desertion of the rest of his followers:

> 'You will all fall away, for the scripture says: *I shall strike the shepherd and the sheep will be scattered . . .*'
>
> MK.14.27

Here is the original version of the passage that Jesus quotes from the book of Zechariah:

> Awake, sword, against my shepherd,
> against the man who is close to me—
> declares Yahweh Sabaoth!
> Strike the shepherd, scatter the sheep!
> And I shall turn my hand against the young!
>
> ZC.13.7

Later in this passage the prophet describes how the true people of God will survive this scattering, and will be tested and refined like gold. This leads into a remarkably detailed description of the battle and the plague of the end times in which all the enemies of Israel shall be defeated. The book of Zechariah concludes that this day will be a day of wonder when "Yahweh will become king of the whole world."[3]

Both Mark and Matthew have Jesus citing this passage about the scattering of the sheep. This is a logical passage for

3 see ZC.14.9.

them to use. They were writing either during or shortly after the destruction of Jerusalem in 70CE, when prejudice against the Christian sect was growing. From their point of view, the sheep were indeed being scattered even as they wrote, and the promise of the coming day of glory was all that kept them going.

Many such details within the gospel stories of Judas's betrayal can be traced, strand by strand, to similar details within the Hebrew Scriptures. Some are more illuminating than others, and some are more immediately evident than others. One of these strands, in Psalm 55, connects to a broader pattern of storytelling that underlies the story of Judas's betrayal. Psalm 55 probably refers to events in King David's lifetime. The "Passion of David" is reflected here, and it bears certain resemblances to the "Passion of Jesus", his descendant. Passion in this context means extreme suffering, and grief.

I would soon find a refuge
    from the storm of abuse,
from the destructive tempest, Lord,
    from the flood of their tongues.

For I see violence
    and strife in the city,
day and night they make their rounds
    along the city walls,

Inside live malice and mischief,
    inside lives destruction,
tyranny and treachery never absent
    from its central square.

Were it an enemy who insulted me,
    that I could bear;
if an opponent pitted himself against me,
    I could turn away from him.

But you, a person of my own rank,
a comrade and dear friend,
to whom I was bound by intimate friendship
in the house of God!

PS.55.10-14

This psalm leads by an intricate route to the bitter aftermath of the story of David and Bathsheba.[4] The story starts when David watches from his palace roof while the beautiful Bathsheba, wife of Uriah the Hittite, has her bath. David decides he must have Bathsheba and sends for her to come to him. She soon discovers she is pregnant. David then becomes embroiled in a devious plot to get rid of Uriah the Hittite. When Uriah is killed, the prophet Nathan gets wind of the plot. He is furious with David for having stolen a man's wife and in effect murdered the man. According to the law David should have been put to death himself.[5] As king he could and did pull rank, but he could not avoid punishment.

'"For this, your household will never be free of the sword, since you showed contempt for me and took the wife of Uriah the Hittite, to make her your wife." Yahweh says this, "Out of your own household I shall raise misfortune for you. Before your very eyes I shall take your wives and give them to your neighbour, who will lie with your wives in broad daylight. You have worked in secret, but I shall work this for all Israel to see, in broad daylight."'

2S.12.10-12

The sword never does leave David's house. To begin with

4 for more on the connections between these texts see Goulder, *The Prayers of David*, chh. 1,2 & 4.
5 for example see EX.21.12 (cp.LV.24.17 & NB.35.16-21). See also NB.35.31ff and DT.19.11ff.

God punishes David by killing his first child by Bathsheba. Then Amnon, David's eldest son by his first wife, betrays and rapes Tamar, David's daughter. She is the sister of Absalom and they are both the children of another of David's wives. Absalom takes his revenge on Amnon by another treachery. He holds a banquet for all his brothers and at the banquet he murders Amnon. Then Absalom turns on David, and spends years undermining the authority of his father, dividing the kingdom between the northern tribes of Israel or "Ephraim", and the two southern tribes of Judah. Finally Absalom sets in motion his final treachery by leading an open rebellion of the northern tribes against the king his father.[6]

The rebellion is so successful that David panics and retreats out of Jerusalem. On his way he spends some time on the road to the Mount of Olives. He and his followers weep over the city:

> David then made his way up the Mount of Olives, weeping as he went, his head covered and his feet bare. And all the people with him had their heads covered and made their way up, weeping as they went.
>
> 2S.15.30[7]

At this point the story starts to fade and the description becomes confused. It sounds rather as if David is leading a large ceremonial pilgrimage out of Jerusalem, reflecting perhaps how the story of his retreat was preserved in subsequent generations. But the focus of the story soon returns. Absalom succeeds in taking the city and with it ten of David's concubines. Nathan's prophecy comes true and David's humiliation seems complete. But David is not to be defeated. As he retreats out of Jerusalem he is met by one Hushai the Archite. Then and there he recruits this man as his spy. With the aid of Hushai the revolt of

6 for more on these stories see 2S.12 and 2S.13.
7 for more on this passage see below p.180.

Absalom is eventually quelled and Absalom is killed.

The connections of this story to the story of the betrayal and sufferings of Jesus are indirect but compelling. The link between Jesus and David was strong proof for a first century Christian/Jewish audience that Jesus was a great leader, one who might restore to Israel the glory of David. The days of King David may have been fraught with scandal and family problems and rebellion, but nonetheless this was the beginning of the most glorious period in the history of Israel. In later centuries, when the dynasty collapsed, a return of David's glory was the constant hope of the people who were left.

The David story carries great authority as a precedent for the gospel writers. They expect Jesus to be the second David. Matthew and Luke make this explicit in their stories of the birth of Jesus, stressing that he is a descendent of David. Later Jesus is betrayed by one of his own closest followers just as David was betrayed by his own family. King David and Jesus are each described walking to the same Mount of Olives while facing the bitter realisation that someone close to them has betrayed them. It seems that each has reached a low point from which he can never recover.

At the beginning of this chapter we quoted two lines from Psalm 41. These lines are cited in John's gospel in the story of Judas's betrayal.[8] In the psalm they are introduced like this:

> All who hate me whisper together about me
> and reckon I deserve the misery I suffer.
> 'A fatal sickness has a grip on him;
> now that he is down, he will never get up again.'
> Even my trusted friend on whom I relied,
> who shared my table, takes advantage of me.
>
> PS.41.7-9

Direct personal betrayal is by no means the only indignity that Jesus shares with David through the language of the psalms.

8 see JN.13.18.

After Jesus is arrested the stories of his final hours are interwoven with persistent themes of abandonment and desertion, themes common to many of the psalms.

All I hear is slander
—terror wherever I turn—
as they plot together against me,
scheming to take my life.

PS.31.13

Friends and companions shun my disease,
even the dearest of them keep their distance.
Those with designs on my life lay snares,
those who wish me ill speak of violence
and hatch treachery all day long.

PS.38.11-12

Such passages from the psalms can be seen not only in the story of Judas's betrayal, but also in the story of Peter's denial. According to Mark the denial story begins with Jesus warning the disciples that they will all fail him that very night:

And Jesus said to them, 'You will all fall away, for the scripture says: *I shall strike the shepherd and the sheep will be scattered*; however, after my resurrection I shall go before you into Galilee.' Peter said, 'Even if all fall away, I will not.' And Jesus said to him, 'In truth I tell you, this day, this very night, before the cock crows twice, you will have disowned me three times.' But he repeated still more earnestly, 'If I have to die with you, I will never disown you.' And they all said the same.

MK.14.27-31

After the betrayal scene in Gethsemane and the arrest of Jesus, Mark tells of Peter following Jesus and the guards that arrested him back to Jerusalem. He goes right into the High

Priest's outer courtyard where there is a fire:

> While Peter was down below in the courtyard, one of the high priest's servant-girls came up. She saw Peter warming himself there, looked closely at him and said, 'You too were with Jesus, the man from Nazareth.' But he denied it. 'I do not know, I do not understand what you are talking about,' he said. And he went out into the forecourt, and a cock crowed. The servant-girl saw him and again started telling the bystanders, 'This man is one of them'. But again he denied it. A little later the bystanders themselves said to Peter, 'You are certainly one of them! Why, you are a Galilean.' But he started cursing and swearing, 'I do not know the man you speak of.' And at once the cock crowed for the second time, and Peter recalled what Jesus had said to him, 'Before the cock crows twice, you will have disowned me three times.' And he burst into tears.
>
> MK.14.66-72

In Mark's gospel this episode is well structured with its three accusations and three denials. It fills a dramatic place in the story, taking us through the long night of the arrest to the next morning. It also provides what the early Christians in Mark's church urgently needed to hear because they themselves were under stress. Peter's denials bring to life in a vivid and personal way what Mark describes elsewhere in his gospel, when he attributes these warning words to Jesus:

> Brother will betray brother to death, and a father his child; children will come forward against their parents and have them put to death. You will be universally hated on account of my name; but anyone who stands firm to the end will be saved.
>
> MK.13.12-13

Peter's temptation to deny Jesus could easily be understood by Mark's audience. They knew what it meant to be afraid of being persecuted for following Jesus. Peter's dilemma was all too familiar and all too human. Having declared he will never desert Jesus Peter then denies him repeatedly, and weeps with grief at what he has done. His weakness, his lack of courage, and his grief have been shared by many throughout the Christian centuries.

Peter disappears from both Mark and Matthew's gospels following his denial of Jesus, but in Luke and John Peter reappears as one of Jesus's leading disciples. He is, effectively, rehabilitated. As a result, in Christian thinking, Peter's denials have not been judged harshly, and his abandonment of Jesus is not ringingly condemned. It is not so with Judas. Yet just like Judas, Peter is to Jesus "a person of my own rank, a comrade and dear friend", and just like Judas he publicly rejects Jesus.

Judas is judged as one of the greatest traitors of all time. Yet over the centuries some people have concluded that Judas has been unfairly condemned. There are many ways of arguing the case for Judas.[9] In general such arguments maintain that Judas has been vilified for an act that any fervent follower of Jesus might have done. Judas is understood as a true supporter of a weakening Jesus, trying in despair to force him to take on the messianic role for which God had preordained him, trying in a desperate move to make Jesus take the responsibility and seize the power that was popularly associated with this role.

Christian history has chosen to judge Judas much more harshly, to follow the lead provided by the gospels, with terrible effect. In Dante's *Inferno*, the three archetypal traitors of the ancient world are in torment at the very centre of hell; they are Cassius, Brutus and Judas. This would have suited the Christian sensibilities of the time very well, because Jews in thirteenth and

9 i an early example is the Cainite sect that had a "Gospel of Judas" in the 2nd.cent.CE.
ii for more on the Judas story see Maccoby, H.; *Judas Iscariot and the Myth of Jewish Evil*; Peter Halban; London; 1992; ch.7, "Judas and the Growth of Antisemitism", pp.101-126.

fourteenth century Europe were widely hated and feared by Christians, and Judas was perceived as the typically treacherous Jew. To see him in agony in hell was considered utterly appropriate. The reported actions of Judas in the gospels have incited centuries of such hatred of Jews by Christians.

In the latter part of the twentieth century we all are aware of the results of this hatred. Millions of Jews were brutally murdered in the Holocaust, and those directly responsible for this were people brought up in the Christian tradition or on its fringes. Christianity inescapably bears this burden, for there is no denying the roots of this hatred. They penetrate the whole of the New Testament, and they were planted there both before and after the time Mark wrote his gospel and introduced the story of the betrayal.[10] The gospel writers and other writers of the New Testament produced documents that have fuelled this continuing disaster. The writers cannot have foreseen this or desired it, but they provided ammunition that fell into the hands of later Christians, and this ammunition is still proving lethal.

Christians were an unpopular minority when the gospels were being written. They perceived themselves as the persecuted ones and the righteous ones. Seeing themselves in this way, Christians did what they thought necessary. They taught doctrines and told stories reflecting badly on the people they saw as their unrighteous persecutors. In this way the seeds of Christian anti-semitism were sown. Successive generations of increasingly powerful Christians fostered these seeds and allowed them to flourish. The persecuted became the persecutors, and history was set on a tragic course. It is now very difficult to read the New Testament without seeing how this tragedy was being set in motion. The most obvious example of this is in the story of Judas as the betrayer of Jesus.

10 i for Paul's role in this see: Gaston, Lloyd; *Paul and the Torah*, University of British Columbia Press, Vancouver, 1987, pp.15ff.
ii for Mark's role see Mack, *A Myth of Innocence*, pp.304f.

CHAPTER ELEVEN

Trials

They led Jesus off to the high priest; and all the chief priests and the elders and the scribes assembled there . . . The chief priests and the whole Sanhedrin were looking for evidence against Jesus in order to have him executed . . .

MK.14.53-55

Jesus, then, was brought before the governor, and the governor put to him this question, 'Are you the king of the Jews?' Jesus replied, 'It is you who say it.' But when he was accused by the chief priests and the elders he refused to answer at all.

MT.27.11-12

(Herod) questioned him at some length, but without getting any reply. Meanwhile the chief priests and the scribes were there, vigorously pressing their accusations. Then Herod, together with his guards, treated him with contempt and made fun of him; he put a rich cloak on him and sent him back to Pilate.

LK.23.9-11

'Here is your king', said Pilate to the Jews. But they shouted, 'Away with him, away with him, crucify him.' Pilate said, 'Shall I crucify your king?' The

> chief priests answered, 'We have no king except Caesar.' So at that Pilate handed him over to them to be crucified.
>
> JN.19.14-16

The gospel stories of Jesus on trial are bewildering. They seem to tell of at least three trials, and possibly two or three interrogations. These include a hearing before the high priest or his father-in-law, a trial before the Jewish religious court the Sanhedrin, a trial before Herod the puppet king of Galilee, a trial before the Roman governor Pilate, and a second hearing before Pilate and the Jewish crowd. The four gospel writers present different versions of how these trials were conducted, and of the sequence of events.

Mark and Matthew each tell of a trial before the Sanhedrin in the dead of night, followed by a trial the next morning before Pilate the Roman governor. Luke also tells of these, although his trial before the Sanhedrin takes place in the morning. Before this trial he tells of Jesus being ill-treated during the night at the high priest's house. Following the trial by the Sanhedrin, Jesus is tried by Pilate, and Luke then adds a third trial. This takes place before Herod, and it is followed by a second appearance before Pilate. John describes an interrogation before the Jewish authorities, and he places the interrogation at the house of Annas, the father-in-law of the high priest Caiaphas. Jesus is then sent to Caiaphas who sends him to Pilate, and John goes on to describe what appear to be two different hearings in front of Pilate.

Taking all of the gospel accounts together it is hard to get a clear picture of what is really going on; which legal procedures are being followed, who is in charge of passing sentence, and under which political or religious jurisdiction certain events are said to have taken place. The processes and legalities involved are not described in a coherent way.

The writers are composing gospels, though, not legal reports. These gospels are collections of committed stories that explain the writers' understanding of the significance of Jesus's life and death. In the trial scenes they are telling stories that try to explain what leads up to the crucifixion of Jesus. They are reconstructing these trial scenes a minimum of three, and as many as six decades after the death of Jesus. During those decades there had been a terrible war and the jurisdictions had changed beyond recognition.

The nature of these jurisdictions at the time of Jesus is blurred. In political and legal terms it is difficult to be sure exactly where the lines of responsibility lay in first century Palestine. The Jewish court, the Sanhedrin, dealt with matters of Jewish law, but the extent and nature of its ability to enforce its own decisions when Palestine was under Roman domination is a matter of debate. According to the gospels, in the case of Jesus when the Sanhedrin is faced with an offense deemed punishable by death, the matter is referred upwards to the Roman authorities. It is unclear if this was normal procedure when the execution of the offender was in question, or if this case was highly unusual. What does seem to be true is that if crucifixion was the desired means of execution, this had to be organized by the Romans, for crucifixion was a Roman, not a Jewish practise.

It is extremely unlikely that any of the gospel writers were witnesses at any of the trials of Jesus that they describe. Time and distance make that virtually impossible. They may have been working from orally transmitted stories, or they may have had access to unknown sources of written information that are now lost. No such sources have ever been traced. What can be traced in the stories of the trials is how the gospel writers turn to the scriptures. In their descriptions of the arrest and the various trials of Jesus the gospel writers tell their stories almost entirely through words and phrases and images from the scriptures.

The gospel writers believed Jesus was the Messiah. In the writings available to them there is a persistent current of allusion that seems to some, but not all people in later ages to refer to a coming messiah. These allusions fed a variety of popular expectations about a great leader who would come to rescue Israel from its oppressors. This means that if Jesus were to be accepted as the Messiah, the gospel writers had a problem. His life had ended in suffering and shame, with no hint of the glory and triumph that was expected of a messiah. Yet the scriptural passages that express such triumphal expectations are not numerous. Most of them are in later writings along with developing ideas about the end times and the resurrection of the dead.[1] These ideas had evolved very gradually.

Leading up to the idea of a triumphal messiah are many stories in the Hebrew Scriptures about leaders of Israel who try to act in the best interests of the nation at great personal cost. These include prophets and kings who often undergo intense suffering and torment for their God and their people. In telling their stories of Jesus, the gospel writers turn to these stories and find in them messianic implications that meet their needs. They find hints and suggestions of a non-triumphal messiah. So it is that when they describe Jesus's sufferings they use the familiar language and images that tell of the sufferings of earlier prophets and kings.

In discovering and developing such a scriptural framework for their stories the gospel writers succeed brilliantly, and their accounts of the various trials of Jesus are a measure of this success. Although these accounts are confusing and contradictory when it comes to legal details, they are rich in scriptural resonances that add both depth and authority to the stories. Because of the use of scriptural material there is a notable consistency of tone in the descriptions of Jesus on trial, despite the inconsistency of detail. The gospel writers speak with one voice in portraying the innocence of Jesus and the villainy of his accusers. Their stories uniformly show his innocence transcending their villainy. Throughout all their descriptions of the various trials, the accusations against Jesus are intended to be seen by the reader as false.

Mark sets this out very clearly:

> The chief priests and the whole Sanhedrin were looking for evidence against Jesus in order to have him executed. But they could not find any. Several,

1 for more about messianic expectations see above, pp.87-89.

> indeed, brought false witness against him, but their evidence was conflicting. Some stood up and submitted this false evidence against him, 'We heard him say, "I am going to destroy this Temple made by human hands, and in three days build another, not made by human hands." But even on this point their evidence was conflicting.
>
> MK.14.55-59

In Mark's account of false witnesses testifying against an innocent victim, there are echoes of the voice of the psalmist. The psalms often speak from the viewpoint of the victim of injustice:

> Yahweh, teach me your way,
> lead me on the path of integrity
> because of my enemies;
> do not abandon me to the will of my foes—
> false witnesses have risen against me,
> and are breathing out violence.
>
> PS.27.11-12

> False witnesses come forward against me
> asking me questions I cannot answer,
> they cross-examine me, repay my kindness with cruelty,
> make my life barren.
>
> PS.35.11-12[2]

The evidence of the false witnesses in Mark's gospel who accuse Jesus of wanting to destroy the temple recalls one of the many misadventures of the prophet Jeremiah. With the voice of his God always ringing in his ears, Jeremiah follows a career of reprimanding his fellow countrymen and prophesying doom

2 for more false witnesses see the stories of Naboth's vineyard in 1K.21.1-16, and the prophet Micaiah in 1K.22.24-28.

for Jerusalem. At one point he predicts that the temple of Jerusalem will be destroyed like the shrine at Shiloh before it.[3] This makes him extemely unpopular, and the temple authorities and a crowd of people seize him and demand that he be put to death. Jeremiah defends himself stoutly, and says:

> 'For myself, I am, as you see, in your hands. Do whatever you please or think right with me. But be sure of this, that if you put me to death, you will be bringing innocent blood on yourselves, on this city and on its inhabitants, since Yahweh has truly sent me to you to say all this for you to hear.'
>
> The chief men and all the people then said to the priests and the prophets, 'This man does not deserve to die: he has spoken to us in the name of Yahweh our God.'
>
> JR.26:14-16

This story of Jeremiah's trial echoes down the centuries to the gospel accounts of Jesus's various trials. Each man is unjustly accused, each is at odds with the temple authorities, and each is arraigned before a crowd. The difference is that the intervention of the people saves the outspoken prophet Jeremiah, while in the gospel stories the intervention of the people ensures that Jesus is condemned.

After the presentation of the false evidence against Jesus, Mark's account of the trial before the Sanhedrin continues:

> The high priest then rose before the whole assembly and put this question to Jesus, 'Have you no answer to that? What is this evidence these men are bringing against you?' But he was silent and made no answer at all.
>
> MK.14.60-61

3 for the rest of the story see above pp.78-80.

This portrayal of Jesus as the falsely accused victim who remains silent appears in all four gospels. The silence of the victim has clear precedents in the scriptures. As always, the voice of the psalmist is heard:

Friends and companions shun my disease,
even the dearest of them keep their distance.
Those with designs on my life lay snares,
those who wish me ill speak of violence
and hatch treachery all day long.

But I hear nothing, as though I were deaf,
as though dumb, saying not a word.
I am like the one who, hearing nothing,
has no sharp answer to make.

PS.38.11-14

There are other silences of other sufferers in the scriptures. The most outstanding of these is the silence of the unnamed victim known as the "suffering servant" of the book of Isaiah:

Ill-treated and afflicted,
he never opened his mouth,
like a lamb led to the slaughter-house,
like a sheep dumb before its shearers
he never opened his mouth.

Forcibly, after sentence, he was taken.
Which of his contemporaries was concerned
at his having been cut off from the land of the living,
at his having been struck dead for his people's
rebellion?

IS.53.7-8 [4]

4 for more on the suffering servant see pp.165- 167.

Another famous sufferer in the scriptures is Job. Although the influence is indirect, the sufferings of the innocent Job are described in a way that is startlingly similar to the sufferings of Jesus. Job's pain is vivid and his bewilderment is terrible:

> When I speak, my suffering does not stop;
> if I say nothing, is it in any way reduced?
> And now it is driving me to distraction;
> you have struck my whole acquaintanceship with horror,
> now it rounds on me, my slanderer has now turned witness,
> he appears against me, accusing me face to face;
> his anger tears and hounds me
> with gnashing teeth.
> My enemies look daggers at me,
> and open gaping jaws.
> Their sneers strike like slaps in the face;
> and they all set on me at once.
> Yes, God has handed me over to the godless,
> and cast me into the hands of the wicked.
>
> JB.16.6-11

Initially, Job accepts his suffering with silence, with patience, and with prayer. But this silence does not last, and his celebrated patience gives way to long outbursts against the injustice of God. Then the voice of God addresses Job from the whirlwind, and having heard this voice, Job falls silent once again.[5]

In Mark's gospel, the silence of Jesus during his trial before the Sanhedrin is broken by the high priest's next question:

> The high priest put a second question to him saying, 'Are you the Christ, the Son of the Blessed One?' 'I

5 for more on Job's silences see above Chapter pp.123-124, and below p.274.

am', said Jesus, 'and you will see the *Son of man seated at the right hand of the power and coming with the clouds of heaven.'* The high priest tore his robes and said, 'What need of witnesses have we now? You heard the blasphemy. What is your finding?' Their verdict was unanimous; he deserved to die. Some of them started spitting at his face, hitting him and saying, 'Play the prophet!' And the attendants struck him too.

MK.14.61-65

This enigmatic reply Mark attributes to Jesus makes use of language and images from one of the visions in the book of Daniel:

I was gazing into the visions of the night,
when I saw, coming on the clouds of heaven,
as it were a son of man.
He came to the One most venerable
and was led into his presence.
On him was conferred rule,
honour and kingship,
and all peoples, nations and languages became his servants.
His rule is an everlasting rule
which will never pass away,
and his kingship will never come to an end.

DN.7.13-14

The book of Daniel in its present form, was written nearly two centuries before the time of Jesus, during the rebellion led by Judas Maccabeus.[6] It is the product of an age in which hopes were taking shape that a powerful messianic leader would emerge for Israel. Expectations of this leader, of the final battle and of the dawning of a new age were becoming more specific,

6 for more see above pp.11-12.

more distinct and more widespread than in earlier times. The book of Daniel expresses all of this in the weird visionary language that eventually became the hallmark of much messianic thought. This is allusive, trance-like, fantastic language that lends itself very readily to imaginative interpretations.

In his response to the high priest, Jesus refers to the "Son of Man coming with the clouds of heaven". This reply is rooted in the passage in the book of Daniel, cited just above. Jesus then adds the detail about being "seated at the right hand of power". This is found in Psalm 110:

> Yahweh declared to my Lord, 'Take your seat at my right hand,
> till I have made your enemies your footstool.'
> Yahweh will stretch out the sceptre of your power;
> from Zion you will rule your foes all around you.
>
> PS.110.1-2

The idea of Jesus as the mysterious Son of Man borne up on the clouds of heaven and enthroned at the right hand of God is the direct result of merging the language of Daniel with the earlier language of the psalmist. Either together or separately, these ideas and images are repeated throughout the New Testament.[7]

None of this explains why Jesus is charged with blasphemy for uttering his reply to the High Priest. To claim to be the "son of man" is far from inflammatory. The phrase "son of man" simply means "man" or "one". The reason for the accusation of blasphemy must lie elsewhere. Jesus does reply "I am" immediately after being asked if he is the Christ, the son of the Blessed One, but again, there is no blasphemy in anyone claiming to be the Christ, or the Messiah. Others did so with apparent

7 for examples of these images see MT.24.29-31; MT.26.64; AC.7.55-56; 1CO.15.24-25; or 1P.3.22.

impunity.[8] This is leaves the possibility that the blasphemy lies in claiming to be the "son of the Blessed One", meaning the son of God. But there are problems here too.

In John's gospel Jesus is repeatedly referred to as "son of God". This title is also used by Paul, and in Mark, Matthew and Luke.[9] Only in John, however, does this title appear in a trial scene. In John's gospel, in the scene when Pilate presents Jesus to the Jewish crowd, the phrase "son of God" is used at a highly charged moment. This is when Pilate presents Jesus to the Jewish crowd:

> Pilate said, 'Here is the man.' When they saw him, the chief priests and the guards shouted, 'Crucify him! Crucify him!' Pilate said, 'Take him yourselves and crucify him: I find no case against him.' The Jews replied, 'We have a Law, and according to that Law he ought to be put to death, because he has claimed to be Son of God.'
>
> JN.19.5B-7

References to "son" or more frequently "sons" of God do occur in the Hebrew scriptures. They can refer to divine beings, or angels:

> One day when the sons of God came to attend on Yahweh, among them came Satan . . .
>
> JB.1.6

8 i for example Judas the Galilean claimed the title Messiah early in the first century CE, and Simon-Bar-Kochba was hailed as the Messiah in 132 CE.
ii for detailed discussion of messianic claims, see Horsley and Hanson, *Bandits, Prophets, and Messiahs,* pps.88-134 and 190-199.

9 for more examples see MK.1.1; MK.3.11; MK.15.39; MT.4.3; MT.8.29; MT.14.33; MT.26.63; MT.27.43; MT.27.54; LK.1.35; LK.3.38; LK.4.41; LK.22.70; JN.1.34,49; JN.3.18; JN.5.25; JN.9.35; JN.10.36; JN.11.4,27; JN.19.7; JN.20.31. see also RM.1.4; 2CO.1.19; GA.2.20.

In the book of Genesis, the phrase "sons of God" appears in one of the early myths of the Hebrew people:

> When people began being numerous on earth, and daughters had been born to them, the sons of God, looking at the women, saw how beautiful they were and married as many of them as they chose . . .
>
> GN.6.1-2

And in one of the psalms, to be a "son of God" refers to the king as the personification of the people of Israel:

> I will proclaim the decree of Yahweh:
> He said to me, You are my son,
> today I have fathered you.
> Ask of me, and I shall give you the nations for your birthright,
> the whole wide world as your possession . . .'
>
> PS.2.7-8[10]

By extension, this usage from Psalm 2 can be taken to imply a future messianic leader, and this is what the gospel writers believe Jesus to be. Yet this still does not explain why the phrase "son of God" is used to condemn Jesus in John's gospel, or why Jesus is charged with blasphemy in Mark's gospel after assenting to the title "son of the Blessed One". Messianic claims were not blasphemous.

What we are left with is a strong element of confusion and uncertainty about the nature of the charges against Jesus. The titles "son of God" and "son of man" do carry overtones from previous usages, but these are not enough to explain the charges. Either the full significance of these titles is not apparent, or they are being used in a heightened manner as false accusations against Jesus; accusations intended by the gospel writers to be seen as false.

10 for more citations of this passage see MT.3.17; MK.1.11; LK.3.22; MT.17.5; MK.9.7; LK.9.35; AC.13.33; HEB.1.5.

There is another title attributed to Jesus in the scenes of his trial. All four gospels use this one. It is "King of the Jews". This title is a potent one, carrying with it implications of rebellious political ambition. To be hailed as King of the Jews was dangerous:

> First thing in the morning, the chief priests, together with the elders and scribes and the rest of the Sanhedrin, had their plan ready. They had Jesus bound and took him away and handed him over to Pilate. Pilate put to him this question, 'Are you the king of the Jews?' He replied, 'It is you who say it.' And the chief priests brought many accusations against him. Pilate questioned him again, 'Have you no reply at all? See how many accusations they are bringing against you!' But, to Pilate's surprise, Jesus made no further reply.
>
> MK.15.1-5

"King of the Jews" has clear political overtones. "Are you King of the Jews?" is repeated in all of the trial scenes before Pilate. Any Roman governor of a troublesome occupied territory would be nervous of a popular local leader who claimed to be, or was acclaimed as a king. Nowhere in the gospels does Jesus lay claim to this title. Yet because the gospels all recognize Jesus as the Messiah and tell stories about him being hailed as the Messiah by large crowds, this carries an implication of kingship. According to the gospels Jesus is of King David's line. They emphasise this repeatedly, and find support for the idea of such a messiah in the scriptures. A passage in the book of the prophet Micah says:

> Now look to your fortifications, Fortress!
> They have laid siege to us;
> the ruler of Israel will be struck
> on the cheek with a rod.

But you (Bethlehem) Ephrathah,
the least of the clans of Judah,
from you will come for me
a future ruler of Israel
whose origins go back to the distant past,
to the days of old.

MI.4.14 - 5.1

A century or so after Micah, the prophet Jeremiah expresses the same kind of hope and expectation for the one who would come to rule Israel:

"Look, the days are coming, Yahweh declares, when I shall fulfil the promise of happiness I made to the House of Israel and the House of Judah:

In those days and at that time,
I shall make an upright Branch grow for David,
who will do what is just and upright in the country.
In those days Judah will triumph
and Israel live in safety.
And this is the name the city will be called:
Yahweh-is-our-Saving-Justice."

'For Yahweh says this: "David will never lack a male descendant to occupy the throne of the House of Israel . . ."'

JR.33.14-17

The book of the prophet Isaiah voices the same idea, speaking of a leader emerging from the stock of Jesse, who was David's father:

A shoot will spring from the stock of Jesse,
a new shoot will grow from his roots.
On him will rest the spirit of Yahweh,
the spirit of wisdom and insight,
the spirit of counsel and power,
the spirit of knowledge and fear of Yahweh:

his inspiration will lie in fearing Yahweh.
His judgement will not be by appearances.
his verdict not given on hearsay.
He will judge the weak with integrity
and give fair sentence for the humblest in the land.

IS.11.1-4

Although the gospels stress that Jesus is of David's kingly line, in their stories of his ministry and preaching they show Jesus consistently rejecting every effort to make him assume the role of a kingly messianic figure. Yet in the trial scenes, and later at the time of the crucifixion this is just what he is accused of, claiming to be "King of the Jews".[11]

In Luke's description of the hearing before Pilate, he has the Jewish authorities accuse Jesus of aspiring to be "Christ, a king". Not only that, they accuse him of threatening the authority of Caesar, the Roman Emperor:

> The whole assembly then rose, and they brought him before Pilate. They began their accusation by saying, 'We found this man inciting our people to revolt, opposing payment of the tribute to Caesar, and claiming to be Christ, a king.' Pilate put to him this question, 'Are you the king of the Jews?' He replied, 'It is you who say it.' Pilate then said to the chief priests and the crowd, 'I find no case against this man.'

LK.23.1-4

Luke's story then goes on to describe how Pilate sends Jesus to Herod, the puppet king of Galilee who held power by grace and favour of the Romans. No other gospel has Jesus appearing before Herod. According to Luke, Jesus is dressed up as a king and mocked by Herod and his guards, then returned to Pilate. Pilate still insists that Jesus is innocent. Three times he addresses

11 for more on "King of the Jews" see below p.174.

the "chief priests and the leading men and the people" because he wants to set Jesus free. They will not allow this, and they demand that Jesus be crucified.

Luke seems intent to reduce the culpability of Pilate, placing the responsibility for Jesus's death squarely on the Jewish crowd. Matthew does the same, even more dramatically. It is in Matthew's gospel that Pilate so emphatically washes his hands of the whole affair. This happens when he despairs of trying to reason with the incensed crowd. He says to them:

> '. . . what am I to do with Jesus who is called Christ?' They all said, 'Let him be crucified!' He asked, 'But what harm has he done?' But they shouted all the louder, 'Let him be crucified!' Then Pilate saw that he was making no impression, that in fact a riot was imminent. So he took some water, washed his hands in front of the crowd and said, 'I am innocent of this man's blood. It is your concern.' And the people, every one of them, shouted back, 'Let his blood be on us and on our children!'
>
> MT.27.22-25

Only Matthew's gospel has this cry "Let his blood be on us and on our children", but the inference can be drawn from all the gospels. The Jewish authorities and the Jewish crowd are held responsible for Jesus's death. Pilate, who has the final authority to order a crucifixion, is largely exonerated. Here again, the preoccupations of the gospel writers are clear. Writing as they were in the latter half of the first century, it was easy to feel hostility to the Jews who by then were increasingly at odds with the Christians. As a result the Jews are blamed for all the ills that befell Jesus, even though it is very clearly the Roman authorities who finally put Jesus to death.

The accounts of Jesus's trial are presented with dramatic flair in the gospels. Jesus as the silent suffering victim, falsely accused, is brilliantly portrayed. The anger of his Jewish accusers is frightening. The vacillations of Pilate add suspense. But although the level of high drama is impressive, the amount of information passed on in these trial scenes is far from great. The accusations are not clear. The legalities are not clear. The circumstances are not clear.

Yet two things are very clear in the trial scenes. First, the writers are weaving into these stories a dense and rich pattern of scriptural resonances. Second, the concerns of the writers are transparent. They are biased in favour of Jesus and against the Jewish authorities. Given their circumstances in the late first century, this is understandable. It does, however, add a certain irony to a question that is raised in John's gospel. When Jesus appears before Pilate, the two men talk together. At the end, Pilate asks about the nature of truth:

> Pilate said, 'So, then you are a king?' Jesus answered, 'It is you who say that I am a king. I was born for this, I came into the world for this, to bear witness to the truth; and all who are on the side of truth listen to my voice.' 'Truth?' said Pilate. 'What is that?'
>
> JN.18.37-38

CHAPTER TWELVE

Mockeries

Throughout the many trial scenes in the gospels Jesus stands alone. He has been deserted by his followers and is at the mercy of his enemies. All four gospels tell how Jesus is tortured during his trials, and they describe derision and mockery as part of this torture. According to Mark this begins at the trial before the Sanhedrin:

> . . . Some of them started spitting at his face, hitting him and saying, 'Play the prophet!' And the attendants struck him too.
>
> MK.14.65

Luke also describes this, placing the scene at the high priest's house before the trial by the Sanhedrin takes place:

> Meanwhile the men who guarded Jesus were mocking and beating him. They blindfolded him and questioned him, saying, 'Prophesy! Who hit you then?' And they heaped many other insults on him.
>
> LK.22.63-65

The mockeries continue through all the trials of Jesus. Probably the best known mockery scene is when Jesus is dressed in a rich cloak and hailed as a king. This is told by all four gospels. Here is Mark's version:

> The soldiers led him away to the inner part of the palace, that is, the Praetorium, and called the whole cohort together. They dressed him up in purple, twisted some thorns into a crown and put it on him. And they began saluting him, 'Hail king of the Jews!' They struck his head with a reed and spat on him; and they went down on their knees to do him homage. And when they had finished making fun of him, they took off the purple and dressed him in his own clothes.
>
> MK.15.16-20

Matthew describes this scene of mockery in much the same way as Mark. Luke's version is shorter and less brutal, and he is the only one who stages this scene before Herod:

> Then Herod, together with his guards, treated him with contempt and made fun of him; he put a rich cloak on him and sent him back to Pilate.
>
> LK.23.11

In John's gospel the scene takes place before Pilate. It occurs just after Pilate has had Jesus flogged:

> . . . the soldiers twisted some thorns into a crown and put it on his head and dressed him in a purple robe. They kept coming up to him and saying, 'Hail, king of the Jews!' and slapping him in the face. Pilate came outside again and said to them, 'Look I am going to bring him out to you to let you see that I find no case against him.' Jesus then came out wearing the crown of thorns and the purple robe. Pilate said, 'Here is the man.'
>
> JN.19.2-5

Much is made of this scene in popular representations of Jesus's last hours. This is so in Sunday School books with their sanitised pictures of Jesus with his crown of thorns and his purple robe, being mocked by the guards. It is so in the savagely comic song in the movie *Jesus Christ Superstar* when a fat and decadent Herod clad only in bathing trunks makes fun of Jesus beside a swimming pool. It is so in the solemn and elaborate crowd scene in the Oberammergau Passion Play when the richly robed Jesus is brought out to face the mob. All presentations of this story elaborate on the different details that appear in the different gospels, and embellish them freely.

The figure of the innocent victim who is set up as a mock king can be found in many different contexts, both political and religious, through many centuries. There is a wealth of such stories. The gospels' presentation of Jesus in this role can be related to a type of popular ritual that was practiced in the countries around the Mediterranean both before and during the time of the Roman Empire. These were rituals associated with religious festivals, and they could be very cruel. They involved making a victim into a mock king for a few hours or for as long as a month, and sometimes executing him. There is some evidence to suggest that on occasion there were two victims, one of whom was eventually released at the pleasure of the mob.

These rituals are discussed in the third edition of James Frazer's massive *The Golden Bough* in relation to the gospel stories of Jesus's death. Frazer, who was writing nearly a century ago, admits that the research into these popular orgies of cruelty is not conclusive, but he insists nonetheless that such stories have a place in any consideration of the stories of the death of Jesus. In his study, Frazer describes one specific mock king ritual in Alexandria. It was held to protest the presence of Herod Agrippa in the city. This was in the year 39 CE when Herod Agrippa had just been appointed King of Judaea by the Roman emperor. He was passing through Alexandria on his way to take possession of his new kingdom. Although he was liked by the Jews, Agrippa was much hated by the Greeks of Alexandria. One group acted out their hatred:

> . . . they laid hold of a certain harmless lunatic named Carabas, who used to roam the streets stark naked, the butt and laughing stock of urchins and idlers. This poor wretch they set up in a public place, clapped a paper crown on his head, thrust a broken reed in his hand by way of a sceptre, and having huddled a mat instead of a royal robe about his naked body, and surrounded him with a guard of bludgeon-men, they did obeisance to him as to a king and made a show of taking his opinion . . .[1]

For the gospel writers there is a strong irony in showing Jesus as a mock king. This is because for them, unlikely as it seems, Jesus really is a king. For them he is the long-awaited leader who comes of King David's line. But instead of being appropriately honoured, he suffers torture and derision from his own people.

It is possible that Jesus was treated as a mock king during his trials, and the gospel writers may have known of this from sources now lost. The only traceable sources for their stories are in the Hebrew scriptures. The tone and the atmosphere as well as some details of the mockery scenes in the gospels appear to derive from specific texts of scripture. The best known of these texts are the "suffering servant" passages in the book of Isaiah.

These passages are found in the section of the book of Isaiah written by an anonymous author known as Second Isaiah, or Deutero-Isaiah. Within his writings there are four poems known as the "Songs of the Servant of Yahweh". [2] These songs provide both form and content for the gospel writers throughout their stories of Jesus's arrest and trial and execution. Like the suffering servant, Jesus is abandoned and tortured and mocked:

1 Frazer, James, *The Golden Bough*, 3rd.Ed., c.1910, vol VI p.418.
2 for the servant songs see IS.42.1-4; IS.49.1-6; IS.50.4-9 and IS.52.13–IS.53.12.

. . . He had no form or charm to attract us,
no beauty to win our hearts;
he was despised, the lowest of men,
a man of sorrows, familiar with suffering,
one from whom, as it were, we averted our gaze,
despised, for whom we had no regard.

. . . .

Forcibly, after sentence, he was taken.
Which of his contemporaries was concerned
at his having been cut off from the land of the living,
at his having been struck dead for his people's
rebellion?
He was given a grave with the wicked,
and his tomb is with the rich,
although he had done no violence,
had spoken no deceit.
It was Yahweh's good pleasure to crush him with
pain;
if he gives his life as a sin offering,
he will see his offspring and prolong his life,
and through him Yahweh's good pleasure will be
done.

IS.53.2-3 & 8-10

These verses are parts of the fourth servant song. Along with the other three songs, its origin and meaning are still much debated, but all four songs appear to tell of the humiliation and suffering of an innocent individual whose sorrow and pain embodies that of his country and his people. The writings of Second Isaiah come from the time of the exile in Babylon, around 580-40 BCE, when the glory days of the kingdom of Israel were emphatically over. The sacrificial system of the temple also seemed to be at an end, for the temple had been destroyed along with most of Jerusalem by King Nebuchadnezzar of Babylon. This meant there was now no acceptable place for the regular sacrifice of animals[3], but the idea persisted of a helpless creature unresistingly taking on the sins of the community, and suffering for the community. In the fourth servant song the sufferer is described as being "like a lamb led to the slaughter-house, like a sheep dumb before its shearers". This idea of the passive victim is expressed in the third servant song by the voice of the sufferer himself:

Lord Yahweh has opened my ear
and I have not resisted,
I have not turned away.
I have offered my back to those who struck me,
my cheeks to those who plucked my beard;
I have not turned my face away
from insult and spitting.

IS.50.5-6

In their trial scenes, the gospels of Mark, Matthew and John all describe Jesus being struck in the face and spat upon. Such details can be traced not only to the writings of Second Isaiah, but to the book of the prophet Micah as well:

. . . They have laid seige to us;
the ruler of Israel will be struck
on the cheek with a rod.

MI.4.14

In the gospels the descriptions of Jesus on trial all share an atmosphere of lonely despair and humiliation, and a sense of unjust persecution. Just as it is in the writings of the Second Isaiah, this is a pervasive theme in a number of psalms:

When I stumble they gather in glee,
    gather around me;
strangers I never even knew

3 for more on animal sacrifice see above pp.105- 106 and pp.118-119.

tear me apart incessantly.
If I fall they surround me,
grinding their teeth at me.

PS.35.15-16

Poor and needy as I am,
my wounds go right to the heart;
I am passing away like a fading shadow,
they have shaken me off like a locust.

My knees are weak from lack of food,
my body lean for lack of fat.
I have become the butt of their taunts,
they shake their heads at the sight of me.

PS.109.22-25 [4]

The same theme surfaces yet again in the book of Job, along with the familiar detail of the persecutors spitting in the face of the sufferer:

My breathing is growing weaker
and the gravediggers are gathering for me.
Scoffers are my only companions,
their harshness haunts my nights.
. . . .
I have become a byword among foreigners,
and a creature on whose face to spit,
since I am nearly blind with grief
and my limbs are reduced to a shadow.

JB.17.1-2,6-7

In all of the gospels Jesus is taunted and knocked about by the guards at one or other of his trials. In Mark, Matthew and

4 for examples of more such psalms see Pss.22; 38; 69; and 88.

John, Jesus is also flogged. This was a normal prelude to a Roman crucifixion.

Although no details about this flogging are provided in the gospels, later imaginations have provided many. Over the centuries a strong tradition has arisen that the flogging of Jesus consisted of precisely 39 lashes.[5] There is no evidence to support this in the gospels, but the number thirty-nine could arise from one of Paul's letters. In this letter he tells how much he has suffered in the course of his missionary work, much more, so he says, than most of his fellow Christians:

> . . . I have been in prison more, I have been flogged more severely, many times exposed to death. Five times I have been given the thirty-nine lashes by the Jews; three times I have been beaten with sticks; once I was stoned . . .
>
> 2CO.11.23-25

The Jewish authorities in charge of synagogues were powerful figures. They carried out the punishments described by Paul with the full sanction of their Roman overlords who allowed them a considerable degree of secular power, and expected them to control their more fractious members. With the exception of the stoning, the penalties Paul describes were an accepted part of the exercise of authority by the synagogues. Stoning, however, was the Jewish form of capital punishment and the Romans may have reserved to themselves the right to carry out death sentences in their occupied territories. The attempt to stone Paul was probably a spontaneous and illegal mob action, not an organized judicial stoning.

Apart from stoning, the worst punishment meted out under Jewish law was flogging. In Jewish law, the number of strokes

5 for more about the flogging of Jesus see Harvey, A.E., "Forty Strokes Save One", in *Alternative Approaches to New Testament Studies*, A.E. Harvey ed., SPCK, London, 1985, pp 79ff.

permitted was limited to forty. The limit is set in the book of Deuteronomy:

> (The judge) may impose forty strokes but no more; otherwise, by the infliction of more, serious injury may be caused . . .
>
> DT.25.3

The number of thirty-nine strokes reported by Paul agrees with this ancient law about flogging. By process of association this same number has come to be applied in the minds of many people to the flogging of Jesus, even though he was flogged by the Romans who did not observe Jewish laws.

As the earliest gospel writer, Mark is the first to tell of Jesus being flogged. Mark is writing almost a generation after Paul and some two generations after the events of Jesus's death. He was writing during or just after the terrible war that disrupted communications, destroyed records and killed or dispersed witnesses. Reliable information about Jesus's trial and death would have been hard to come by. Probably all Mark could be sure of was that Jesus had been crucified, and that this crucifixion was a Roman act. Knowing this, Mark incorporates into his story the trial before Pilate and the flogging, for these were normal Roman practices before a crucifixion.

How Mark came to know that Jesus had been crucified is uncertain. Stories about the life and death of Jesus were no doubt circulating amongst his followers, but it is impossible to know the details of such an oral tradition. Equally it is impossible to be certain if there were earlier written stories, for none have survived. There is a possibility that Mark knew the letters of Paul that mention Jesus's death by crucifixion.[6] for by Mark's time Paul's letters were probably beginning to be circulated amongst the churches. Mark also could have learned from Paul

6 for example see RM.6.6; 1CO.1.17-18,23; 1CO.2.2; 1CO.2.8; 2CO.13.4; GA.2.20; GA.3.1; GA.6.14 and PH.2.7-8. Compare COL.1.20 and COL.2.14 that might also be written by Paul.

how he was "five times given the thirty-nine lashes", and this would have had a familiar ring to Mark. Such floggings were becoming an increasingly real threat to the followers of Jesus. This is evident earlier in Mark's gospel, when he has Jesus comment on this practice:

> 'Be on your guard: you will be handed over to sanhedrins; you will be beaten in synagogues; and you will be brought before governors and kings for my sake . . .'
>
> MK.13.9

The story in Mark's gospel of the flogging of Jesus makes sense on at least three different levels. It was a usual punishment inflicted on those who were condemned to be crucified. It reflects contemporary anxieties about the persecution of Christians in Mark's time. And the account of such punishment also recalls the sufferings of the unknown victim in the servant songs of Second Isaiah:

> As many people were aghast at him
> —he was so inhumanly disfigured
> that he no longer looked like a man—
> so many nations will be astonished
> and kings will stay tight-lipped before him,
> seeing what had never been told them,
> learning what they had not heard before.
>
> IS.52.14-15

In the gospel accounts of Jesus on trial, another accused and convicted character has a role to play. This is Barabbas, whose story is part of the trial scene before Pilate. Here is Mark's version:

> At festival time Pilate used to release a prisoner for them, any one they asked for. Now a man called Barabbas was then in prison with the rebels who had

> committed murder during the uprising. When the crowd went up and began to ask Pilate the customary favour, Pilate answered them, 'Do you want me to release for you the king of the Jews?' For he realised it was out of jealousy that the chief priests had handed Jesus over. The chief priests, however, had incited the crowd to demand that he should release Barabbas for them instead. Then Pilate spoke again, 'But in that case, what am I to do with the man you call king of the Jews?' They shouted back, 'Crucify him!' Pilate asked them, 'What harm has he done?' But they shouted all the louder, 'Crucify him!' So Pilate, anxious to placate the crowd, released Barabbas for them and, after having Jesus scourged, he handed him over to be crucified.
>
> MK.15.6-15

There are some intractable problems with this story of the release of Barabbas. There is very little support for the contention that there was an established custom of freeing a Jewish prisoner at festival time. By the same token, there is no precedent to be found in the scriptures that accounts either for this custom or for the role of Barabbas. There is also no satisfactory explanation for the behaviour of Pilate in this story. Several independent accounts of the man exist, and they agree that he was a merciless and cruel person, not at all likely to be "anxious to placate the crowd", as Mark puts it.[7] But although the whole Barabbas story is problematic as history, it does emphasise very sharply the humiliation of Jesus; how he is mocked and belittled, an innocent man rejected by the crowd in favour of a convicted criminal.

As Jesus's death approaches, the title "King of the Jews" becomes the focus for even more mockery. In the gospels of

7 for more about Barabbas and Pilate see Nineham, D.E., *The Gospel of St. Mark*, Pelican New Testament Commentaries, Penguin, London, 1963, p. 413.

Mark and Matthew this is particularly evident. They tell of jeering and sadistic taunts about kingship continuing even when Jesus is on the cross. Mark's version goes like this:

> It was the third hour when they crucified him. The inscription giving the charge against him read, 'The King of the Jews'. And they crucified two bandits with him, one on his right and one on his left. The passers-by jeered at him; they shook their heads and said, 'Aha! So you would destroy the Temple and rebuild it in three days! Then save yourself; come down from the cross!' The chief priests and the scribes mocked him among themselves in the same way with the words, 'He saved others, he cannot save himself. Let the Christ, the king of Israel, come down from the cross now, for us to see it and believe.'
>
> MK.15.25-32

Here the people who are mocking Jesus are given words that come directly from Psalm 22:

> . . . all who see me jeer at me,
> they sneer and wag their heads,
> 'He trusted himself to Yahweh, let Yahweh set him free!
> Let him deliver him, as he took such delight in him.'
>
> PS.22.7-8

Luke also tells of Jesus being mocked while he is on the cross. His version is different:

> The people stayed there watching. As for the leaders, they jeered at him with the words, 'He saved others, let him save himself if he is the Christ of God, the Chosen One.' The soldiers mocked him too, coming up to him, offering him vinegar, and saying, 'If

> you are the king of the Jews, save yourself.' Above him there was an inscription: 'This is the King of the Jews'.
>
> LK.23.35-38

The inscription "King of the Jews" above Jesus on the cross is an extension of how he is treated as a mock king in the trial scenes. In all of the gospels the use of the title "King of the Jews", and the mockery of Jesus as a king is profoundly ironic. When Jesus is on trial, and later when he is dying on the cross, he looks nothing like a king. He looks instead like a helpless victim entirely at the mercy of his persecutors, derided by the use of a title that only emphasises his powerlessness. Yet despite all this, for the gospel writers Jesus is a king, because he is, for them, the Messiah.

Expectations of the Messiah included the idea that this leader should be a king. In how they link Jesus to King David the gospels assert a royal lineage for him, connecting him directly to the kings of Israel. On the face of it, though, there is a deep conflict between the gospels' presentation of Jesus and the idea of a messianic king. They appear to be completely contradictory.[8] Given this apparent contradiction, the way in which Jesus is hailed as "king" could only be expected to attract both mockery and doubt.

Such mockery and doubt have an important dramatic function in the gospels, for in the end the mockery will be silenced and the doubt resolved. In the end, paradoxically, they serve to emphasise who Jesus really is, and they help to vindicate him in the eyes of his followers. In addition, these accounts of the tormenting of Jesus can also be understood to reflect the sufferings of Christians in the first century, at the time the gospels were being written. This was when Christians were facing increasing harassment in the synagogues. The stories of the mockery of Jesus provided a model of unmerited suffering that could both inspire and comfort.

8 see above pp.157-159.

The mockery of Jesus is described in language and images that belong to a scriptural tradition in which defenseless and innocent victims are cruelly treated. And this tradition provides far more than mere language and images. It also provides hope. In previous stories from the scriptures the undeserved suffering of the helpless victim is usually vindicated:

> After the ordeal he has endured,
> he will see the light and be content.
> By his knowledge, the upright one, my servant will justify many
> by taking their guilt on himself.
>
> Hence I shall give him a portion with the many,
> and he will share the booty with the mighty,
> for having exposed himself to death
> and for being counted as one of the rebellious,
> whereas he was bearing the sin of many
> and interceding for the rebellious.
>
> IS.53.11-12 [9]

The gospel writers believe that Jesus is the Messiah, that he is a king. Their stories are written with the conviction that despite all the ill-treatment and mockery Jesus suffers, he will be vindicated. The stories also encourage the belief that this vindication will be shared by all his followers.

9 see also PS.35.27-28; PS.109.30-31; PS.22.22- 31; JB.42.7-17.

CHAPTER THIRTEEN

Crucified

They led him out to crucify him. They enlisted a passer-by, Simon of Cyrene, father of Alexander and Rufus, who was coming in from the country, to carry his cross. They brought Jesus to the place called Golgotha, which means the place of the skull. They offered him wine mixed with myrrh, but he refused it. Then they crucified him, and shared out his clothing, casting lots to decide what each should get. It was the third hour when they crucified him. The inscription giving the charge against him read, 'The King of the Jews'. And they crucified two bandits with him, one on his right and one on his left.

MK. 15.21-27

Mark's description of the crucifixion of Jesus is the shortest and the least elaborate of all four gospel accounts, as well as being the earliest. In the letters of Paul there are even earlier references to the death of Jesus, written roughly twenty years before Mark. Unlike Mark and the other gospel writers, Paul does not provide descriptions of the death. Instead, he provides lengthy explanations about what the death means. In the course of these explanations, Paul sometimes makes glancing references to the way Jesus died. This passage from his first letter to the Corinthians is one example:

> It is of the mysterious wisdom of God that we talk, the wisdom that was hidden, which God predestined to be for our glory before the ages began. None of the rulers of the age recognised it; for if they had recognised it, they would not have crucified the Lord of glory . . .
>
> 1CO.2.7-8 [1]

The most detail Paul ever provides about the death of Jesus is in his letter to the Philippians, when he quotes what is believed to be an early Christian hymn:

> . . . he emptied himself,
> taking the form of a slave,
> becoming as human beings are;
> and being in every way like a human being,
> he was humbler yet,
> even to accepting death, death on a cross.
>
> PH.2.7-8

All that can be concluded from these references to the death of Jesus is that Paul is affirming that Jesus died by crucifixion, and that this appears to have been common knowledge amongst early Christians. In the quagmire of historical uncertainties that arise in the New Testament stories of Jesus, one thing that can be said with some confidence is that Jesus was crucified. Paul's early references to the crucifixion, scant as they are, carry considerable authority. They transmit the beliefs and assumptions of Christians from much earlier in the first century than the gospels. It is very likely that early references such as these led Mark to tell his story of the crucifixion. In turn, out of Mark's story came the other accounts of crucifixion.

Despite all of the stories told in the gospels, details of the crucifixion of Jesus are very uncertain. The gospels provide

1 for more examples see above p.170, footnote #6.

vivid descriptions from which highly coloured and highly emotional images of the crucifixion have developed. These have been presented in painting and in sculpture, in stained glass, in mosaics and in movies. Yet despite what appears to be a wealth of detailed images, to be certain of any single detail or incident that is reported as part of the crucifixion of Jesus is virtually impossible.

A good example is the story of the soldiers gambling for the clothing of Jesus at the foot of the cross. This dramatic little incident is reported in all the gospels, and it is popular in paintings, passion plays, and Hollywood productions. But it is extremely unlikely, verging on impossible, that Mark, as the first gospel writer, actually witnessed this. The incident is not a reliably reported event. Instead it is part of a pattern of storytelling in which incidents and details from earlier sources are borrowed and used in later stories. So it comes as no surprise to discover that the men gambling for the clothes of a suffering victim are familiar figures. They appear in one of the psalms:

> My strength is trickling away,
> my bones are all disjointed,
> my heart has turned to wax,
> melting inside me.
> My mouth is dry as earthenware,
> my tongue sticks to my jaw.
> You lay me down in the dust of death.
>
> A pack of dogs surrounds me,
> a gang of villains is closing in on me
> as if to hack off my hands and my feet.
> I can count every one of my bones,
> while they look on and gloat;
> they divide my garments among them
> and cast lots for my clothing.

PS.22.16-18

In their stories of the crucifixion, perhaps more clearly than anywhere else in their writings, the gospel writers use old material to tell new stories. Most of all, they use the ancient laments of Israel, especially the measured words of the psalms. Their very use of such material implies a realization that everything they write must function on two levels. First, they must tell good stories. Second, these stories must be written and understood "according to the scriptures". The scriptures provide a frame of reference that is essential if the stories of the gospel writers are to carry weight and authority.

In looking at the gospel accounts of the crucifixion of Jesus, as far as possible we will stay with Mark's gospel, using it as our base text. But because each gospel writer adds his own characteristic and well-known additions to the story, it will often be necessary to look at passages in the other gospels as well. For instance, on the way to the place of crucifixion, Luke has much more to say than the other gospel writers. Mark and Matthew say only that one Simon of Cyrene is made to carry the cross for Jesus. John says only that Jesus carries his own cross. Luke agrees about Simon of Cyrene, but he then adds another episode to the story:

> As they were leading him away they seized on a man, Simon from Cyrene, who was coming in from the country, and made him shoulder the cross and carry it behind Jesus. Large numbers of people followed him, and women too, who mourned and lamented for him. But Jesus turned to them and said, 'Daughters of Jerusalem, do not weep for me; weep rather for yourselves and for your children. For look, the days are surely coming when people will say, "Blessed are those who are barren, the wombs that have never borne children, the breasts that have never suckled!" Then they will *say to the mountains, "Fall on us!"; to the hills, "Cover us!"* For if this is

> what is done to green wood, what will be done when the wood is dry?'
>
> LK.23.26-31

This passage brings together many elements. First of all, there is the story of the lamentation of the women. On the surface this is a typically Lucan touch, sympathetic and kindly in tone, but it is much more than that. It recalls another more ancient lamentation at the time of another more ancient procession out of Jerusalem. This is a reminder of the lowest point of the career of Jesus's ancestor King David, who as a betrayed and broken man was driven out of Jerusalem. As the king departed, he wept over his city:

> David then made his way up the Mount of Olives, weeping as he went, his head covered and his feet bare. And all the people with him had their heads covered and made their way up, weeping as they went.
>
> 2S.15.30 [2]

In Luke's description of the women weeping as Jesus walks from Jerusalem to his place of execution, there are still more layers of scriptural references. When Jesus replies to these "daughters of Jerusalem" in foreboding tones about how they should weep for themselves rather than for him and tells them to rejoice if they have not borne children, this is language of the end times. The implication is that Jerusalem will soon be destroyed and everything will end in a terrible last battle. In Jesus's words to the women, Luke is bringing together two separate passages from the book of Hosea.

Hosea was writing in the second half of the eighth century BCE, a very gloomy time for the northern kingdom of Israel, a time of great political upheaval, complete with rebellions, assassinations and invasions by the Assyrians. There seemed to be

2 for more on this passage see above p.139.

little hope left for Israel, called "Ephraim" by Hosea, and the prophet spoke in a voice of despair:

> It was like finding grapes in the desert when I found Israel,
> like seeing early fruit on a fig tree when I saw your ancestors;
> but when they reached Baal-Peor, they devoted themselves to Shame
> and became as loathsome as the thing they loved.
> The glory of Ephraim will fly away like a bird:
> no giving birth, no pregnancy, no conceiving.
> If they rear their children, I shall take them away
> before they grow up!
> Woe to them indeed when I leave them!
> Ephraim looked to me like Tyre, planted in a meadow,
> so Ephraim will present his children to the slaughterer.
> Give them, Yahweh - what are you to give? —
> give them wombs that miscarry and dried-up breasts.
>
> HO.9.10-14

Not long after this lament Hosea goes on to describe how Bethel, one of Israel's greatest shrines, will be destroyed and its altars abandoned. Hosea not only foretells its destruction, he also deliberately insults the great shrine by calling it "Aven" or "Beth-Aven", which means "house of sin".

> The high places of Aven, the sin of Israel,
> will be destroyed;
> thorns and thistles will grow over their altars.
> Then they will say to the mountains, 'Cover us!'
> and to the hills, 'Fall on us!'
>
> HO.10.8[3]

3 for more use of this passage in the gospels see MK.13.14- 23; MT.24.15-25; and LK.21.20-24.

Luke has Jesus repeat this doom-filled language of the prophet Hosea as he approaches his death. This language can be understood to recall not only the ancient history of Hosea's time, but the recent history of a particular group of Christians. During the years of the war leading up to the destruction of Jerusalem in 70 CE, many Christians had left or been driven out of Jerusalem. Some of them spent years as refugees, moving from place to place in the mountains of Judaea. Finally they settled at a place called Pella on the east bank of the river Jordan. The trials and dangers they had faced in the hostile countryside seem to have been known in some parts of the early church, but little about them is reliably known today.[4]

Luke was writing about fifteen years after the Romans had destroyed Jerusalem, about fifty years after the crucifixion, and some eight hundred years after Hosea had called despairingly to the mountains "Fall on us". In his story of Jesus walking to his execution, when he repeats these words of Hosea, past and present and future are brought together by Luke. History is foreshortened, and the end is very near in more senses than one. Jesus is about to die and in Luke's own time Jerusalem had been destroyed. Luke speaks in the language of a prophet foreseeing doom. A terrible end is in sight. Hills and mountains will fall and the laments of women will ring out over the ruins of Jerusalem. Hosea said all this centuries earlier; it could be seen in the destruction of Jerusalem and in the recent hardships of Christian refugees in the desert. It is also a reminder of the promised end times that were expected so imminently by early Christians.

It is not only Hosea who prophesies that the women of Jerusalem will lament. The same idea appears later in the scriptures in the book of Zechariah. Written by the unknown prophet whose writings were added to those of Zechariah himself, this passage stresses the grief of the women when Jerusalem faces its end:

4 for more see Carrington, Philip; *The Early Christian Church*; C.U.P.; Cambridge; 1957; pp.227f.

'When that day comes, I shall set about destroying all the nations who advance against Jerusalem. But over the House of David and the inhabitants of Jerusalem I shall pour out a spirit of grace and prayer, and they will look to me. They will mourn for the one whom they have pierced as though for an only child, and weep for him as people weep for a first-born child. And the country will mourn clan by clan:

The clan of the House of David by itself,
and their women by themselves;
the clan of the House of Nathan by itself,
and their women by themselves;
the clan of the House of Levi by itself,
and their women by themselves;
the clan of the House of Shimei by itself,
and their women by themseves;
the rest of the clans, every clan by itself,
and their women by themselves.'

ZC. 12:9-14

Mark and Matthew and John do not have Jesus speak explicitly about the coming end on the way to his crucifixion. This end is evident in the very events they describe at the hour of Jesus's death. After Jesus has been mocked by the onlookers as he hangs on the cross, Mark continues:

When the sixth hour came there was darkness over the whole land until the ninth hour. And at the ninth hour Jesus cried out in a loud voice, '*Eloi, eloi, lama sabachthani?*' which means, '*My God, my God, why have you forsaken me?*'

MK. 15.33-34

These words from the cross are repeated by Matthew, though not by Luke or John. They are a direct citation from Psalm 22, one of the psalms usually ascribed to King David:

My God, my God, why have you forsaken me?
The words of my groaning do nothing to save me.
My God, I call by day but you do not answer,
at night, but I find no respite.

Yet you, the Holy One,
who make your home in the praises of Israel,
in you our ancestors put their trust,
they trusted and you set them free.
To you they called for help and were delivered;
in you they trusted and were not put to shame.

PS.22.1-5 [5]

When Mark tells of Jesus crying out in the words of Psalm 22, he also describes a darkness falling over the land at midday. This darkness can be understood in many different ways. Earlier in Mark's gospel, another darkness is mentioned in apocalyptic language that Mark attributes to Jesus himself:

> 'But in those days, after that time of distress, the sun will be darkened, the moon will not give its light, the stars will come falling out of the sky and the powers in the heavens will be shaken. And then they will see the Son of man coming in the clouds with great power and glory . . .'

MK.13.24-26 [6]

In contrast to this idea of an apocalyptic darkness signifying the coming end of the world, there is another tradition of darkness falling on the land as a sign of God's favour. When the sky had darkened at another time in the history of Israel, it was a sign that God was trying to save his people. This story is told in the book of Exodus and it describes how dark falls over Egypt as Moses tries to free the Israelites from slavery:

5 for more on the words from the cross see below p.195-196.
6 for related passages see above p.5, footnote #1.

> Yahweh then said to Moses, 'Stretch out your hand towards heaven, and let darkness, darkness so thick that it can be felt, cover Egypt.' So Moses stretched out his hand towards heaven, and for three days there was thick darkness over the whole of Egypt. No one could see anyone else or move about for three days, but all the Israelites did have light where they were living.
>
> EX.10.21-23

This darkness was the ninth of the ten plagues that preceded the liberating journey of the Israelties from Egypt to the promised land. Many centuries later, in the stories of the crucifixion of Jesus, another darkness precedes the beginning of a new day for the followers of Jesus.

During the time of the prophet Amos the looked-for day of deliverance and new life was called "the day of the Lord". Amos had witnessed many false hopes and expectations about this coming day. He was the keeper of an orchard turned prophet, and he lived very near the time of Hosea. At one point in his prophetic career Amos goes from his orchard in Judaea to speak to the neighbouring Hebrews at Bethel. He delivers a dire warning about their desire for this new day, this "day of the Lord". This warning comes across best in the sonorous prose of the King James Bible:

> Woe unto you that desire the day of the Lord! to what end is it for you? The day of the Lord is darkness, and not light.
>
> As if a man did flee from a lion, and a bear met him; or went into the house, and leaned his hand on the wall, and a serpent bit him.
>
> Shall not the day of the Lord be darkness, and not light? even very dark, and no brightness in it?
>
> AM.5.18-20 (AV)

Later on Amos again speaks of this ominous darkness:

> On that Day—declares the Lord Yahweh—
> I shall make the sun go down at noon
> and darken the earth in broad daylight.
> I shall turn your festivals into mourning
> and all your singing into lamentation; . . .
>
> AM.8.9-10

In describing darkness at noon when Jesus is dying on the cross, Mark is providing the clearest evidence he can find that something cataclysmic is happening. This darkness is the dawning of the "day of the Lord". It is a sign that something new is emerging, and for Mark this is the promised glory for the people of Israel and for the whole world.

This darkness also signifies the despair of the sufferer who has been abandoned. It is comparable to the dark that envelopes the despairing psalmist in Psalm 88.

> But, for my part, I cry to you, Yahweh,
> every morning my prayer comes before you;
> why, Yahweh, do you rebuff me,
> turn your face away from me?
>
> Wretched and close to death since childhood,
> I have borne your terrors — I am finished!
> Your anger has overwhelmed me,
> your terrors annihilated me.
>
> They flood around me all day long,
> close in on me all at once.
> You have deprived me of friends and companions,
> and all that I know is the dark.
>
> PS.88.13-18 [7]

7 for more on Psalm 88 see above pp.119-120.

Although Mark's account of unnatural darkness at the time of the death of Jesus is dramatic, it does not satisfy Matthew. His description of what happens includes the darkness, but it goes much further:

> And suddenly, the veil of the Sanctuary was torn in two from top to bottom, the earth quaked, the rocks were split, the tombs opened and the bodies of many holy people rose from the dead, and these, after his resurrection, came out of the tombs, entered the holy city and appeared to a number of people. The centurion, together with the others guarding Jesus, had seen the earthquake and all that was taking place, and they were terrified and said, 'In truth this man was son of God.'
>
> MT.27.51-54

Even the most generous reader of Matthew might raise an eyebrow here. Keen to prove a point about the earth-shaking nature of the events taking place, Matthew overstates his case. His description of the dead arising and wandering about stretches the limits of belief. The resurrection of the dead was a contentious issue amongst both Christians and Jews during the first century. This belief had been evolving slowly for several centuries and although it had become widespread its roots are sparse within the Hebrew Scriptures. There are few direct references to resurrection, and most of them are imprecise and confusing. [8] Matthew creates his ghostly scenario from the much debated beliefs that had developed from these scattered allusions. With imaginative flair, he builds on these beliefs to produce a scene that is unmatched elsewhere in the gospels.

None of the other gospel writers reproduce Matthew's list of extraordinary phenomena and manifestations at the time of Jesus's death. John mentions nothing of the kind, not even the

8 see above, pp.61-69 *passim* for more on "resurrection" and the scriptures.

darkness. Luke agrees with Matthew and Mark that darkness fell, but he expresses this differently, saying "the sun's light failed", using the Greek word that means an eclipse.

Far more than the other gospel writers, in his crucifixion scene Luke concentrates on the human drama of those who are suffering. Only he pays any attention to the other men who are crucified with Jesus. In doing so he recounts a conversation as they are all dying:

> One of the criminals hanging there abused him: 'Are you not the Christ? Save yourself and us as well.' But the other spoke up and rebuked him. 'Have you no fear of God at all?' he said. 'You got the same sentence as he did, but in our case we deserved it: we are paying for what we did. But this man has done nothing wrong.' Then he said, 'Jesus, remember me when you come into your kingdom.' He answered him, 'In truth I tell you, today you will be with me in paradise.'
>
> LK.23.39-43

This exchange establishes once again that Jesus is an innocent man who has done no wrong. It acknowledges Jesus as the Christ, the Messiah, whose kingdom is still to come. This passage also picks up on Luke's earlier hints of how Jesus knows he will be counted amongst wrongdoers:

> '. . . I tell you these words of scripture are destined to be fulfilled in me: *He was counted as one of the rebellious . . .*'
>
> LK.22.37

Here Jesus is quoting one of the servant songs from the book of Isaiah:

> Hence I shall give him a portion with the many,
> and he will share the booty with the mighty,

for having exposed himself to death
and for being counted as one of the rebellious,
whereas he was bearing the sin of many
and interceding for the rebellious.

IS.53.12

Crucified as he is with two other convicted men, Jesus is indeed "counted as one of the rebellious". Having emphasised this point Luke brings his crucifixion scene to an end:

> It was now about the sixth hour and the sun's light failed, so that darkness came over the whole land until the ninth hour. The veil of the Sanctuary was torn right down the middle. Jesus cried out in a loud voice saying, 'Father, *into your hands I commit my spirit.*' With these words he breathed his last.

LK.23.44-46

Luke and Matthew and Mark all agree that at the time of Jesus's death the "veil of the Sanctuary" is torn down the middle. The history of this veil, or curtain, of the Sanctuary goes back a very long way.

The veil first appears in the holy tent which, according to the book of Exodus, was set up in the desert after the Israelites had crossed over the Red Sea on their way to the promised land. The God of Israel gives detailed instructions to Moses about how this "Dwelling" is to be fitted out:

> You will make a curtain of finely woven linen, dyed violet-purple, red-purple and crimson, and embroidered with great winged creatures, and put it on four poles of acacia wood overlaid with gold, with golden hooks for them, set in four sockets of silver. You will put the curtain below the clasps, so that inside behind the curtain, you can place the ark of the Testimony, and the curtain will mark the division

> for you between the Holy Place and the Holy of Holies.
>
> EX.26.31-34

This curtain sets apart the holiest sanctuary from the rest of the dwelling. When Solomon, son of David, later builds his magnificent temple in Jerusalem, the same kind of curtain reappears:

> He (Solomon) also made the Curtain of violet, scarlet, crimson and fine linen, working a design of winged creatures on it.
>
> 2CH.3.14

The curtain or veil later becomes a feature of the grandiose third temple that Herod the Great began to build nearly fifty years before the death of Jesus. It is this veil of the third temple that is "torn in two from top to bottom" according to Mark.

Mark's story about the temple veil, later reiterated by Matthew and Luke, can best be understood in light of the events of his time. He was writing at the time of the war against the Jews when the temple in Jerusalem was levelled to the ground. The tearing of the curtain can be seen as a symbol for this destruction of the temple. Mark is showing that the "Day of the Lord" is at hand, the old world order is in its death throes and a new age is dawning. His story of the destruction of the temple veil is a dramatic sign of this painful process, and it also signifies the cosmic disorder that accompanies the death of Jesus.

Matthew is even more emphatic about the tearing of the veil as a portent of an old age dying and a new age dawning. To state his case more powerfully, Matthew adds the earthquake, and for good measure describes rocks splitting, tombs opening and the dead coming to life. Luke and John do not share these extremes. Although Luke tells of the temple veil being torn and the darkness at noon, he does not dwell on these. John, who wrote more than a decade later than Luke, does not include either the darkness at noon or the tearing of the temple veil.

According to both Mark and Matthew, shortly before he dies Jesus cries out loud. In both gospels onlookers think he is calling on Elijah:

> When some of those who stood by heard this, they said, 'Listen, he is calling on Elijah.' Someone ran and soaked a sponge in vinegar and, putting it on a reed, gave it to him to drink saying, 'Wait! And see if Elijah will come to take him down.'
>
> MK.15.34-37[9]

This is not the first reference to Elijah in the gospels of Mark and Matthew. Time and again Jesus is compared to, or seen as a reincarnation of Elijah, who was one of the greatest of all the prophets.[10] Elijah led an exciting life and his adventures are reported in the First Book of Kings starting at Chapter 17, with some additional material about Elijah's death in the first two chapters of the Second Book of Kings. This is how Elijah is first introduced:

> Elijah the Tishbite, of Tishbe in Gilead, said to Ahab, 'By the life of Yahweh, God of Israel, whom I serve, there will be neither dew nor rain these coming years unless I give the word.'
>
> 1K.17.1

In this terse statement Elijah is threatening King Ahab, one of the most powerful monarchs the Hebrews ever produced. Elijah's blunt challenge to this mighty monarch is entirely in character, for Elijah is a man of fiery courage, who never doubts that God is on his side. His confidence seems justified. His threat to Ahab is carried out, and the prophet miraculously

9 see also MT.27.45-50.
10 for example see MT.11.14; MT.16.14; MT.17.3ff; MT.27.47,49; MK.6.15; MK.9.4ff; MK.15.36; LK.1.17; LK.4.25; LK.9.8,19; LK.9.30ff; and JN.1.21,25.

survives the calamitous drought that follows.

All stories of Elijah are reported by admiring partisans of the prophet. Their admiration of Elijah is almost equalled by their hatred of King Ahab, and this hatred of Ahab is almost but not quite equalled by the hatred felt for his wife Jezebel. Elijah and Jezebel are always at daggers drawn and their conflicts are on an epic scale. Elijah is a prophet of the old Hebrew religion; Jezebel is the daughter of Ethbaal, king of Sidon. Her marriage to Ahab was a political alliance between two powerful nations. These nations had their differences, not the least of which was that Jezebel and her people followed Baal, the fertility god of the Canaanites. When she marries, Jezebel brings her religion with her to the land of Israel, and together she and Ahab build a temple to Baal. Jezebel has influence and money and the power that go with them; Elijah has only the conviction that when he threatens a drought, his God will provide a drought, and when he calls for fire his God will provide fire.

Elijah is so sure of his God that he sets up a show of strength on Mount Carmel. There are two rival sacrifices. Jezebel's prophets of Baal, all four hundred and fifty of them, slaughter an ox, set it on the pyre and call on Baal to provide the fire to roast it. There is no result. Meanwhile Elijah, working alone, repairs a broken-down altar of Yahweh, sets another ox on another pyre and then calls for help. He has some of his people pour a great quantity of water over the sacrifice until the water runs in all directions. Then he prays for fire:

> '... let them know today that you are God in Israel, and that I am your servant ... Answer me, Yahweh, answer me, so that this people may know that you, Yahweh, are God and are winning back their hearts.'
>
> Then Yahweh's fire fell and consumed the burnt offering and the wood and licked up the water in the trench ...
>
> 1K.18.37-38

After this Elijah calls for the people to seize the prophets of Baal and he slaughters all four hundred and fifty of them, apparently single-handedly, on the banks of the river called Kishon. But Elijah's triumph is brief, he is no match for the enraged Jezebel. She is determined to do away with him and he is forced to flee into the desert. This leads to his vision of God on the holy mountain of Horeb, also called Sinai. [11]

After his return from the desert Elijah anoints his successor Elisha. King Ahab carries on to win notable victories in battle, but he continues to antagonise the God of Israel and Elijah continues to expostulate. Before Elijah's death, he repeats the miracle of Moses and parts the waters, not of the Red Sea but of the Jordan river. He and Elisha cross the river dryshod, and there on the other side of Jordan Elijah is swept up to heaven in a chariot of fire, in a death scene as flamboyant as his life.

The gospel writers often describe Jesus in light of what they know about Elijah. The influence is very clear. Elijah is renowned as a great miracle worker and a great disturber of the status quo, and so is Jesus. Elijah is described being raised to glory in the full sight of onlookers, and so is Jesus. According to Mark, when Jesus is on the cross he cries out in Aramaic "Eloi, eloi, lama sabachthani?". These are the words from Psalm 22 translated as "My God, My God, why have you forsaken me?". Matthew closely follows Mark's lead in his gospel, but he has the Hebrew word "Eli" in place of the Aramaic "Eloi". In both gospels the bystanders seem to mishear what Jesus has said, for they declare that Jesus is calling on Elijah. Given the important place held by Elijah in the scriptures, it is quite logical that Jesus might be understood to be calling on Elijah to rescue him. This reflects a widespread belief that Elijah offers help and solace to those in despair.[12] And the role of Elijah carries even

11 for more on Elijah on Mount Horeb see below pp.254-255, 273-274.

12 for more on Elijah see: Wiener, Aharon, *The Prophet Elijah in the Development of Judaism*, Routledge and Kegan Paul, London, 1978, pp.1-37, 136- 151 *passim*.

more significance than that. He is the prophet expected to return when the "day of the Lord" is near. This expectation is clearly expressed in the book of the prophet Malachi:

> 'Look, I shall send you the prophet Elijah before the great and awesome Day of Yahweh comes. He will reconcile children to their parents and parents to their children, to forestall my putting the country under the curse of destruction.'
>
> ML.3.23-24

In the story of Elijah in the book of Kings, Elijah himself knows despair. When he has fled to the desert even this great prophet knows what it is to feel abandoned by his God and in despair:

> 'Yahweh,' he said, 'I have had enough. Take my life; I am no better than my ancestors.'
>
> 1K.19.4

When he is dying on the cross, Jesus too speaks words of total despair. His despair recalls that of Elijah, but it is expressed in the powerful words of the psalmist. Such is the world of text of the gospel writers.

CHAPTER FOURTEEN

Dead

As Jesus is dying the gospels all report his final words. These words are memorable, but they vary from one gospel to another:

> '*My God, my God, why have you forsaken me?*'
>
> MK.15.34 and MT.27.46

> 'Father, forgive them; they do not know what they are doing.'
>
> LK.23.34

> 'In truth I tell you, today you will be with me in paradise.'
>
> LK.23.43

> 'Father, *into your hands I commit my spirit.*'
>
> LK.23.46

> 'Woman, this is your son' . . 'This is your mother.'
>
> JN.19.26-27

> '*I am thirsty.*'
>
> JN.19.28

'It is fulfilled.'

JN.19.30

Only Mark and Matthew include that bleak phrase from the opening of Psalm 22 "My God, my God why have you forsaken me?". Luke and John present entirely different words. The variations in the words from the cross demonstrate the different styles of the writers; they also draw on different sources and they emphasise different points.

In his crucifixion scene Luke has Jesus say, "Father forgive them; they do not know what they are doing". This is not repeated in any other gospel, and there is some doubt about the authenticity of the text.[1] This phrase is, however, consistent with Luke's usual style. Throughout his gospel he shows a gentler side than the other gospel writers, and tends to be more forgiving and more sympathetic.

The next words Luke has Jesus say from the cross are addressed to one of the men being crucified with him: "In truth I tell you, today you will be with me in paradise." Once again, this is a phrase unique to Luke's gospel, and once again it can be understood as an indication of Luke's sympathetic approach. He invests the two men crucified beside Jesus with personalities and individual points of view, and he is the only gospel writer to do so. In the words he attributes to these men Luke stresses both the identity and the innocence of Jesus, and in the reply a message of hope and mercy is extended.[2]

The final words Luke has Jesus say on the cross are uttered just after the temple veil is torn in half:

> Jesus cried out in a loud voice saying, 'Father, *into your hand I commit my spirit.*' With these words he breathed his last.

LK.23.46

1 Some early manuscripts omit this sentence entirely. The problem is noted in many modern English versions. For example see notes in NJB, NRSV, REB & NIV.

2 for more on the words of the dying men see above pp.188-89.

These words are from Psalm 31:

> Draw me out of the net they have spread for me,
> for you are my refuge;
> to your hands I commit my spirit,
> by you have I been redeemed.
>
> PS.31.4-5

In John's gospel, the final moments of Jesus's life are described in very different terms:

> Near the cross of Jesus stood his mother and his mother's sister, Mary the wife of Clopas, and Mary of Magdala. Seeing his mother and the disciple whom he loved standing near her, Jesus said to his mother, 'Woman, this is your son.' Then to the disciple he said, 'This is your mother.' And from that hour the disciple took her into his home.
>
> JN.19.25-27

Only in this scene of John's is there a group of Jesus's followers standing "near the cross". In the other accounts the onlookers stand at a distance. Only here does Jesus speak from the cross to his mother and to the disciple he loves.

For Christians who attach great significance to the role of Mary the mother of Jesus, this is a very important scene. These words of Jesus are believed to express far more than the love of a son who, even in his agony, wants to care for his grieving mother. Rather they are understood as a declaration that Mary is to be cherished as the spiritual mother of all followers of Jesus, who are represented by the beloved disciple.[3]

John was writing at the end of the first century. By this time, both Matthew and Luke had asserted the virginity of Mary in their stories about the birth of Jesus. In his gospel, although John says nothing about the virginal conception and includes

3 see NJB, p. 1787, note L.

very few references to Mary, what he does say confirms the centrality of Mary in the eyes of many Christians. This is almost entirely due to the prominent role John assigns her at the time of Jesus's death.

After John tells of Jesus speaking to his followers at the foot of the cross, he goes on to describe the death of Jesus:

> After this, Jesus knew that everything had now been completed and, so that the scripture should be completely fulfilled, he said: '*I am thirsty.*' A jar full of sour wine stood there; so, putting a sponge soaked in the wine on a hyssop stick, they held it up to his mouth. After Jesus had taken the wine he said, 'It is fulfilled'; and bowing his head he gave up his spirit.
>
> JN.19.28-30

In having Jesus say "I am thirsty", John echoes two of the psalms:

> My mouth is dry as earthenware,
> my tongue sticks to my jaw.
> You lay me down in the dust of death.
>
> PS.22.15

> You know well the insults,
> the shame and disgrace I endure.
> Every one of my oppressors is known to you.
> Insult has broken my heart past cure.
> I hoped for sympathy, but in vain,
> for consolers - not one to be found.
> To eat they gave me poison,
> to drink, vinegar when I was thirsty.
>
> PS.69.19-21

The other gospels also report Jesus being offered a bitter drink while he is on the cross. In Mark and in Matthew, Jesus refuses this, but according to John after Jesus tastes the drink he dies with the words that are traditionally translated as "It is finished". Again, these words echo the despair of one of the psalms:

> ... why, Yahweh, do you rebuff me,
> turn your face away from me?
>
> Wretched and close to death since childhood,
> I have borne your terrors — I am finished!
> Your anger has overwhelmed me,
> your terrors annihilated me.
>
> They flood around me all day long,
> close in on me all at once.
> You have deprived me of friends and companions,
> and all that I know is the dark.
>
> PS.88.14-18[4]

Another powerful cry of despair comes in Psalm 69:

> Save me, God, for the waters
> have closed in on my very being.
>
> I am sinking in the deepest swamp
> and there is no firm ground.
>
> PS.69.1-2

Psalm 69, like Psalm 88, resonates in the stories of the crucifixion. These two psalms have a lot in common. As we suggested in Chapter 9, the sufferer of Psalm 88 may be a priest or shaman figure, whose fear and agony is thought to be for the greater good of the agricultural community and whose suffering

4 PS.88.16B is translated here as "I am finished". It appears differently in other translations. For example: "I am desperate"(NRSV); "your terrors have destroyed me"(NIV) and "your onslaughts have overwhelmed me"(REB).

became stylised as part of an annual fertility rite. In Psalm 69 the sufferer may be a king whose fear and pain is thought to be for the greater good of Israel and whose suffering became stylised as a much-repeated lament. This king could be King David himself, the great leader who is claimed as Jesus's ancestor.[5]

According to this theory about Psalm 69, penance and suffering were required of King David. This goes back to early in his career when the king had grievously offended his God by taking the wife of another man and doing away with her husband. When the fiery prophet Nathan hears of this he foretells dire and long-term consequences for the entire nation and declares that the king will be punished. Although the reign of David is hailed in the scriptures as a golden age for Israel, his kingdom appears to have lurched from one crisis to another. As Nathan said, because of David's sin, "For this, your household will never be free of the sword . . .".[6]

Some of the laments of the psalms appear to describe the atonement of David in response to the succession of crises in his kingdom. Psalm 69 is one such lament. Here David can be seen to be lowered into a cistern beside a spring in a manner similar to the fertility offering of the shaman in Psalm 88. Michael Goulder, in his study of these psalms, says that in Psalm 69 we can see "the wretched old man . . . let down into the spring of Gihon, scrabbling to find a footing in the mud, conscious of the unplumbed waters beneath, fearful lest their welling force should take away his breath . . ."[7]

Rescue me from the mire before I sink in;
so I shall be saved from those who hate me,
from the watery depths.
Let not the waves wash over me,

5 for more on these readings of Pss. 88 and 69 see above pp.119-121 with footnotes #2 and #3.
6 for more on this story see above pp.138-139.
7 Goulder, *The Prayers of David*, p.224.

> nor the deep swallow me up,
> nor the pit close its mouth on me.
>
> PS.69.14-15

The tone of despair in this psalm and others was familiar to the gospel writers. In the first century these psalms were accessible as well as popular. They were rich with well-known associations that expressed both the glory and the despair of Israel. The language and images of such associations provide a kind of code that helps the gospel writers say what they want to say about Jesus. They firmly believe that he is the leader who has come to fulfil earlier hopes, and in his suffering they see both purpose and direction. They are convinced that this suffering serves the greater good of all, just as the sufferings of Jesus's predecessors in the psalms served a larger purpose.

In John's gospel, after the death of Jesus, the story of the crucifixion continues:

> It was the Day of Preparation, and to avoid the bodies' remaining on the cross during the Sabbath—since that Sabbath was a day of special solemnity—the Jews asked Pilate to have the legs broken and the bodies taken away. Consequently the soldiers came and broke the legs of the first man who had been crucified with him and then of the other. When they came to Jesus, they saw he was already dead, and so instead of breaking his legs one of the soldiers pierced his side with a lance; and immediately there came out blood and water. This is the evidence of one who saw it—true evidence, and he knows that what he says is true—and he gives it so that you may believe as well. Because all this happened to fulfil the words of scripture: '*Not one bone of his will be broken*;' and again, in another place scripture says: '*They will look to the one whom they have pierced.*'
>
> JN.19.31-37

The breaking of the bones and the wounding of Jesus with a lance are only described by John. These are plausible details. Crucifixion was a protracted death and sometimes after bodies had hung on the cross for some time, bones would be broken or wounds inflicted to hasten the death. But John's descriptive interests are incidental. His real concerns are indicated by the two direct quotations in the above passage. The first of these, about bones not being broken, comes from another psalm:

> They cry in anguish and Yahweh hears,
> and rescues them from all their troubles.
> Yahweh is near to the broken-hearted,
> he helps those whose spirit is crushed.
>
> Though hardships without number beset the upright,
> Yahweh rescues them from them all.
> Yahweh takes care of all their bones,
> not one of them will be broken.
>
> PS.34.17-20

This phrase about no bones being broken also appears in a different context in the book of Exodus. Here it is part of the detailed rules governing the Passover sacrifice of animals:

> Yahweh said to Moses and Aaron, 'This is the ritual for the Passover: no alien may eat it, but any slave bought for money may eat it, once you have circumcised him. No stranger and no hired servant may eat it. It must be eaten in one house alone; you will not take any of the meat out of the house; nor may you break any of its bones . . .'
>
> EX.12.43-46

It is only in John's gospel that Jesus is described as the "lamb of God", a phrase that equates him with the sacrificial animal killed at Passover.[8] It is also only in John's gospel that the quotation appears about bones not being broken. More than the other gospel writers, John focuses on the sacrificial nature of the death of Jesus.

After the quotation about the breaking of bones, John cites a passage from the book of Zechariah, "They will look to the one whom they have pierced". This comes from the latter section of the book, full of apocalyptic predictions about the approaching "Day of the Lord".

> 'When that day comes, I shall set about destroying all the nations who advance against Jerusalem. But over the House of David and the inhabitants of Jerusalem I shall pour out a spirit of grace and prayer, and they will look to me. They will mourn for the one whom they have pierced as though for an only child, and weep for him as people weep for a first-born child.'
>
> ZC.12.9-10

A few verses later the prophet adds:

> 'When that day comes, a fountain will be opened for the House of David and the inhabitants of Jerusalem, to wash sin and impurity away . . .'
>
> ZC.13.1

This fountain that washes away sin and impurity is associated in some forms of Christian doctrine with the water John describes flowing from the side of Jesus, which is understood to be referring to the water used in the ritual of baptism.

Obscure symbolism like this does consistently underlie John's narrative. When he speaks of the piercing of Jesus's side, John is taking a scriptural reference and transforming it into a story about the crucified Jesus. In describing Jesus as a source

8 see JN.1.29, JN.1.35.

of water, and then quoting a passage that speaks of washing sin away, John provides scriptural background for an already existing practice. In the ritual of baptism, water is used to wash sin away, and by the time John was writing this was the established initiation rite amongst Christians.

The sufferings of Jesus as described by John also recall a passage in the book of Job. Here is another reference to the piercing through of an innocent sufferer:

> My enemies look daggers at me,
> and open gaping jaws.
> Their sneers strike like slaps in the face;
> and they all set on me at once.
> Yes, God has handed me over to the godless,
> and cast me into the hands of the wicked.
>
> I was living at peace, until he made me totter,
> taking me by the neck to shatter me.
> He has set me up as his target:
> he shoots his arrows at me from all sides,
> pitilessly pierces my loins,
> and pours my gall out on the ground.
>
> JB.16.9-13

Another outcry from Job is that he has been deserted by his friends and abandoned by those that love him in his time of greatest need.

> . . . my relatives take care to avoid me,
> my intimate friends have gone away
> and the guests in my house have forgotten me.
> . . . .
>
> Even the children look down on me,
> whenever I stand up, they start jeering at me.
> All my dearest friends recoil from me in horror:
> those I loved best have turned against me.
>
> JB.19.13-14, 18-19

Similarly, in the book of Isaiah one of the many sorrows of the suffering servant is that he is abandoned; that he is despised and rejected. This theme is also dominant in many of the laments of the psalms:

> Friends and companions shun my disease,
> even the dearest of them keep their distance . . .
>
> PS.38.11

> The sheer numbers of my enemies
>   makes me contemptible,
> loathsome to my neighbours,
>   and my friends shrink from me in horror.
>
> When people see me in the street
>   they take to their heels.
> I have no more place in their hearts than a corpse,
>   or something lost.
>
> PS.31.10-12

In the stories leading up to Jesus's death the theme of abandonment is powerful. Jesus prays alone in Gethsemane; he is denied, he is betrayed, and he faces his accusers alone. But as the gospel stories develop, from Mark through to John, the insistence on this abandonment becomes less strong. It is only the earlier gospels, Mark and Matthew, who say that after the arrest of Jesus all of the disciples deserted him and ran away.[9] Equally, it is Mark and Matthew who make it clear that none of Jesus's followers are close at hand either before or during the crucifixion. Luke, on the other hand, tells of the women following Jesus on the way to the crucifixion, and also suggests rather vaguely that all of Jesus's friends were standing by at a distance while he was crucified. Then there is John, who tells of several of Jesus's followers being very close to him as he is dying.

Even in Mark's unelaborate account, however, the aban-

9 see MK.14.50 & MT.26.56.

donment of Jesus at the time of the crucifixion is qualified. There are a few faithful followers standing a distance away. They are women. Nothing is said of them until after the death of Jesus:

> There were some women watching from a distance. Among them were Mary of Magdala, Mary who was the mother of James the younger and Joset, and Salome. These used to follow him and look after him when he was in Galilee. And many other women were there who had come up to Jerusalem with him.
>
> MK.15.40-41[10]

Following the death of Jesus, Matthew also tells of women "watching from a distance". His list of the women is different:

> And many women were there, watching from a distance, the same women who had followed Jesus from Galilee and looked after him. Among them were Mary of Magdala, Mary the mother of James and Joseph, and the mother of Zebedee's sons.
>
> MT.27.55-56

Luke is less specific about the onlookers to the crucifixion than either Mark or Matthew. On the way to Golgotha he tells of Jesus speaking to "large numbers of people . . . and women too, who mourned and lamented for him."[11] After Jesus has died Luke refers generally to all of his friends being nearby, typically giving the followers of Jesus the benefit of the doubt. Luke does not emphasise their fear or absence as Mark and Matthew do:

> . . . And when all the crowds who had gathered for the spectacle saw what had happened, they went

10 the NJB translators refer to "Mary who was the mother of . . . Joset." In most translations the name is spelled "Joses".
11 LK.23.27; also see above pp.179-80.

> home beating their breasts. All his friends stood at a distance; so also did the women who had accompanied him from Galilee and saw all this happen.
>
> LK.23.47-49

Here Luke names no women and he seems to imply that men were also present, watching the crucifixion from a distance.

John tells a much more vivid story. In his version a number of people were close to Jesus:

> Near the cross of Jesus stood his mother and his mother's sister, Mary the wife of Clopas, and Mary of Magdala . . .
>
> JN.19.25

John goes on to add at least one male follower to the group gathered by the cross. He is known only as "the disciple whom Jesus loved", and it is to this man that Jesus entrusts the care of his mother, in the phrase "Woman, this is your son . . ." and "This is your mother."

The presence of Mary the mother of Jesus at the foot of the cross is unique to John's gospel. This has fired many an artistic imagination. Through centuries of Christian art Mary has been represented grieving at the foot of the cross, and mourning over the body of Jesus when he has been removed from the cross. John fails to, in fact, describe any of this. Neither Mary's actions nor her grief are mentioned.

Only Luke fails to identify the women who are said to have been present at the crucifixion. Mark, Matthew and John each name these women, although the names vary from one gospel to the next. The one name that is common to all three gospels is Mary of Magdala, or Mary Magdalene as she is also called. Mark's gospel includes her along with Salome and another Mary who is "the mother of James the younger and Joset". Matthew's gospel has Mary Magdalene along with a Mary "the mother of James and Joseph", and the mother of Zebedee's sons; John's gospel has Mary Magdalene, Mary the mother of

Jesus, her sister, and Mary "the wife of Clopas".[12] That the names of these women change from one gospel to another is hardly surprising. The gospels were written generations after the event. What is surprising about these lists of women's names is that they are included at all.

The attention that is paid to the presence of the women is unprecedented. Almost every other detail of the crucifixion scenes can be related to and understood in light of the Hebrew Scriptures, but this is not so with the women. Nothing foreshadows their presence. Yet they are there as faithful onlookers to the death of Jesus, and in the two earliest gospels they are the only onlookers from amongst all his followers.

One factor that may explain their presence is that women in first century Jerusalem could attend such a crucifixion in relative safety, whereas it would be risky for the men. This is because women were not regarded as politically significant. Because they were women their presence did not matter and their allegiance to a condemned man did not endanger them. Even so, except in John's gospel, they are said to have stood at a distance.

At the crucifixion the role of the women is that of passive witnesses. But as the stories surrounding Jesus's death continue to unfold, the role of the women develops and grows stronger. They do not remain passive, nor do they continue to keep their distance. The stories in the gospels all agree that after Jesus's body has been removed from the cross and buried, it is the women who are the first to be aware that something odd is going on. They are also the first to react.

12 It is possible to understand this passage to mean only three women.

CHAPTER FIFTEEN

Buried

It was now evening, and since it was Preparation Day—that is, the day before the Sabbath—there came Joseph of Arimathaea, a prominent member of the Council, who himself lived in the hope of seeing the kingdom of God, and he boldly went to Pilate and asked for the body of Jesus. Pilate, astonished that he should have died so soon, summoned the centurion and enquired if he had been dead for some time. Having been assured of this by the centurion, he granted the corpse to Joseph who bought a shroud, took Jesus down from the cross, wrapped him in the shroud and laid him in a tomb which had been hewn out of the rock. He then rolled a stone against the entrance to the tomb. Mary of Magdala and Mary the mother of Joset took note of where he was laid.

MK.15.42-47

In this way, according to Mark, Jesus is buried. A man named Joseph of Arimathaea organises a hurried burial that takes place without ceremony. There is no mention of Jesus's followers. The only familiar figures who witness the burial are Mary of Magdala and Mary the mother of Joset, two of the three women Mark has earlier named as onlookers to the crucifixion.

The stories told about the burial of Jesus in all four gospels are, at first glance, similar one to another. All of the writers tell of Jesus being buried in something of a hurry by Joseph of Arimathaea. They all mention women coming to the tomb on the morning after the burial. All except Matthew refer to the preparation of spices. Finally, they all tell of the tomb being empty when the women arrive, and of angelic figures or a young man dressed in white telling the women that Jesus is not there. Within these broadly similar stories there are many differences of detail. In this chapter we will look first at the similarities, then at some of the more notable differences.

In all of the stories of the burial, Joseph of Arimathaea appears. He is a new character, dropped into the action from nowhere. He claims the body of Jesus, removes it from the cross, and buries it. He is first mentioned in Mark's gospel, written over thirty years after the death of Jesus. The obvious question is how Mark would have known about Joseph in the first place. Did he know of him from a tradition or reminiscence that circulated amongst Christians? Did he invent the character just as a fiction writer might invent a character for dramatic purposes? Or did Mark have some other source to draw on?

The answer seems to be that Mark is drawing on the most substantial sources he knows. As always, these are in the Hebrew Scriptures. Here another Joseph buries another great man and involves himself in the intimate details of burial. This is the Joseph of old who became an eminent counsellor to the Pharaoh of Egypt. He buries his father Jacob, the man whose other name is Israel; Jacob, who is son of Isaac, who is son of Abraham.

The burial of Jacob is perhaps the most elaborate description of a burial that can be found in the scriptures. He dies in exile from his own land, in Egypt, attended by his other sons and by Joseph. As Jacob lies dying he instructs his sons how to bury him:

> 'Bury me with my ancestors, in the cave that is in the field of Ephron the Hittite . . . There Abraham and his wife Sarah were buried. There Isaac and his

wife Rebekah were buried; and there I buried Leah . . .'

When Jacob had finished giving his instructions to his sons, he drew his feet up into the bed, and breathing his last was gathered to his people.

At this Joseph threw himself on his father's face, covering it with tears and kisses. Then Joseph ordered the doctors in his service to embalm his father. The doctors embalmed Israel, and it took them forty days, for embalming takes forty days to complete. The Egyptians mourned him for seventy days.

GN.49.29-33,50.1-3

After the seventy days of mourning comes the burial of Jacob. This means travelling from Egypt to Caanan with a large retinue of mourners, complete with chariots and horses. Once in Caanan Joseph mourns his father for seven more days, and buries Jacob in the assigned cave as instructed. Then Joseph returns to Egypt.

The story of Jacob's death comes near the end of the book of Genesis, the first book of the Hebrew Scriptures. It marks, in other words, the end of the beginning of the story of a people. Israel is now identified; its territory is being defined; its leaders are being established. The history of a people is about to unroll, a history that will chronicle many hundreds of years of political and religious developments, leading up to the glory of Israel under David and Solomon and on through the loss of that glory in subsequent centuries.

This rise and fall of Israel was alive in the minds of first century Jews; they were living it, hoping for a revival of the glory and power their ancestors had known. The gospel writers knew this; for them this knowledge of past glory was bred in the bone and it is reflected in all they write. This knowledge of Israel, past and present, was their literature, their religion, their entire frame of reference. So inevitably, in telling how Jesus is buried by Joseph of Arimathaea, the burial of Jacob by Joseph of Egypt is recalled. This is because in the scriptures the burial of Jacob marks the end of one era and the beginning of another, and in this new era the people of Israel are to define themselves more clearly as a people and as a nation, and they are to know glory. The same process is expected following the death and burial of Jesus.

According to Mark and to the other gospels Joseph of Arimathaea was a well respected citizen, a wealthy man and "prominent member of the council". He is presented as someone who has the confidence to ask the authorities for the body of an executed and disgraced prophet from Galilee without fearing reprisals. He ensures for Jesus exactly what was provided for the suffering servant of God in the book of Isaiah:

> He was given a grave with the wicked,
> and his tomb is with the rich,
> although he had done no violence,
> had spoken no deceit.
>
> IS.53.9

Anointing with spices and ointments was part of the usual process of laying out a body, but the gospels do not agree about the anointing of Jesus's dead body. According to Mark and Matthew and Luke, Joseph of Arimathaea simply wraps the body in a shroud and places it in the tomb. Mark and Luke then go on to say that when the women come to the tomb on the following day they come with spices and ointments to anoint the body.

In John's gospel the anointing falls to Joseph of Arimathaea and a man called Nicodemus. Nicodemus is a leading Pharisee who has been mentioned earlier in John's gospel.[1] He brings an ample supply of spices and the two men do what is required:

> They took the body of Jesus and bound it in linen cloths with the spices, following the Jewish burial custom. At the place where he had been crucified

1 see JN.3.1. and JN.7.50

> there was a garden, and in this garden a new tomb in which no one had yet been buried. Since it was the Jewish Day of Preparation and the tomb was nearby, they laid Jesus there.
>
> JN.19.40-42

Here the place name "Arimathaea" provides yet another coded scriptural message. For Joseph of Arimathaea anoints the body of Jesus before burial, and to be anointed by one from Arimathaea recalls an earlier story. This is because Samuel, the prophet who anointed the great king David, was the son of one Elkana, a man of Armathaim, or Ramathaim- Zophim.[2] The name Armathaim, when translated into Greek and then into English, becomes "Arimathaea". So Joseph who anoints Jesus is a man of the same place as Samuel, the prophet who recognised and anointed David as the king of Israel.

It is, however, only in John's gospel that Joseph anoints the body of Jesus. In the other accounts the body is buried without being anointed. Following the death of Jesus, on the morning of the first day of the week, the day after the sabbath, the women come to do the anointing. Here is Mark's version of the story:

> When the Sabbath was over, Mary of Magdala, Mary the mother of James, and Salome, bought spices with which to go and anoint him. And very early in the morning on the first day of the week they went to the tomb when the sun had risen. They had been saying to one another, 'Who will roll away the stone for us from the entrance to the tomb?' But when they looked they saw that the stone—which was very big—had already been rolled back.
>
> MK.16.1-4

"Who will roll away the stone . . ." is a question asked only in Mark's gospel. This question is entirely practical, for such a

2 see 1S.1.1

stone would have been heavy. Large stones made very effective seals for tombs or caves or wells, and such stone seals or covers are referred to several times in the scriptures. These stones were not easily moved.

The question of who would move the stone carries with it a reminder of another story about Jacob, who was Israel. In the book of Genesis Jacob emerges as a redoubtable roller of stones. Just before he first meets Rachel, who will later become his wife, Jacob comes across a stone that usually requires the strength of several men to move it:

> Continuing his journey, Jacob reached the Land of the Easterners. And there, out in the open, he saw a well with three flocks of sheep lying beside it; this well was used for watering the flocks. Now the stone on the mouth of the well was a large one, and only when all the flocks had collected there, did they roll the stone off the mouth of the well and water the sheep; then they would replace the stone over the mouth of the well.
>
> GN.29.1-3

After introducing himself and chatting to the shepherds, Jacob asks why they are delaying watering their sheep. They explain:

> 'We can't, until all the shepherds have assembled to roll the stone off the mouth of the well; then we can water the sheep.' He was still talking to them, when Rachel arrived with her father's flock, for she was a shepherdess. As soon as Jacob saw Rachel, his uncle Laban's daughter, with his uncle Laban's flock, he went up and, rolling the stone off the mouth of the well, watered his uncle Laban's sheep.
>
> GN.29.8-10

When Jacob eventually marries Rachel, she becomes the mother of Joseph, the same Joseph who eventually buries Jacob with such aplomb.

The connection here between Jacob as the roller of great stones and the stone that has been rolled away from Jesus's tomb in the gospel stories is neither obvious nor direct. It is like a distant, familiar chord; no more. Yet when any story in the gospels recalls Jacob, however faintly, the connection is always important. For Jacob was Israel; it was to him and his descendants that God promised their own land. The story of Jacob's life and wanderings all lead up to the story of his people in this promised land. When Jacob is described rolling a great stone from the mouth of the well, this is part of the history of Israel. It is one of those strangely detailed episodes of no obvious significance that proves to have a lasting influence. Stories like this come together to establish and define the consciousness of a people.

In his gospel Mark offers no explanation about the rolling away of the stone in front of Jesus's tomb. He simply asserts that the stone has gone and lets his story stand. Luke and John do much the same, saying very little about the stone. Matthew, on the other hand, appears to be fascinated by the stone. He seems to feel impelled to provide abundant and graphic detail:

> After the Sabbath, and towards dawn on the first day of the week, Mary of Magdala and the other Mary went to visit the sepulchre. And suddenly there was a violent earthquake, for an angel of the Lord, descending from heaven, came and rolled away the stone and sat on it.
>
> MT.28.1-2

Even by the most lenient standards of storytelling, Matthew's angel is an improbable figure. The ground shakes, the angel appears, the angel rolls away the stone, and then the angel sits on it. Matthew's story of the empty tomb is decisive and complete; it attempts to provide explanations, to allay fear and doubt. It is not so in Mark's story of the empty tomb. Here there is no attempt to explain the mystery. Mark's gospel ends with questions unanswered; it ends with doubts and with fear[3] The gospel writers who follow Mark respond to the questions and doubts and fears that are raised in his story of the empty tomb in their own characteristic fashions, each reflecting the preoccupations and concerns of his own time and place.

Matthew is certainly preoccupied and concerned with the stone covering Jesus's tomb. From the outset in describing Jesus's burial he tells detailed stories about this stone, stories found nowhere else. After Joseph of Arimathaea buries Jesus, Matthew tells of the chief priests and Pharisees going to Pilate and requesting that a guard be posted on the grave so that the disciples could not steal Jesus's body.

> '. . . give the order to have the sepulchre kept secure until the third day, for fear his disciples come and steal him away and tell the people, "He has risen from the dead." This last piece of fraud would be worse than what went before.' Pilate said to them, 'You may have your guard; go and make all as secure as you know how.' So they went and made the sepulchre secure, putting seals on the stone and mounting a guard.
>
> MT.27.64-66

In emphasising the seal and the guards, Matthew is responding to contemporary doubt and disbelief like that expressed by the Pharisees. He is effectively strengthening his astonishing story about the discovery of the empty tomb with some familiar and telling details from the scriptures.

The story of a seal on a stone cover is found in the story of Daniel in the lion's den. Daniel was a heroic figure [4]. He is best known as one of the advisors to the Persian King Darius in

3 for more on Mark's ending see below pp.261-263, 275- 276, 277, 279. See also Appendix One, p.281.

4 for more see EZK.14.14-20 & 28.3: the name is sometimes read 'Danel'.

Babylon several hundred years before the time of Jesus. In this story, his fellow counsellors and other high ranking civil servants have become jealous of Daniel's influence on the king, and they plot against him so successfully that the king has no choice but to condemn Daniel to death. This means being thrown to the lions.

> The king then ordered Daniel to be brought and thrown into the lion pit. The king said to Daniel, 'Your God, whom you have served so faithfully, will have to save you.' A stone was then brought and laid over the mouth of the pit; and the king sealed it with his own signet and with that of his noblemen, so that there could be no going back on the original decision about Daniel.
>
> DN.6.17-18

But King Darius knows that he is being manipulated and he does not like what is happening to Daniel. He hopes, against all the odds, that Daniel will somehow survive his ordeal in the sealed lions' pit:

> Sleep eluded him, and at the first sign of dawn he got up and hurried to the lion pit. As he approached the pit he called in anguished tones to Daniel, 'Daniel, servant of the living God! Has your God, whom you serve so faithfully, been able to save you from the lions?' Daniel answered the king, 'May Your Majesty live for ever! My God sent his angel who sealed the lions' jaws; they did me no harm, since in his sight I am blameless; neither have I ever done you any wrong, Your Majesty.' The king was overjoyed and ordered Daniel to be released from the pit.
>
> DN.6.20-24

With the release of Daniel, a sealed pit is opened to reveal a miracle. In another much earlier story in the scriptures, another sealed enclosure has a quite different role to play. First it is a secure prison, then a grave. Here again, the influence on Matthew can be seen.

This earlier story comes in the book of Joshua. Joshua was the great military leader who repeatedly led the Israelite tribes into victory. This particular story tells of a battle between his forces and those of five kings of southern Palestine. The five kings are defeated:

> As regards the five kings, these had fled and hidden in the cave of Makkedah, and news of this was brought to Joshua. 'The five kings have been found hiding in the cave at Makkedah.' Joshua said, 'Roll great stones over the mouth of the cave and post men there to keep guard . . .'
>
> JOS.10.16-18

Later, Joshua has to decide what to do with the five kings. His decision is quick and brutal:

> . . . Joshua assembled all the men of Israel and said to the chiefs of the warriors who had fought with him, 'Come forward and put your feet on the necks of these kings!' They came forward and put their feet on their necks. 'Be fearless and undaunted,' Joshua went on, 'be strong and stand firm, for this is how Yahweh will deal with all the enemies you fight.' With this, Joshua struck and killed them and had them hanged on five trees; they hung there till evening.
>
> At the hour of sunset, on Joshua's orders, they were taken down from the trees and thrown into the cave where they had been hiding. Great stones were laid over the mouth of the cave, and these are still there to this very day.
>
> JOS.10.24-27

In telling how the tomb of Jesus is guarded and the stone sealed Matthew's gospel carries echoes of these earlier stories of guarded tombs and sealed stones. He builds on these to tell a story far more memorable than its predecessors. For in Matthew's gospel, in the face of all precautions to make the tomb secure, it is found to be empty. The precautions, with all their scriptural background and authority, serve to emphasise the wonder of what Matthew is describing.

The scriptural influences on Matthew's story of the burial become even clearer as events unfold. He provides, for example, a vivid picture of the angel who sits so decisively on the stone:

> . . His face was like lightning, his robe white as snow . . .
>
> MT.28.3

Comparing this to one of the apocalyptic visions of Daniel provides very straightforward parallels:

> On the twenty-fourth day of the first month, as I stood on the bank of that great river, the Tigris, I raised my eyes to look about me, and this is what I saw:
> A man dressed in linen, with a belt of pure gold round his waist:
> his body was like beryl,
> his face looked like lightning,
> his eyes were like fiery torches,
> his arms and his face had the gleam of burnished bronze,
> the sound of his voice was like the roar of a multitude.
>
> DN.10.4-6

Just like the powerful angel in this vision, Matthew's angel has a face "like lightning", and is dressed in white. The other gospel writers also draw on this very well-known passage in Daniel for their descriptions of the angelic appearances at the tomb of Jesus. Mark speaks of a "young man in a white robe"; Luke speaks of "two men in brilliant clothes"; and John has "two angels in white".

In the gospels of Mark, Matthew and Luke, the mysterious figures at the tomb of Jesus speak to the women. At this point of the story Mark and Matthew say much the same thing. Here is Mark:

> On entering the tomb they saw a young man in a white robe seated on the right-hand side, and they were struck with amazement. But he said to them, 'There is no need to be so amazed. You are looking for Jesus of Nazareth, who was crucified: he has risen, he is not here. See, here is the place where they laid him. But you must go and tell his disciples and Peter. "He is going ahead of you to Galilee; that is where you will see him, just as he told you."'
>
> MK.16.5-7

After the women are commissioned to go and tell the disciples to meet Jesus in Galilee, Mark and Matthew part company in the stories they tell. Matthew, who has only two women at the tomb, goes on to provide detail of what the women do, and what they see. Mark's account is very different, as we will see in the final chapter of this book.

Luke and John also tell of angels speaking to the women at the tomb, although in John's gospel only one woman is there, Mary of Magdala. These two gospels go on to describe the arrival of male disciples at the tomb, an incident missing in both Mark and Matthew. In Luke's gospel it is Peter who goes running to the tomb:

> Peter, however, went off to the tomb, running. He bent down and looked in and saw the linen cloths but nothing else; he then went back home, amazed at what had happened.
>
> LK.24.12

This verse in Luke's gospel is disputed. Although it is omitted in several early manuscripts it is valued by many people, and biblical translators cannot agree on how to deal with it. Many modern Bibles completely omit this description of Peter running to the tomb, while others include it[5] However, later in the gospel there is an allusion to the disciples visiting the empty tomb. In the story of Jesus on the road to Emmaus, two disciples are discussing what has happened, and they say that "Some of our friends went to the tomb and found everything exactly as the women had reported . . ."[6] This is in line with what John later describes in his gospel. He tells of both Peter and the unnamed beloved disciple running to the tomb. Again, all they see are the linen cloths that had wrapped the body.

In Luke's gospel when the angels, the "two men in brilliant clothes" appear to the women, they do not repeat what was said in Mark and Matthew. Instead, they remind the women that Jesus was due all along to rise from the dead on the third day:

> . . . the two said to them, 'Why look among the dead for someone who is alive? He is not here; he has risen. Remember what he told you when he was still in Galilee: that the Son of man was destined to be handed over into the power of sinful men and be crucified, and rise again on the third day.' And they remembered his words.
>
> LK.24.5-8

This reference to Jesus saying he would rise on the third day recalls an earlier saying of Jesus reported by Luke:

> 'The Son of man is destined to suffer grievously, to be rejected by the elders and chief priests and

5 LK.24.12 appears in AV, Good News, NRSV, NIV and NJB. The verse is omitted in RV, RSV, NEB and REB. In all cases except AV and NIV there is a note about the problem.

6 see LK.24.24.

scribes and to be put to death, and to be raised up on the third day.'

LK.9.22

This is the first of three prophecies of his death that Luke attributes to Jesus, and in two of these Jesus is quoted as saying he will rise on the third day. The other gospels also repeatedly refer to Jesus rising on the third day.[7] Much earlier in the first century Paul was the first writer of the New Testament to mention Jesus rising on the third day:

> . . . that Christ died for our sins, in accordance with the scriptures, and that he was buried; and that on the third day he was raised to life, in accordance with the scriptures . . .

1CO.15.3-4

"In accordance with the scriptures", says Paul, Jesus was raised on the third day. This claim is problematic, for there are no clear references in the scriptures to such a resurrection on the third day. The most likely passage in the scriptures that Paul is referring to appears in the book of the prophet Hosea, written around the year 850 BCE. Here, being raised up on the third day is a hope shared by everyone who looks for a new life in harmony with God:

> Come, let us return to Yahweh.
> He has rent us and he will heal us;
> he has struck us and he will bind up our wounds;
> after two days he will revive us,
> on the third day he will raise us up
> and we shall live in his presence.
> Let us know, let us strive to know Yahweh;
> that he will come is as certain as the dawn.

7 for examples see MT.12.40; MT.17.22-23; MT.20.17-19; MK.8.31; MK.9.31; MK.10.32-34; LK.13.33; LK.18.31; and JN.2.21-22.

He will come to us like a shower,
like the rain of springtime to the earth.

HO.6.1-3

The only other story from the Hebrew Scriptures that even remotely mentions being raised on the third day is the tale popularly known as "Jonah and the whale".[8] Jonah was a prophet and the hero of an undated story that was probably recorded some time in the fourth century BCE. The story opens with Jonah receiving a divine command to tell the people of the great city of Nineveh how wicked they are. Jonah is so unhappy at the prospect that he tries to run away. He goes to Jaffa, pays his fare and gets on a ship bound for Tarshish. On the way there is a great storm and everyone is terrified and starts praying. After a while the sailors go down below to lighten the ship by throwing the cargo overboard. There they find Jonah asleep. They are furious and tell him he should at least be praying.

When things get no better they draw lots to find out if anyone is to blame for the ship's bad luck. The lot falls on Jonah, and he explains to them that he is a Hebrew trying to escape from his God. He tells them that if they want the sea to be still they must throw him overboard. The sailors make a last effort and try to row the ship to safety, but it is no use. The storm gets worse, so they stop rowing and cast Jonah to the waves. The sea immediately calms down, but meanwhile . . .

. . . Yahweh ordained that a great fish should swallow Jonah; and Jonah remained in the belly of the fish for three days and three nights.

JON.2.1

In the belly of this great fish, during these three days and nights, Jonah at last decides he had better start praying, and he does. Then the creature vomits and Jonah is thrown up on dry land. He realizes he has no choice but to go to Nineveh and the

8 "Whale" is more correctly translated as "great fish". See MT.12.39-40 for a direct reference to Jonah's story.

rest of the book of Jonah tells how he manages to do what God wanted him to do in the first place.

So there are two places in the Hebrew Scriptures where three days is specified as the waiting time before some form of new life is granted. It is on the strength of these passages that the gospel writers and Paul are able to say that Jesus rose from the dead after three days "according to the scriptures".

Broadly speaking, the gospels agree about the progress of events during the final days of Jesus's life, up to and including the death and burial. Their accounts of the arrest and trial and crucifixion present different details, but the outlines of the stories have a great deal in common, and the tone and atmosphere are very similar. This remains true in the stories of the burial of Jesus and in the stories of the women discovering the empty tomb. But from this point onwards, everything changes. As the gospels tell their stories about what followed the death of Jesus, they move further and further apart. Their differences become dramatic.

CHAPTER SIXTEEN

Disbelief

The stories in the gospels that follow the discovery of the empty tomb are known as the resurrection appearance stories. With more or less detail Matthew and Luke and John describe Jesus appearing to his followers after his death. Their accounts rarely agree. Matthew tells of two appearances; Luke also tells of two; John, writing much later, has four. Mark, the earliest gospel writer, describes no resurrection appearances at all.[1] By contrast Paul, who wrote well before any of the gospel writers, provides a list of no fewer than six resurrection appearances.

In the next two chapters we will be looking at these different accounts of the risen Jesus. We will discuss their major themes and patterns and look at related stories in the Hebrew Scriptures. Before considering the resurrection appearance stories of Matthew, Luke and John it is necessary to look at the writings of Paul. This is because Paul's writings came first, predating the gospels by as much as fifty years.

Paul's life and travels and teachings are described in the book of Acts, written by Luke.[2] Although the book of Acts is not a reliable guide to the details of Paul's life and travels, it does

1 i for more on the ending of Mark's gospel see below pp.261-263, 277, 279. See also Appendix One, p.281.
2 for more on the background to Paul's writings see above pp.18-23 *passim.*

provide a broad indication of the issues and problems facing early Christians, and it shows the way in which Paul and other leaders of the early church responded to these.

In one of the stories in Acts, Paul runs into problems when he is preaching about the resurrection of Jesus to a gathering in Athens. Quite simply, no one believes him. His listeners are a group of philosophers known as the council of the Areopagus. This was the Oxford or Harvard of the world of Greek culture. Paul's sermon is rolling along very well until he makes a statement about Jesus rising from the dead:

> '... God is telling everyone everywhere that they must repent, because he has fixed a day when the whole world will be judged in uprightness by a man he has appointed. And God has publicly proved this by raising him from the dead.'
>
> At this mention of rising from the dead, some of them burst out laughing ...
>
> AC.17.30-32

Or as the King James Bible puts it, "And when they heard of the resurrection of the dead, some mocked". In the face of such mockery and laughter Paul leaves Athens, though not before making several converts. From Athens Paul goes to Corinth, where he stays for eighteen months and establishes a Christian church. After leaving Corinth, he remains in touch with this new church by writing letters in which he dispenses advice and tries to monitor the problems arising in the church.

In one of his letters to Corinth Paul emphatically reasserts his belief that Jesus rose from the dead, and he tries to clarify the nature of this belief for the church at Corinth. In the process he provides the earliest writing about the resurrection of Jesus to appear anywhere: [3]

3 PH.2.9 is written a year or so earlier, but does not claim a bodily resurrection.

> The tradition I handed on to you in the first place, a tradition which I had myself received, was that Christ died for our sins, in accordance with the scriptures, and that he was buried; and that on the third day he was raised to life, in accordance with the scriptures . . .
>
> 1CO.15.3-4

After this statement Paul lists a number of people who he claims saw Jesus after his death. This list of witnesses is very specific and it is not found anywhere else in the New Testament:

> . . . and that on the third day, he was raised to life, in accordance with the scriptures; and that he appeared to Cephas; and later to the Twelve; and next he appeared to more than five hundred of the brothers at the same time, most of whom are still with us, though some have fallen asleep; then he appeared to James, and then to all the apostles. Last of all he appeared to me too . . .
>
> 1CO.15.4-8 [4]

Paul goes on to say that because of the life and death and resurrection of Jesus, all Christians can now expect to be resurrected from the dead "when the last trumpet sounds". He tries to explain what this means:

> Someone may ask: 'How are dead people raised, and what sort of body do they have when they come?' How foolish! What you sow must die before it is given new life; and what you sow is not the body that is to be, but only a bare grain, of wheat I dare say, or some other kind . . .

4 for more on this list of witnesses see below pp.267-268.

> . . . what is sown is perishable, but what is raised is imperishable; what is sown is contemptible but what is raised is glorious; what is sown is weak, but what is raised is powerful; what is sown is a natural body, and what is raised is a spiritual body . . .
>
> . . . The trumpet is going to sound, and then the dead will be raised imperishable, and we shall be changed, because this perishable nature of ours must put on imperishability, this mortal nature must put on immortality.
>
> from 1CO.15.35-53

Some of these phrases have been used in Christian burial services for generations, and they are greatly valued by many people. But this passage becomes problematic when a clear explanation of the concept of resurrection is being sought. This is dense and difficult theological territory, and at best Paul's meaning is obscure. What this passage does show very clearly, though, is that even in the earliest days of Christianity efforts were being made to explain ideas about resurrection. Paul, who was raised as a Pharisee, was keenly aware of how contentious and divisive this subject was in the first century.[5] In this letter to the Corinthians he is trying to set the record straight, but the subject overwhelms his capacities as a preacher and writer. It has overwhelmed many others since.

The gospels, written well after Paul's time, do not even attempt to explain the idea of resurrection. Instead, Matthew and Luke and John tell a variety of stories about Jesus appearing after his death. They attempt to satisfy curiosity, answer questions and provide detail about the resurrection of Jesus without long and difficult explanations. Their stories are designed to meet the needs of early Christians, assuring them that Jesus did indeed rise from the dead. The stories can also be understood

5 for a story about this see above pp.64-66.

to imply that a general resurrection awaits some or even all people.

In telling of the resurrection of Jesus the gospel writers face the problem of disbelief and incredulity head on. Just like Paul, they knew resurrection was a highly controversial subject. This is clear in how they write of Jesus's resurrection, for their stories appear to respond to specific doubts and questions. These doubts and questions very probably reflect those of the gospel writers' own congregations.

A good example of this can be found in Matthew's gospel. At the time of the burial, Matthew introduces the idea that the authorities are fearful of a claim that Jesus would rise from the dead. In a scene that appears only in his gospel, Matthew tells of the Jewish leaders asking Pilate to take decisive measures to prevent such a claim ever being made:

> . . . the chief priests and the Pharisees went in a body to Pilate and said to him, 'Your Excellency, we recall that this impostor said, while he was still alive, "After three days I shall rise again." Therefore give the order to have the sepulchre kept secure until the third day, for fear his disciples come and steal him away and tell the people, "He has risen from the dead." . . .'
>
> MT.27.62-64

Matthew here may be reacting to an existing rumour that Jesus's body had been stolen out of the tomb by his followers so that they could falsely claim he had risen from the dead. In his story, even though the tomb is made secure with a seal and guards at the request of the Pharisees, the tomb is found to be empty.[6] After reporting the discovery of the empty tomb, Matthew tells how the rumour that the body was stolen was set in motion:

6 for more on the sealing of the tomb and the guard see above pp.216-218.

> . . . some of the guards went off into the city to tell the chief priests all that had happened. These held a meeting with the elders and, after some discussion, handed a considerable sum of money to the soldiers with these instructions, 'This is what you must say, "His disciples came during the night and stole him away while we were asleep." And should the governor come to hear of this, we undertake to put things right with him ourselves and to see that you do not get into trouble.' So they took the money and carried out their instructions, and to this day that is the story among the Jews.
>
> MT.28.11-15

Luke addresses the problem of disbelief in the resurrection even more directly than Matthew. On the very morning when the women visit the tomb and find it empty . . .

> . . . they returned from the tomb and told all this to the Eleven and to all the others. The women were Mary of Magdala, Joanna, and Mary the mother of James. And the other women with them also told the apostles, but this story of theirs seemed pure nonsense, and they did not believe them.
>
> LK.24.9-11

Luke's story of the men dismissing what the women say is not found in the other gospels. In telling his story this way, Luke must now respond to the disbelief of the disciples. As a skilled storyteller he is setting up dramatic tensions and problems in the narrative, problems that are designed to be overcome.

Up until this point in Luke's account of the death and burial of Jesus, the women have been consistently faithful witnesses of record. They mourn for Jesus on the road to Golgotha, they watch from a distance as he is crucified, they take note of where he is buried, and they are the first to return to the tomb the day after the burial with spices and ointments to anoint the body.

Through all this the men are conspicuous by their absence. Yet when the women return to tell the men what they have seen, their story is dismissed as hysterical nonsense.

Although everything Luke subsequently relates in his gospel is a verification that the women are faithful and reliable witnesses, he does present something of a hostage to fortune in this story. The disciples' dismissal of what the women say is sometimes taken literally, rather than being understood as a dramatic device that moves the story along. Critics of Christian beliefs, particularly male critics, have found it only too easy to agree with the disciples' initial reaction and discount the women as credulous and unreliable witnesses.

A particularly well known example of this attitude was expressed by a second century philosopher called Celsus, who took a firm stand against Christianity. Celsus had nothing good to say about this young and growing religion. Unfortunately no original records of his criticisms have survived, but some of these were recorded in a work by Origen. Origen was a third century Christian scholar who set out to rebut Celsus in a work known as *Contra Celsum*. In the process of disputing Celsus, Origen provides the only record of his arguments. Celsus did not mince his words about Jesus rising from the dead:

> While (Jesus) was alive he did not help himself, but after death he rose again and showed the marks of his punishment and how his hands had been pierced. But who saw this? An hysterical female, as you say, and perhaps some other one of those who were deluded by the same sorcery, who either dreamt in a certain state of mind and through wishful thinking had a hallucination due to some mistaken notion (an experience which has happened to thousands) or, which is more likely, wanted to impress the others by telling this fantastic tale . . .[7]

7 *Origen: Contra Celsum*, H. Chadwick trans., Cambridge University Press, first published 1953, reprinted 1979, Book 2, section 55, p. 109.

Celsus is fairly even-handed here. He finds the male witnesses no more convincing than the women. But that there are "hysterical females" cited as witnesses to such an incredible event weakens the story even further as far as he is concerned.

According to some biblical translations, after Luke describes the disciples refusing to believe the women, he tells of Peter running to the tomb and finding it empty.[8] But even this is not enough to prove to the disciples that Jesus has risen from the dead. Their incredulity continues. Then comes Luke's story of Jesus appearing on the road to Emmaus.

Two of the disciples are walking to the village of Emmaus, some seven miles from Jerusalem. As they go they discuss the events of the past few days, and Jesus appears and walks with them as a fellow traveller. They do not recognise him and they tell him the whole troubled story of the crucifixion. Then they come to the most perplexing part of their tale:

> '. . . And this is not all: two whole days have now gone by since it all happened; and some women from our group have astounded us: they went to the tomb in the early morning, and when they could not find the body, they came back to tell us they had seen a vision of angels who declared he was alive. Some of our friends went to the tomb and found everything exactly as the women had reported, but of him they saw nothing.'
>
> Then he said to them, 'You foolish men! So slow to believe all that the prophets have said! Was it not necessary that the Christ should suffer before entering into his glory? ' Then, starting with Moses and going through all the prophets, he explained to them the passages throughout the scriptures that were about himself.
>
> LK.24.21-27

8 for more on how various Bibles handle this episode see above p.221 footnote #5.

Here, by referring to Moses and all the prophets, Luke is on territory that is familiar to his audience. At this stage of the narrative something reassuring is needed, and Luke tells of the risen Jesus giving explanations from the scriptures to the puzzled disciples, making it quite clear to them that they should believe the story of the women. Jesus is setting the record straight for the disciples, and he is using the scriptures to prove what he is saying.

In speaking of Moses and all the prophets, a vast world of text and story is being opened out by Luke. He is having Jesus go back to the very origins of the world in the process of explaining who he is. "Moses" in this context means the so-called "books of Moses" or the Torah, the first five books of present day Jewish or Christian Bibles. "Moses" starts with the creation of the world and the story of Adam and Eve in the garden.

In this story the first man and woman are in the garden of Eden. There they have everything they need and some things they do not need, like the tree of the knowledge of good and evil, the fruit of which they are told not to eat. The serpent appears, and this serpent is subtle and subversive. The serpent tempts the woman to eat the forbidden fruit. She takes some and eats and gives some to the man. Then with the knowledge of the tree of good and evil, for the first time they see they are naked, so they cover themselves with fig leaves. They try to hide from their creator God, but they are found and the man is asked if they have eaten the fruit. The man blames the woman saying she gave him the fruit. The woman says that the serpent tricked her. This is followed by the curse; a terrible primeval curse. The serpent is cursed and condemned to crawl on its belly, the woman is cursed and condemned to the pain of child bearing, the man is cursed and condemned to labour. The man and the woman are then expelled from the garden and an angel with a flaming sword guards the gates of the garden so they can never return.[9]

9 see GN. chh. 2-3 for the full story of the garden of Eden.

Curses are, however, a form of negative prayer; they are blessings turned on their heads. Within a very few chapters of the story of Eden there is also the great blessing that is partner to the great curse. This blessing is given into the care of Abraham:

> . . . I shall make you a great nation, I shall bless you
> and make your name famous; you are to be a blessing!
> I shall bless those who bless you,
> and shall curse those who curse you,
> and all clans on earth
> will bless themselves by you.
>
> GN.12.2-3

This same blessing is reaffirmed and amplified after the sacrifice of the ram that is caught by its horns in the bushes in time to save Abraham's son Isaac from the same fate.[10]

This curse and its corresponding blessing resurface with another appearance of the serpent in the books of Moses. In one of the stories of the Israelites going to the promised land, the serpent brings both death and life. The Israelites have been complaining to Moses about how hungry they are, and their God punishes them by sending poisonous serpents among them. Many people die from being bitten, and the others then repent for speaking against God and ask Moses to intercede on their behalf. Moses does so, and God tells him what he must do:

> 'Make a fiery serpent and raise it as a standard.
> Anyone who is bitten and looks at it will survive.'
> Moses then made a serpent out of bronze and raised
> it as a standard, and anyone who was bitten by a serpent and looked at the bronze serpent survived.
>
> NB.21.8-9[11]

10 for this story see above p.105.
11 for more about the serpent see 2K.18.4.

Centuries later, after the death of Jesus, this same serpent resurfaces yet again in the understanding of some early Christians. A symbol of evil again becomes a symbol of salvation in John's gospel:

> . . . as Moses lifted up the snake in the desert,
> so must the Son of man be lifted up
> so that everyone who believes may have eternal life
> in him.
> JN.3.14

John wrote this several generations after Jesus had been "lifted up" on the cross. He wrote it believing that Jesus was the Son of Man, sacrificed to save the whole world. According to John, Jesus on the cross brings salvation, just as the serpent Moses had put on a pole in the desert brought salvation to the Israelites. Millions of Christians to this day are sure they can look at Jesus on the cross and be saved from the effects of the primeval curse.

The books of Moses in the Bible express how the people of Israel, all of them descendents of the "blessed" Abraham and the "cursed" Adam, hold to the belief that because of the blessing they will be delivered from whatever trials or curse they suffer. Their great prophet Moses helps to deliver them from Egypt to a new life in the promised land, and Moses announces to all Israel that their God will raise up another prophet like himself and that they are to listen to that prophet[12].

This is the background to the story Luke tells of Jesus appearing to the disciples on the road to Emmaus. When Jesus exclaims at their disbelief and proceeds to explain his role to them through "Moses and the prophets", Luke is telling his story in the most powerful and hopeful way open to him. He only hints at what this means. A generation later John makes it explicit, by having Jesus say that he is the prophet promised by Moses:

12 see DT.18.15.

Do not imagine that I am going to accuse you before the Father:
you have placed your hopes on Moses,
and Moses will be the one who accuses you.
If you really believed him
you would believe me too,
since it was about me that he was writing;
but if you will not believe what he wrote,
how can you believe what I say?

JN.5.45-47

Luke's story of the events on the road to Emmaus is full of allusions and hidden references to the prophets as well as to Moses. Most of these are to do with the failure to recognize God or God's messenger because of blindness or disbelief.[13]

The story of Jesus appearing on the road to Emmaus is a very long one, told only by Luke. It culminates in the two disciples eventually recognising Jesus when he breaks the bread at mealtime. Then he vanishes from their sight, and they return to Jerusalem to the rest of the disciples and tell their story of seeing Jesus. But the excitement is not over, nor has Luke abandoned his storytelling technique of arousing and then resolving disbelief:

> They were still talking about all this when he himself stood among them and said to them, 'Peace be with you!' In a state of alarm and fright, they thought they were seeing a ghost. But he said, 'Why are you so agitated, and why are these doubts stirring in your hearts? See by my hands and my feet that it is I myself. Touch me and see for yourselves; a ghost has no flesh and bones as you can see I have.' And as he said this he showed them his hands and his feet. Their joy was so great that they still could not

13 for more about failure to recognise the divine see below p.243ff.

> believe it, as they were dumbfounded; so he said to them, 'Have you anything here to eat?' And they offered him a piece of grilled fish, which he took and ate before their eyes.
>
> LK.24.36-43

In a different translation of this passage, the King James Bible has a particularly memorable phrase. The disbelief of the disciples is shown as part of a process that leads in the end to recognition "... they yet believed not for joy, and wondered ...".

In this second story of Jesus appearing to his disciples, Luke emphasises his physical nature. Jesus manifests himself as a creature of flesh and bone, as one who can eat. This physical emphasis is another response to disbelief for as Luke says, the disciples "thought they were seeing a ghost". This is not good enough for Luke. He wants to show Jesus as a living, functioning being.

In stories from the scriptures, when God or the representative of God appears, food is frequently offered to the appearing one. In the book of Genesis, when God appears to Abraham in the guise of three angels, Abraham offers them food, and they eat.[14] In other stories, when the one who appears does not eat, this becomes a matter for comment.

In having Jesus eat, Luke takes his story one step further than a story found in the book of Tobit. This is part of the Apocrypha and was written about 200 years before the time of Jesus. It tells the amazing adventures of the good Tobit and his kinsfolk, especially his son Tobias. The background to these adventures is that there has been a run of bad luck in Tobit's family. Tobit has been blinded and his kinsman Raguel, who lives some distance away, has suffered a strange series of catastrophes. Raguel's daughter Sarah has lost seven bridegrooms in succession, all of them killed on the wedding night by a demon.

14 GN.18.1-15:—for more on this story see above p.109, and below, p.243.

The blind Tobit is in despair and decides he is going to die. But first he resolves that he must send Tobias to collect some money he is owed by a relative in the town of Media. Tobias sets out to Media in the company of a mysterious travelling companion, quite unaware that this companion is really the angel Raphael who has been sent by God to ensure everything works out for the best in this blighted family. Tobias and his angelic friend have many high adventures on their travels. In the end they return to Tobit having not only collected the money, but having resolved the problems of the unfortunate Sarah, married her to Tobias, and eaten a few hearty meals in the bargain. To top everything off, when Tobias and Tobit are reunited, the sight of the older man is restored. At this point, the angel Raphael decides it is time to reveal himself:

> 'I am Raphael, one of the seven angels who stand ever ready to enter the presence of the glory of the Lord.' They were both overwhelmed with awe; they fell on their faces in terror. But the angel said, 'Do not be afraid; peace be with you. Bless God for ever. As far as I was concerned, when I was with you, my presence was not by any decision of mine, but by the will of God; he is the one whom you must bless as long as you live, he the one that you must praise. You thought you saw me eating, but that was appearance and no more. Now bless the Lord on earth and give thanks to God . . .'
>
> TB.12.15-20

The appearance of the angel Raphael ends with his disavowal about eating. "You thought you saw me eating", says Raphael, "but that was appearance and no more". Then the angel disappears. This idea that an angel of God does not eat is also found in a story in the book of Judges. Here, an angel appears to a man called Manoah, and to his wife. These are soon to be the parents of the strong man of Israel called Samson. The angel, who is unrecognized, delivers detailed instructions to Manoah's wife about how to behave during her pregnancy and how to raise the yet unborn Samson. Before the angel disappears Manoah tries to offer hospitality:

> Manoah then said to the Angel of Yahweh, 'Allow us to detain you while we prepare a kid for you'— for Manoah did not know that this was the Angel of Yahweh. The Angel of Yahweh said to Manoah, 'Even if you did detain me, I should not eat your food; but if you wish to prepare a burnt offering, offer it to Yahweh.'
>
> JG.13.15-16

When, in Luke's gospel, the appearing Jesus eats before his followers, Luke is stressing something important. Angels of the Lord might appear and refuse to eat, but Jesus is quite different. He appears in the tradition of God appearing to Abraham. Luke offers no loopholes here and allows for no shade of disbelief. This is not, according to him, an illusion, an apparition, or a vision. Above all, it is not a ghost. The Jesus who appears to the disciples in Luke's story is a living sentient being, and Luke insists that this be believed.

The same insistence can be found in John's gospel. In what is probably the best known of his resurrection appearance stories John very deliberately stresses the physical reality of Jesus's body. He does this to lay to rest the disbelief of the disciple called Thomas. Thomas is a doubter. When Jesus appears to the other disciples, Thomas is not there, and when they tell him what he has missed, he refuses to believe them:

> Thomas, called the Twin, who was one of the Twelve, was not with them when Jesus came. So the other disciples said to him, 'We have seen the Lord,'

> but he answered, 'Unless I can see the holes that the nails made in his hands and can put my finger into the holes they made, and unless I can put my hand into his side, I refuse to believe.' Eight days later the disciples were in the house again and Thomas was with them. The doors were closed, but Jesus came in and stood among them. 'Peace be with you,' he said. Then he spoke to Thomas, 'Put your finger here; look, here are my hands. Give me your hand; put it into my side. Do not be unbelieving any more but believe.' Thomas replied, 'My Lord and my God!'
>
> JN.20.24-28

John's portrayal of the risen Jesus is oddly contradictory in this story. On the one hand he shows a Jesus who is solid and real, whose wounds can be touched. On the other hand, he presents a Jesus who can materialize through closed doors. John's readers, like Luke's before, are expected to believe extraordinary things of the risen Jesus. John is clearly aware, as Luke is, that the first and the logical reaction to such extraordinary things is disbelief. Like Luke, he tells a complex story designed to overcome this disbelief. But disbelief is not easily put to rest, and John knows this.

Having just shown the resurrected Jesus responding to the disbelief of one of his followers, John carries on to emphasise the importance of belief. After Thomas acknowledges Jesus, Jesus says to him:

> 'You believe because you can see me.
> Blessed are those who have not seen and yet believe.'
>
> JN.20.29

And then John concludes his gospel by saying:

> There were many other signs that Jesus worked in the sight of the disciples, but they are not recorded in this book. These are recorded so that you may

> believe that Jesus is the Christ, the Son of God, and
> that believing this you may have life through his
> name.
>
> JN.20.30-31[15]

"These are recorded so that you may believe". In this phrase, John summarizes the purpose of his stories. When he describes the disbelief of Jesus's followers, he is telling stories designed to inspire and strengthen belief. His stories of disbelief are dramatic and memorable, and as in Luke's gospel, this is particularly true of the stories that insist on the physical reality of Jesus's resurrected body.

But this insistence on Jesus's physical resurrection does cause problems. Reaction to these stories is very mixed. Some people manage to believe every word of them, fiercely and literally. Others understand them symbolically, or take them as a kind of inspired allegory. Others find such passages uncomfortable and embarrassing. For some readers such stories do encourage various forms of belief. For others they promote only argument and scepticism.

15 The rest of the text of John's gospel is epilogue, added either by John or one of his colleagues. See NJB note a, p.1789.

CHAPTER SEVENTEEN

Recognition

In the previous chapter we looked at Luke's story of Jesus appearing to two of his followers on the road to Emmaus. This is one of the best known of all resurrection appearance stories. In this story Jesus is not recognised. He appears to two of the disciples as a fellow traveller and walks along with them discussing the recent events in Jerusalem and discoursing on the scriptures. When they reach Emmaus, the two disciples invite this stranger to eat with them:

> Now while he was with them at table, he took the bread and said the blessing; then he broke it and handed it to them. And their eyes were opened and they recognised him; but he had vanished from their sight. Then they said to each other, 'Did not our hearts burn within us as he talked to us on the road and explained the scriptures to us?'
>
> LK.24.30-32

Perhaps more than any other of Luke's stories, the road to Emmaus narrative shows his skills as a storyteller. It can be read and understood on many different levels. First of all, it is an appealing and human story. It makes good sense that the disciples would look back on what had just happened and say to each other that they knew all along there was something special about the stranger walking with them. Wise hindsight such as this is a common experience; it is totally understandable and almost comically predictable. Secondly, in Luke's church the breaking of bread and the sharing of a cup of wine was a normal part of Christian meetings, and Luke is emphasising that in this practice it is possible to see and know Jesus. Thirdly, Luke is telling a familiar story in a familiar manner. Anyone who knows the Hebrew Scriptures is aware that even the greatest figures in the history of Israel have been known to "entertain angels unawares".[1]

Probably the best known example of this occurs in the book of Genesis. This tells of the time when Abraham had three visitors:

> Yahweh appeared to him at the Oak of Mamre while he was sitting by the entrance to the tent during the hottest part of the day. He looked up, and there he saw three men standing near him . . .
>
> GN.18.1-2[2]

Abraham welcomes these strangers and provides them with rest and food. They return his hospitality by pronouncing the strange prophecy that Abraham and his aged wife Sarah will have a son. Sarah overhears this and laughs to herself, knowing it is impossible. "Why did Sarah laugh?" God asks Abraham. ". . . Nothing is impossible for Yahweh." The prophecy of the three strangers proves true, and it leads to the birth of Isaac.

The angels who had visited Abraham carry on in their travels and two of them go to the city of Sodom. There they visit Lot, the brother of Abraham. Like Abraham before him, Lot does not know who they are and he takes them to be travellers. He welcomes them and asks them in and entertains them. Meanwhile a riot is brewing in the streets of Sodom, a city of very ill repute. The men of Sodom gather outside Lot's

1 This phrase comes from the unknown author of the letter to the Hebrews, see Heb.13.2 (AV).
2 for more on this story see above pp.108-109.

house, curious and angry about the unknown visitors inside. They demand that Lot send these visitors out to satisfy both their curiosity and their lust.

> Calling out to Lot they said, 'Where are the men who came to you tonight? Send them out to us so that we can have intercourse with them.' Lot came out to them at the door and, having shut the door behind him, said, 'Please brothers, do not be wicked . . .'
>
> GN.19.5-7

But the men of Sodom have every intention of being wicked. Their idea seems to be to gang-rape Lot's visitors. Lot attempts to defend his guests. He even tries to appease the mob by suggesting an alternative. He generously offers his two virgin daughters for them to rape instead. But the Sodomites do not want his daughters and continue to demand the men inside the house, threatening Lot with violence:

> Then they forced Lot back and moved forward to break down the door. But the men reached out, pulled Lot back into the house with them, and shut the door. And they dazzled those who were at the door of the house, one and all, with a blinding light, so that they could not find the doorway.
>
> GN.19.10-11

After this the angelic guests tell Lot that they are about to destroy the city and they urge him to escape with his family. Lot lingers, so they seize him by the hand, and lead him from the city along with his wife and his two daughters. Then God rains brimstone and fire upon Sodom and upon the other condemned city Gomorrah, and nothing further is heard of the two angels.

Such unrecognised and mysterious beings who appear from nowhere are often described in the scriptures. Stories telling of their appearances follow a predictable pattern. First, the mysterious being appears to a specially chosen person or group of people and is not recognised. There is then conversation or some kind of activity, and in the course of this the divine nature of the one who appears is recognised. The onlookers are struck with awe, often prostrating themselves on the ground. The appearing one then passes on some kind of instruction or blessing, and disappears from sight.

In the more dramatic and memorable stories of Jesus appearing after his death, the same pattern is followed. Jesus appears and is not recognised, disbelief and incredulity are expressed by people who see him, Jesus speaks to them and reassures them, he then is recognised, and he then disappears.[3]

The resurrection appearance stories that follow this pattern of non-recognition and disbelief being resolved in recognition and belief are found only in Luke and John. Mark does not tell any resurrection appearance stories at all [4] and Matthew's very brief stories of Jesus being seen after his death provide little detail. The nearest Matthew gets to describing either disbelief or non-recognition is in his short account of Jesus appearing to the eleven disciples on an unspecified mountain in Galilee. When they see Jesus most of them recognise him right away, but some have reservations. As Matthew says:

> When they saw him they fell down before him,
> though some hesitated . . .
>
> MT.28.17

Luke and John are much more forthcoming and far less cautious in their descriptions of how Jesus's followers react when he appears to them after his death. They tell colourful and memorable stories about how these friends of Jesus resolve their

3 for more on this pattern, see Alsup, John E., *The Post-Resurrection Appearance Stories of the Gospel Tradition*, SPCK, London, 1974, pp. 239-263 *passim*, 268-270.
4 for more on Mark's ending see below pp.261-263.ff

doubts and eventually come to recognise that Jesus is indeed there before them.

In the Hebrew Scriptures, stories of how God or a heavenly messenger appear are sometimes interwoven with the ancient idea that to look directly at God is a dangerous thing to do. In the earlier writings, to see God means risking death. This is made very clear to Moses.

> (Moses) then said, 'Please show me your glory.' Yahweh said, 'I shall make all my goodness pass before you, and before you I shall pronounce the name Yahweh; and I am gracious to those to whom I am gracious and I take pity on those on whom I take pity.' 'But my face,' he said, 'you cannot see, for no human being can see me and survive.' Then Yahweh said, 'Here is a place near me. You will stand on the rock, and when my glory passes by, I shall put you in a cleft of the rock and shield you with my hand until I have gone past . . .'
>
> EX.33.18-23[5]

Perhaps because of the danger of seeing God face to face, encounters with the divine in the scriptures are often described as encounters with the angel of God, rather than with God directly. The word "angel" comes from the Greek "angelos" meaning "messenger". It is an angel of God that appears to the wife of Manoah, in the book of Judges[6]

> The Angel of Yahweh appeared to this woman and said to her, 'You are barren and have had no child, but you are going to conceive and give birth to a son. From now on, take great care . . .'
>
> JG.13.3-4

5 see also, EX.3.6; GN.32.30; DT.5.24; JG.6.24; JG.13.22; IS.6.5.
6 for more on this story see above p.239.

The angel tells Manoah's wife in great detail how she must nurture the child she is carrying. This child is to be the champion of Israel who will "start rescuing Israel from the power of the Philistines." After hearing this Manoah's wife goes in search of her husband, and she says:

> 'A man of God has just come to me, who looked like the Angel of God, so majestic was he. I did not ask him where he came from, and he did not tell me his name . . .
>
> JG.13.6

Manoah is anxious to see this "man of God" himself, and he prays that he will come again. Not long after, the angel returns to the woman as she is sitting in a field. She runs to get her husband and they both speak with the angel who repeats his detailed instructions to Manoah's wife and affirms that an important child has been conceived.[7] Manoah is grateful for this news and asks the angel to stay and share in a sacrificial offering. The angel explains that he cannot eat with them and when Manoah asks for his name he says only that his name is a "name of wonder." Manoah then places a sacrificial kid on a rock and makes his offering to God:

> . . . as the flame rose heavenwards from the altar, the Angel of Yahweh ascended in this flame before the eyes of Manoah and his wife, and they fell face downwards on the ground. After this, the Angel of Yahweh did not appear any more to Manoah and his wife, but Manoah understood that this had been the Angel of Yahweh. And Manoah said to his wife, 'We are certain to die, because we have seen God.' His wife replied, 'If Yahweh had meant to kill us, he would not have accepted a burnt offering and obla-

7 for the relationship between this story and the story of the birth of Jesus see *Beyond Bethlehem*, pp.73-74.

tion from us, he would not have let us see all this
and, at the same time, have told us such things.'

JG.13.20-23

A few chapters earlier in the book of Judges, the great warrior Gideon has a similar encounter with the angel of God. Like Manoah and his wife, he does not know that this is an angel and he too makes an offering to God while the angel is with him. This time the angel becomes actively involved in the process:

> ... the Angel of Yahweh said to him, 'Take the meat and unleavened cakes, put them on this rock and pour the broth over them.' Gideon did so. The Angel of Yahweh then stretched out the tip of the staff which he was carrying, and touched the meat and unleavened cakes. Fire sprang from the rock and consumed the meat and unleavened cakes, and the Angel of Yahweh vanished before his eyes. Gideon then knew that this was the Angel of Yahweh, and he said, 'Alas, my Lord Yahweh! Now I have seen the Angel of Yahweh face to face!' Yahweh answered, 'Peace be with you; have no fear; you will not die.'

JG.6.20-23

The story of Tobias and the angel Raphael in the book of Tobit follows a similar pattern. Here again, an angel appears, is not recognized, and later disappears before the eyes of witnesses. As we mentioned in the previous chapter, the story Luke tells about Jesus on the road to Emmaus has certain similarities with the book of Tobit.[8] The two disciples on the road to Emmaus are accompanied by a stranger they do not recognise, just as Tobias on the road to Media is accompanied by a stranger he does not recognise:

8 for more on this see above pp.237-238.

> Tobias went out to look for a man who knew the way to go with him to Media. Outside he found Raphael the angel standing facing him, though he did not guess he was an angel of God. He said, 'Where do you come from, friend?' The angel replied, 'I am one of your brother Israelites; I have come to these parts to look for work.'
>
> TB.5.4-5

After much travelling and many adventures, Tobias and the angel Raphael return to where they began their journey. They meet up once again with Tobit, the father of Tobias, and the old man's blindness is cured. The angel Raphael then decides it is time to declare who he is. When he does this, both Tobit and Tobias prostrate themselves in front of him. Raphael continues talking:

> '. . . Now bless the Lord on earth and give thanks to God. I am about to return to him who sent me from above. Write down all that has happened.' And he rose in the air. When they stood up again, he was no longer visible. They praised God with hymns; they thanked him for having performed such wonders; had not an angel of God appeared to them?'
>
> TB.12.20-21

"And he rose in the air"—thus Raphael departs. Similarly the angel of God vanishes in front of Manoah and his wife, and in front of Gideon. The heavenly ones who appear in the scriptures seem able to materialize and disappear at will. This is also evident in the resurrection appearance stories in Luke's gospel. Jesus vanishes at the meal at Emmaus, and later he vanishes in front of the disciples. This second disappearance follows the story in which Jesus eats to prove to the disciples that he is a real person of flesh and blood:

> Then he took them out as far as the outskirts of Bethany, and raising his hands he blessed them. Now as he blessed them, he withdrew from them and was carried up to heaven . . .
>
> LK.24.50-51

This disappearance of Jesus upwards into heaven is a story Luke develops further in another account in the book of Acts. This account is known as the ascension:

> Now having met together, they asked him, 'Lord, has the time come for you to restore the kingdom to Israel?' He replied, 'It is not for you to know times or dates that the Father has decided by his own authority, but you will receive the power of the Holy Spirit which will come on you, and then you will be my witnesses not only in Jerusalem but throughout Judaea and Samaria, and indeed to earth's remotest end.'
>
> As he said this he was lifted up while they looked on, and a cloud took him from their sight. They were still staring into the sky as he went when suddenly two men in white were standing beside them and they said, 'Why are you Galileans standing here looking into the sky? This Jesus who has been taken up from you into heaven will come back in the same way as you have seen him go to heaven.'
>
> AC.1.6-11

It is only Luke who tells of the ascension of Jesus. The other gospels do not mention it, although John does have Jesus talking about "ascending to his father."[9] But although they do not tell

9 There are very few allusions to the ascension. See JN.20.17, cp. JN.3.13, and 1TH.4.17. In the book of Ephesians (by an unknown author) see EP.4.8-10 which cites PS.68.18. Not all translations agree that the psalm is relevant.

the story of the ascension, Mark and Matthew do describe the "transfiguration", an event that occurs during Jesus's lifetime. This is also described by Luke. All three accounts of the transfiguration share certain qualities with the story of the ascension:

> . . . (Jesus) took with him Peter and John and James and went up to the mountain to pray. And it happened that, as he was praying, the aspect of his face was changed and his clothing became sparkling white. And suddenly there were two men talking to him; they were Moses and Elijah appearing in glory, and they were speaking of his passing which he was to accomplish in Jerusalem. Peter and his companions were heavy with sleep, but they woke up and saw his glory and the two men standing with him. As these were leaving him, Peter said to Jesus, 'Master it is wonderful for us to be here; so let us make three shelters, one for you, one for Moses and one for Elijah.' He did not know what he was saying. As he was saying this, a cloud came and covered them with shadow; and when they went into the cloud the disciples were afraid. And a voice came from the cloud saying, 'This is my Son, the Chosen One. Listen to him.' And after the voice had spoken, Jesus was found alone. The disciples kept silence and, at that time, told no one what they had seen.
>
> LK.9.28-36 [10]

Luke's accounts of both the transfiguration and the ascension insist that the disciples are able to recognise Jesus; he is the one "taken up", he is the "Chosen One". In these stories no doubt is left, no incredulity. Supernatural intervention and overwhelming visions are accepted without question.

10 see also MK.9.2-13 and MT.17.1- 13.

Here once again an ancient tradition is reflected, a tradition of powerful experiences and visions in which the divine is revealed in a way that leaves no question or doubt. The scriptures tell of many such visionary experiences, and as Luke well knew the most influential visions are those anchored in the physical surroundings and in the psychic roots of the people involved. It is no accident that Luke's stories of the transfiguration and the ascension of Jesus are firmly anchored in both.

The Mount of Olives is named as the site of the ascension. An anonymous mountain is named as the site of the transfiguration. In the Hebrew Scriptures, mountains are time-honoured places to receive visions and to see God. This applies particularly to Mount Sinai, where Moses received the ten commandments:

> Yahweh said to Moses, 'Come up to me on the mountain. Stay there, and I will give you the stone tablets—the law and the commandment—which I have written for their instruction.' Moses made ready, with Joshua his assistant, and they went up the mountain of God . . .
>
> Cloud covered the mountain. The glory of Yahweh rested on Mount Sinai and the cloud covered it for six days. On the seventh day Yahweh called to Moses from inside the cloud. To the watching Israelites, the glory of Yahweh looked like a devouring fire on the mountain top. Moses went right into the cloud and went on up the mountain. Moses stayed on the mountain for forty days and forty nights.
>
> EX.24.12-18

In the scriptures there are at least three descriptions of Moses meeting his God on the mountain.[11] In one of these,

11 see EX.19.2-25; EX.24.1-18; EX.31.18ff; parts of EX.34 1-35. In NB.11.24ff the vision is in the tent of meeting.

when Moses comes down from his encounter his face is shining.

> When Moses came down from Mount Sinai with the two tablets of the Testimony in his hands, as he was coming down the mountain, Moses did not know that the skin of his face was radiant because he had been talking to him. And when Aaron and all the Israelites saw Moses, the skin on his face was so radiant that they were afraid to go near him.
>
> EX.34.29-30

Centuries later, in the same tradition, Luke tells how Jesus's face and his entire being are transformed as he prays on a mountain, and "the aspect of his face was changed and his clothing became sparkling white."

Mount Sinai, where Moses so radiantly meets his God, is also called Mount Horeb. Horeb is where the great prophet Elijah has his extraordinary encounter with the divine, also known as his "theophany". Elijah was a young prophet when Ahab became king of Israel about 850 BCE. Although Ahab was a very powerful king, Elijah was not impressed, nor were the later writers who recorded the history of Ahab and Elijah. They were particularly unimpressed by Ahab's choice of a wife, and their displeasure is recorded in the first book of Kings.

> Ahab son of Omri did what is displeasing to Yahweh, and was worse than all his predecessors . . . he married Jezebel daughter of Ethbaal, king of the Sidonians, and then proceeded to serve Baal and worship him . . .
>
> 1K.16.30-32

This was provocation. Elijah was a prophet of Yahweh, the God of the Hebrews, and he rises to this provocation. He has already established himself by predicting a three year drought,[12]

12 see above pp.61- 62 and 191-193.

and now he engages in a momentous struggle for ascendancy with Jezebel. At first he has some miraculous victories but soon Elijah is driven away by Jezebel, and he retreats to the desert.

Elijah cannot cope with life in the desert, and after a few days he sits down under a furze bush and decides to die. There he has his first vision and in his vision he is given food and water. On the strength of this he travels all the away to Horeb. Forty days later he is on the mountain and he stays in a cave where he has the vision for which he is so famous:

> . . . the word of Yahweh came to him saying, 'What are you doing here, Elijah?' He replied, 'I am full of jealous zeal for Yahweh Sabaoth, because the Israelites have abandoned your covenant, have torn down your altars and put your prophets to the sword. I am the only one left, and now they want to kill me.' Then he was told, 'Go out and stand on the mountain before Yahweh.' For at that moment Yahweh was going by. A mighty hurricane split the mountains and shattered the rocks before Yahweh. But Yahweh was not in the hurricane. And after the hurricane, an earthquake. But Yahweh was not in the earthquake. And after the earthquake, fire. But Yahweh was not in the fire. And after the fire, a light murmuring sound. And when Elijah heard this, he covered his face with his cloak . . .
>
> 1K.19.9-13

In the "light murmuring sound", more memorably translated in the King James Bible as "a still, small voice", Elijah recognises his God. Like Moses in earlier stories, and like the disciples of Jesus in later stories, he is filled with awe. This vision of his God strengthens Elijah and enables him to carry on with his usual zeal. He recruits his successor Elisha and many others who join him in the struggle against Ahab and Jezebel, a struggle that lasts for the rest of Elijah's life.

The story of the death of Elijah is spectacular. Rich with echoes of earlier stories, it reaches out and in turn influences countless later stories. The story begins with the phrase "This is what happened when Yahweh took Elijah up to heaven in the whirlwind", and it tells how Elijah and Elisha cross the River Jordan:

> Elijah took his cloak, rolled it up and struck the water; and the water divided to left and right, and the two of them crossed over dry-shod. When they had crossed, Elijah said to Elisha, 'Make your request. What can I do for you before I am snatched away from you?' Elisha answered, 'Let me inherit a double share of your spirit.' 'Your request is difficult,' Elijah said. 'If you see me while I am being snatched away from you, it will be as you ask; if not, it will not be so.' Now as they walked on, talking as they went, a chariot of fire appeared and horses of fire coming between the two of them; and Elijah went up to heaven in the whirlwind. Elisha saw it, and shouted, 'My father! My father! Chariot of Israel and its chargers!' Then he lost sight of him . . .
>
> 2K.2.8–12

This story fits into the tradition of visions and mountaintop revelations that are granted to Moses and Elijah and many others. Luke's story of the ascension of Jesus on the Mount of Olives can be seen as a response to and a reiteration of this tradition.

An integral part of this tradition is the cloud. When Jesus so surprisingly disappears from the disciples in Luke's story in the book of Acts, it is a cloud that "took Jesus from their sight". Mysterious clouds that shelter the divine and protect the righteous, and are found throughout the scriptures. These can be dark or bright clouds; they can be brooding or portentous or joyous. A cloud protects the Israelites while they cross the Red Sea to escape from Egypt, on Mount Sinai the Lord God encounters Moses inside an awesome cloud, a cloud covers the holy "tent of meeting" in the desert and broods over the sanctuary of the first temple, and early in Luke's gospel "the power of the Most High" overshadows Mary when she is told that she will bear a child who will be the Messiah.[13] Given the strength of this tradition it is not surprising that when Luke wants to tell of Jesus departing from his disciples, the cloud appears yet again.

In the ascension scene in the book of Acts there is another strong influence at work. It is revealed in the question Luke puts in the mouths of the disciples, "has the time come for you to restore the kingdom to Israel?". The hope expressed in this phrase recalls the obstinate hope that is recorded in the book of the prophet Micah, nearly a century after Elijah's visit to Horeb. Micah watched in dismay from Jerusalem in the southern "kingdom of Judah" as the "kingdom of Israel" to the north disintegrated.[14] This was the beginning of the long downhill slide for both "Israel" and "Judah" as political powers in the ancient world. The Assyrians from what is present day Iraq were on the offensive. They conquered Samaria, which had been Ahab's citadel in Israel, and Micah could see nothing to stop the victorious Assyrian army advancing south to Jerusalem. But against all the odds, the prophet was still able to look to the future, and he hoped against hope:

But in days to come
Yahweh's Temple Mountain
will tower above the mountains,
rise higher than the hills,
Then the peoples will stream to it,
then many nations will come and say,
'Come, we will go up to Yahweh's mountain,

13 i for example see EX.13.21-22; EX.14.19-20,24; EX.16.10; EX.19.9; EX.24.15-18; EX.34.5; EX.40.34 -38; NB.11.25; 1K.8.10-12; and LK.1.35.
ii for further discussion see *Beyond Bethlehem* pp.74-76.

14 David's kingdom had splintered when Solomon died. Kings of David's line were in Jerusalem, in "Judah". King Ahab and his father Omri were notables of the northern kings in Samaria, in "Israel".

> to the Temple of the God of Jacob,
> so that he may teach us his ways
> and we may walk in his paths . . .'
>
> MI.4.1-2

This passage goes on to express the hope that all wars will end, that swords will be hammered into ploughshares, and that each man will sit in peace under his vine and fig tree. Micah assumes that when all this comes to pass the kingdom shall be restored to its former power and glory. This assumption prevails in everything Micah writes, despite a very unpromising political climate.

In his stubborn hopefulness for the kingdom to be restored, Micah looks to the "Tower of the Flock". This was Ophel, one of the hills of the city.

> And to you, Tower of the Flock,
> Ophel of the daughter of Zion,
> to you your former sovereignty will return,
> the royal power of the daughter of Jerusalem.
>
> MI.4.8

Micah is expressing some of the earliest hopes and expectations for the restoration of all Israel. When from century to century, and generation to generation these hopes fail to be realized, another set of hopes begins to evolve. These are eventually expressed as the hope for coming of the Messiah, variously expected to be a prophetic, a priestly, a warlike, or a kingly figure. By the time of Jesus, this Messiah is expected to conquer the abhorred occupying forces of Israel in a great battle, and to usher in a new age that offers salvation to the faithful. This complex network of ideas underlies the apocalyptic visions and fantastical imagery of such writings as the book of Daniel and the book of Revelation. Such ideas are also implicit in the hope expressed in the question Luke has the disciples ask Jesus in the story of the ascension. When will the kingdom be restored? when will the ancient glories of all Israel be recovered? This is what everyone wanted to know; for this recurring hope had been fundamental in the hearts and minds of the Jewish people ever since the divided kingdoms began to fail during the time of Micah.

Mysteriously, Micah's hope for the kingdom seems to reside in Ophel, the "Tower of the Flock". As he says: " . . . to you, Tower of the Flock, Ophel of the daughter of Zion, to you your former sovereignty will return . . ." That a tower should be the focus of Micah's hope is natural. The scriptural significance of the tower is clear, along with its later influence. The roots go back to Moses, and the later influence extends to Mary Magdalene.

When Moses leads the people out of slavery in Egypt towards salvation in the promised land of Israel, the route lies "between Migdol and the sea."[15] Migdol was a watchtower or blockhouse. Through the centuries the name changed and the place shifted until Migdol became Magdala, the village by the sea of Galilee that is the home of Mary, the disciple of Jesus. She is one of the faithful women who witness the crucifixion and the burial. In the gospels of Luke and John she also is a witness to the resurrection of Jesus, the first witness according to John. Her name "Magdala" recalls the watchtower that saw the salvation of Israel, and also recalls the stubborn hope of the prophet Micah that "the tower" would see the return of the glory of Israel. In the gospels, Mary of Magdala is a witness, a watchtower. She sees the death of Jesus and the resurrection. In terms of the gospels' message, this makes her a witness to the great glory of a new salvation.

In John's gospel Mary of Magdala comes to the tomb early on the "first day of the week" and sees that the stone has been rolled away. She then runs to get help and on the way meets Peter and the beloved disciple. She tells the two men that the body is missing and the two men run to the tomb. The beloved

15 see EX.14.2.

disciple arrives first and sees the grave cloths but no body. Peter then arrives and goes inside the tomb only to see the same thing. Mary's turn comes next. She is left alone outside the tomb, weeping. When she stoops to look inside, she sees two angels in white who ask her why she is crying:

> 'They have taken my Lord away,' she replied, 'and I don't know where they have put him.' As she said this she turned round and saw Jesus standing there, though she did not realise that it was Jesus. Jesus said to her, 'Woman, why are you weeping? Who are you looking for?' Supposing him to be the gardener, she said, 'Sir, if you have taken him away, tell me where you have put him, and I will go and remove him.' Jesus said, 'Mary!' She turned round then and said to him in Hebrew, 'Rabbuni!'—which means Master. Jesus said to her, 'Do not cling to me, because I have not yet ascended to the Father. But go and find my brothers, and tell them: I am ascending to my Father and your Father, to my God and your God.' So Mary of Magdala told the disciples, 'I have seen the Lord,' and that he had said these things to her.
>
> JN.20.13-18

By the time John was writing, at least sixty years had passed since the death of Jesus. In that time Jesus had not returned in glory to usher in the end times. "The Day of the Lord" had not yet come. Christians of the late first century needed to be encouraged by positive and reassuring stories that Jesus was the Messiah, and that he would return. The resurrection appearance stories told by John and Luke provide such encouragement.

The storytelling pattern followed in these stories is designed to transform uncertainty into certainty and disbelief into belief. Ever since they were written, countless people have found that the resurrection appearance stories have this effect;

that uncertainties and doubts are somehow resolved in these stories in a way that is entirely convincing and profoundly reassuring. For others this is not so, and this resolution of uncertainty and disbelief seems completely implausible. It is very striking that not all the gospel writers attempt such resolution of uncertainties and doubts. It is very striking that Mark ends his gospel in an entirely different way.

CHAPTER EIGHTEEN

Fear

In this final chapter we return to Mark's gospel and to his scene of the women coming to the tomb on the morning after the burial. Mary of Magdala is there, not a lonely figure weeping by the tomb as in John's gospel, but one of three women who arrive at the tomb with a supply of spices to anoint the body of Jesus.

> When the Sabbath was over, Mary of Magdala, Mary the mother of James, and Salome, bought spices with which to go and anoint him.
>
> MK.16.1

These are the same women who witness the crucifixion:

> There were some women watching from a distance. Among them were Mary of Magdala, Mary who was the mother of James the younger and Joset, and Salome.
>
> MK.15.40

And two of these women also witness the burial:

> ... He then rolled a stone against the entrance to the tomb. Mary of Magdala and Mary the mother of Joset took note of where he was laid.
>
> MK.15.46-47

When these three women go to visit the tomb of Jesus they find his body is not there. Instead, in the tomb they see a mysterious figure in white:

> . . . On entering the tomb they saw a young man in a white robe seated on the right-hand side, and they were struck with amazement. But he said to them, 'There is no need to be so amazed. You are looking for Jesus of Nazareth, who was crucified: he has risen, he is not here. See, here is the place where they laid him. But you must go and tell his disciples and Peter. "He is going ahead of you to Galilee; that is where you will see him, just as he told you." And the women came out and ran away from the tomb because they were frightened out of their wits; and they said nothing to anyone, for they were afraid.
>
> MK.16.5-8

Here, at verse 8 of Chapter 16, Mark's gospel comes to an abrupt end. It ends with the women who, finding the tomb empty ". . . ran away from the tomb because they were frightened out of their wits; and they said nothing to anyone, for they were afraid." After this flight of the women, and their silence, and their fear Mark's gospel has no more to say.

Mark tells no stories of Jesus appearing after his death. The women at the tomb do not see the risen Jesus, nor does anyone else. Mark has nothing to say that is even remotely comparable to Matthew's account of Jesus appearing to the eleven, or Luke's story of the appearance on the road to Emmaus, or John's story of the appearance to Thomas. Mark's silence on this subject is deafening.

Yet Mark's gospel as it is printed in many Bibles does appear to continue beyond verse 8 of Chapter 16. It appears to carry on for another twelve verses, and in these twelve verses no fewer than three resurrection appearances of Jesus are briefly described. These descriptions seem like short versions of appearances described in the other gospels. But these three resurrection appearances at the end of Mark's gospel are problematic. Many modern translations of the Bible take the precaution of placing this section of the gospel in parentheses, or they add an explanatory note. [1] This is because most biblical scholars agree that this last section of Chapter 16 of Mark's gospel is not written by Mark at all. The most reliable early manuscripts of the gospel do not have this section. It is a later addition to Mark's gospel and its author is not known.

How this last section became attached to Mark's gospel and where it comes from is uncertain. It is possible that it was summarized from later New Testament writings and added to Mark's text in an attempt to resolve his apparently incomplete story. Early Christian copyists and editors of the gospels may have found the ending at verse 8 of Chapter 16 harsh and hard to accept in the light of subsequent colourful stories about the resurrected Jesus. But the evidence is very strong that this original abrupt ending is Mark's original ending. It is in keeping with his usual terse and abrupt style.

Given this understanding of the ending of Mark's gospel, readers are left with an empty tomb, flight, silence, and fear. To make matters worse, Mark's story not only seems unfinished, but the events he describes lack convincing witnesses. He only has the three women, and the testimony of women carried little authority in first century Palestine. The other gospel writers also have women as witnesses at the empty tomb, and they even have women witnessing the resurrected Jesus, but the testimony of these women is consistently backed up by that of men. For example, in Matthew's gospel when the women encounter the

1 i for more on the ending of Mark in various English translations see Appendix One, p.281.
ii For two discussions of the ending of Mark's gospel see:
(a) Metzger, Bruce M., *A Textual Commentary of the Greek New Testament: A Companion Volume to the United Bible Societies' Greek New Testament (third edition)*, United Bible Societies, 1971, pp.122-126.
(b) Lane, William L., *The Gospel According to Mark* in the series *New International Commentaries on the New Testament*, William B. Eerdmans, Grand Rapids, 1974, pp. 590-92.

angel at the tomb, the story is at first similar to Mark's, but it soon takes a very different turn. As in Mark's gospel, the women are instructed by the angel to tell the disciples what they have seen, but according to Matthew the women are filled with "awe and great joy" rather than with fear, and as they leave the tomb they meet the risen Jesus:

> Filled with awe and great joy the women came quickly away from the tomb and ran to tell the disciples. And suddenly, coming to meet them, was Jesus. 'Greetings,' he said. And the women came up to him and, clasping his feet, they did him homage. Then Jesus said to them, 'Do not be afraid; go and tell my brothers that they must leave for Galilee; there they will see me.'
>
> MT.28.8-10

After Matthew tells of Jesus appearing to the women he wraps up his gospel very quickly. The eleven disciples meet Jesus on an appointed mountain in Galilee and he speaks to them, exhorting them to go and "make disciples of all nations". The women fade from sight completely and it is the male disciples who are sanctioned by Jesus to preach and proseletize. Matthew makes it quite clear that the male witnesses are the important witnesses to the resurrection, the ones who will carry the story to a wider audience.

To be a witness to the resurrection of Jesus is perceived by all the gospel writers as an extremely important role. In the final verses of his gospel Luke has Jesus tell his disciples that their role is to be witnesses both to his identity as the Christ and to his resurrection. In the book of Acts Luke emphasises this even more strongly and ascribes these words to Peter:

> 'God raised this man Jesus to life, and of that we are all witnesses . . . the whole House of Israel can be certain that the Lord and Christ whom God has made is this Jesus whom you crucified.'
>
> AC.2.32,36

John is also preoccupied with the role of witnesses. This is evident very early in his gospel in the brief story about the man called Nathanael. Jesus has been selecting disciples, and he chooses a man called Philip as one of his followers. Philip then finds Nathanael, and brings him to Jesus. When he sees Nathanael, Jesus appears to know a lot about him and Nathanael recognises Jesus instantly:

> Nathanael asked, 'How do you know me?' Jesus replied, 'Before Philip came to call you, I saw you under the fig tree.' Nathanael answered, 'Rabbi, you are the Son of God, you are the king of Israel.' Jesus replied, 'You believe that just because I said: I saw you under the fig tree. You are going to see greater things than that.' And then he added, 'In all truth I tell you, you will see heaven open and the angels of God ascending and descending over the Son of man.'
>
> JN.1.48-51

This reference to angels ascending and descending suggests that Nathanael will be a very important witness whose experience will be comparable to that of the patriarch Jacob, who was Israel. When Jacob was a witness to the glory of God he too saw angels ascending and descending:

> (Jacob) had a dream: there was a ladder, planted on the ground with its top reaching to heaven; and God's angels were going up and down on it. And there was Yahweh, standing beside him and saying, 'I, Yahweh, am the God of Abraham your father, and the God of Isaac. The ground on which you are lying I shall give to you and your descendants . . .'
>
> GN.28.12-13

In his resurrection appearance stories John describes in

detail how his witnesses perceive the risen Jesus [2]. His stories always allay the doubts of these witnesses and affirm their belief. Mary of Magdala's grief at the tomb is resolved when she recognizes Jesus. When he next appears Jesus shows the wounds on his hands and feet to the disciples to prove who he is and they are "filled with joy". The next time they see Jesus he satisfies the doubts of Thomas. Then comes the final appearance of Jesus in the epilogue of John's gospel. This tells of a meeting between Jesus and the disciples on the shore of the Sea of Tiberias, which is another name for the Sea of Galilee.

In this story the disciples are out fishing and Jesus appears on the shore. They do not recognize him at first but when he tells them how to set their nets and at once they catch a lot of fish, they realize who he is. They come to shore as he is preparing a meal that they all share. The conversation that follows has Jesus paying particular attention to Peter and to the beloved disciple. After repeatedly asking Peter if he loves him, Jesus predicts Peter's death. This death had already occurred in the mid-sixties, decades before the writing of John's gospel. Jesus then indicates to the aggrieved Peter that the beloved disciple will see the time of his second coming. This was the great hope of all the gospels; that the return of Jesus was imminent, and that his followers would live to witness it.

As time passed in the first century, the gospels' interest in witnesses to the resurrection seems to increase. As decade after decade passed with no sign of Jesus returning, Matthew, Luke and John make ever stronger affirmations that Jesus had indeed risen from the dead and would indeed come again. Christianity was building on this belief and on this hope, and it fell to the gospels to provide detailed stories with reliable witnesses to the resurrection and with firm assurances about the second coming.

Many years before the gospels were written, Paul recognized an earlier form of this need for affirmation and assurance.

2 JN.20.11-29; cp.JN.21, the epilogue, for more such appearances.

He responded to it differently, not by telling stories, but by trying to define the nature of Christian belief:

> I want to make quite clear to you, brothers, what the message of the gospel that I preached to you is . . . that Christ died for our sins, in accordance with the scriptures, and that he was buried; and that on the third day, he was raised to life, in accordance with the scriptures; . . .
>
> 1CO.15.1-4

Paul wrote this in the mid fifties in his first letter to the new Christian church he had established in the Greek city of Corinth. After he states the belief that Jesus rose from the dead, he affirms this by providing a list of witnesses to Jesus's resurrection:

> . . . he appeared to Cephas; and later to the Twelve; and next he appeared to more than five hundred of the brothers at the same time, most of whom are still with us, though some have fallen asleep; then he appeared to James, and then to all the apostles. Last of all he appeared to me too . . .
>
> 1CO.15.5-8

This is an interesting list.[3] It was written well before the gospels and it provides very different information. Here Paul cites over five hundred witnesses to a single resurrection appearance. He also names Cephas, which is another name for Peter, and James as witnesses to other appearances, he specifies "all the apostles" as witnesses, and last of all he names himself as a witness. Any first century audience would understand that this is a solemn and authoritative list of witnesses to the resurrection, for here is a great number of men.

But there are problems with this list. Although it provides

3 see above pp.227-228.

an impressive array of witnesses to the resurrection, it is short on background evidence. Paul does not, for instance, indicate when any of these appearances occurred, though the appearance to himself is believed to have taken place some months or possibly even years after the death of Jesus. By contrast, the appearances described by Matthew and Luke seem to have occurred within just a few days of the death, while in the main body of John's gospel the appearances occur within about ten days of the death, and in Acts the final appearance occurs forty days after the first resurrection appearance.

More importantly, when Paul provides his list of witnesses to the resurrection, he produces no accompanying evidence about the death and burial of Jesus, nor does he cite any witnesses to that death and burial. All he says is that Jesus . . .

> . . . died for our sins, in accordance with the scriptures, and that he was buried; and that on the third day, he was raised to life, in accordance with the scriptures . . .
>
> 1CO.15.4 [4]

Paul is a Pharisee, and in this letter he is preoccupied with the idea of resurrection. His business is not to tell stories about the death of Jesus, but to explain its aftermath and significance. Consequently the letter gives no supporting evidence about the death, and tells of no witnesses to the death. Paul supports his statement that Jesus rose from the dead by listing hundreds of witnesses to this resurrection, but such a list means little without firm evidence that Jesus died and was buried.

If the assertion of the resurrection of Jesus was to carry authority, witnesses were needed to the death and burial. Mark, who was writing some fifteen or twenty years after Paul, understood this need. There are scholars who argue that Mark simply invented the story of the burial of Jesus and the empty tomb in

4 for other examples of Paul referring to the death of Jesus see above p.19, footnote #2, and p.170, footnote #6.

order to meet this need, and that the later gospel writers then constructed their stories around Mark's.[5]

A more generous attitude towards Mark's story of the death and burial and empty tomb is that it was not widely known before he recorded it because it was based on the testimony of women. This story may have reached Mark through sources that are now lost, sources that would have been questionable in the first century because they relied on the evidence of women. In making known the story of these female witnesses, Mark could be recording stories that were not widely accepted earlier in the century. Because the witnesses were women, and because the evidence of women carried little if any weight, such a story would have been almost impossible to credit.

Yet the women Mark provides as witnesses are women of note. Although they are described fleeing from the tomb, too frightened to discuss what they have seen, they have a pivotal role to play in his gospel. They also have the status and background required for such a role. This is evident in their names, names rich with associations. The three women are Mary of Magdala, Mary the mother of James and Joset, and Salome.

The name Mary derives from Miriam. In the Hebrew Scriptures Miriam is the sister of Aaron and Moses, a prophetess who plays a leading role in helping the Israelites escape from slavery in Egypt. Miriam first appears as a young girl watching over her brother Moses when he is an infant. Moses is threatened with death when the Pharaoh of Egypt decides to slaughter all first-born male children of the Israelites. In a desperate move to save him, his mother and Miriam place Moses in a basket in the river. When he is found by the sister of the Pharaoh Miriam is watching from a distance. She offers to get a nurse for the baby, and brings their own mother to care for him. Later when

5 i See Mack, *A Myth of Innocence*, pp.251 and 308 passim.
ii For further discussion see Butts, James R., *Probing the Polling, Jesus Seminar Results on the Kingdom Sayings*, in *Foundations and Facets Forum*, Vol.3, No.1, November 1987, p.111 and passim.

Moses leads the Israelites out of Egypt, Miriam leads the women across the Red Sea when the waters are parted. Playing her tambourine, dancing, and singing, she shows the way to the salvation promised them in a new land. [6]

Mark has two Marys. The first, Mary of Magdala, is named after the place of her birth, the place of the watchtower.[7] The other Mary is identified by the names of her two sons, James the younger and Joset. James is an equivalent of the name Jacob, and Jacob of old was Israel. It was Jacob who, when he saw Rachel for the first time, single-handedly rolled away a great stone from the mouth of a well that normally was opened by several men. It was Jacob who saw the glory of God in a dream of angels ascending and descending a ladder, and in that dream Jacob was told of a land promised to his descendants forever. The name Joset, spelled Joses in most translations, is an equivalent of Joseph. And Joseph of old was the son of Jacob by that same Rachel, his favourite wife. It was Joseph who saw to the burial of his father with great honour, embalming him and taking his body back to the land of Israel from Egypt.[8]

Mark's third female witness is Salome. She is mentioned twice without any patronymic or place-name to explain who she is. But her name itself supplies this lack, for it is the female version of the name "Solomon", and Solomon is one of the celebrated lovers in the Song of Songs. The language of the Song is redolent of exotic spices and ointments:[9]

> What is this coming up from the desert
> like a column of smoke,
> breathing of myrrh and frankincense
> and every exotic perfume?
> Here comes Solomon's litter . . .
>
> . . . .

6 for the stories of Miriam see EX.2.1-10 & EX.15.20-21.
7 for more on this name see above pp.256-258.
8 for more on the burial Joseph's father see above pp.210-211.
9 for more on the Song of Songs see above pp.95-96.

Before the day-breeze rises,
before the shadows flee,
I shall go to the mountain of myrrh,
to the hill of frankincense . . .

. . . .

His cheeks are beds of spices,
banks sweetly scented,
His lips are lilies,
distilling pure myrrh.

SG.3.6-7A; 4.6; 5.13

In the middle of the Song, the beloved cannot find the lover:

I opened to my love,
but he had turned and gone.
My soul failed at his flight,
I sought but could not find him,
I called, but he did not answer.

SG.5.6

Salome's name is a distant reminder of the extravagant language and the devoted love of the Song of Songs. Her name evokes its aromatic oils and fragrant spices, and recalls also the haunting sense of loss when the loved one cannot be found.

These then are Mark's witnesses; Salome, Mary and Mary. The story of what they do at the empty tomb brings Mark's gospel to a close.

. . . And very early in the morning on the first day of the week they went to the tomb when the sun had risen.

They had been saying to one another, 'Who will roll away the stone for us from the entrance to the tomb?' But when they looked they saw that the stone—which was very big—had already been rolled

> back. On entering the tomb they saw a young man in a white robe seated on the right-hand side, and they were struck with amazement.
>
> MK.16.2-5

Or as the King James Bible says, "they were affrighted". Their fear and amazement at the empty tomb is fundamental to the dramatic power of Mark's gospel. The fear of these three women provides the unsettling and disturbing tone that so radically distinguishes the ending of Mark's gospel from the other gospels. Matthew and Luke and John do not allow the fear of their witnesses to dominate. In their accounts such fear is appeased and qualified by further stories and explanations. Mark offers no appeasement, no qualifications.

Yet in telling of the fear of the women, Mark is telling a story full of a profound excitement, and the tone of this story is familiar. Mark is writing within a tradition in which fear can signal the overwhelming presence of God. In the Hebrew Scriptures great fear is often the response to extraordinary visions, and direct encounters with the divine. Such fear is part of the process of recognizing God or the greatness of God. Far from being a negative experience that must be overcome, such fear is a legitimate and necessary response to an overpowering revelation. It is a positive response, an affirmation.

The examples of this are many. They are found throughout the Hebrew Scriptures. When Jacob has his dream of the glory of God, complete with angels ascending and descending a ladder, he wakes full of fear:

> Then Jacob awoke from his sleep and said, 'Truly, Yahweh is in this place and I did not know!' He was afraid and said, 'How awe-inspiring this place is! This is nothing less than the abode of God, and this is the gate of heaven!'
>
> GN.28.16-17

"Please show me your glory", Moses says to his God in one of their encounters on Mount Sinai. His God warns him that such a revelation may be too much for Moses to bear:

> '. . . my face,' he said, 'you cannot see, for no human being can see me and survive.' Then Yahweh said, 'Here is a place near me. You will stand on the rock, and when my glory passes by, I shall put you in a cleft of the rock and shield you with my hand until I have gone past . . .'
>
> EX.33.20-22

In another encounter with his God on Mount Sinai, when Moses comes down with his face radiant, he is the one who inspires fear. The Israelites are afraid to approach this man who has been so close to his God.[10] And earlier in the book of Exodus, well before the stories of Moses on Mount Sinai, the story of the very first encounter between Moses and his God tells how Moses is afraid:

> Moses looked; there was the bush blazing, but the bush was not being burnt up . . . God called to him from the middle of the bush. 'Moses, Moses!' he said. 'Here I am,' he answered. 'Come no nearer,' he said. 'Take off your sandals, for the place where you are standing is holy ground. I am the God of your ancestors,' he said, 'the God of Abraham, the God of Isaac and the God of Jacob.' At this Moses covered his face, for he was afraid to look at God.
>
> EX.3.2-6

It is the same for the prophet Elijah on Mount Horeb when his God appears to him. This is an encounter only for the strong of heart, and it leaves Elijah beyond words:

10 see EX.34.29-35.

> A mighty hurricane split the mountains and shattered the rocks before Yahweh. But Yahweh was not in the hurricane. And after the hurricane, an earthquake. But Yahweh was not in the earthquake. And after the earthquake, fire. But Yahweh was not in the fire. And after the fire, a light murmuring sound. And when Elijah heard this, he covered his face with his cloak . . .
>
> 1K.19.11-13[11]

To be overwhelmed by the mystery of God or the glory of God often means being reduced to silence in the scriptures. This was the experience of Job. After many long chapters of berating his God, Job has little left to say when the voice "from the whirlwind" reveals the extent of the glory of God:

> You have told me about great works that I cannot understand,
> about marvels which are beyond me, of which I know nothing.
>
> . . . .
>
> Before, I knew you only by hearsay
> but now, having seen you with my own eyes,
> I retract what I have said,
> and repent in dust and ashes.
>
> JB.42.3-6

Much later in the scriptures, in the book of Daniel, a different vision of the divine fills Daniel with a similar holy dread:

> I, Daniel, alone saw the apparition . . . I was left alone, gazing on this great vision; I was powerless, my appearance was changed and contorted; my

11 for more on this passage see above p.254.

> strength deserted me. I heard a voice speaking, and at the sound of the voice I fell fainting, face downwards on the ground. I felt a hand touching me, setting my knees and my hands trembling. He said, 'Daniel, you are a man specially chosen; understand the words that I am about to say; stand up; I have been sent to you now.' He said this, and I stood up trembling. He then said, 'Daniel, do not be afraid . . .'
>
> DN.10.7-12

Daniel is not the only awestruck witness in the scriptures to be offered reassurance and encouragement when he is overwhelmed by an encounter with God or a heavenly messenger. The same happens to Gideon in the prehistory of Israel, and to Tobit and his son Tobias whose story is nearer the time of Daniel's. In a less direct but comparable way, it is the same for Moses of old, for Manoah and his wife, and for Elijah.[12] Much later it is so for the followers of Jesus.

"Do not be afraid", the angels tell the women at the tomb, and in Matthew and Luke and John this instruction is later repeated by Jesus when he appears to his followers. But the witnesses in these stories are afraid, just as their predecessors in the scriptures were, and nowhere is this fear more stark than in Mark's gospel:

> . . . And the women came out and ran away from the tomb because they were frightened out of their wits; and they said nothing to anyone, for they were afraid.
>
> MK.16.8

From the outset we have said that as far as possible Mark would be our control text in looking at the gospel stories of the

12 for more on each story see: Gideon, JG.6.23; Tobit/Tobias, TB.12.16; Daniel, DN.10.2-21; Moses, EX.3.1-12; Manoah, JG.13; Elijah, 1K.19,11-18.

death and resurrection of Jesus. This is because Mark's is the earliest of the gospels, and the most authoritative. With stories of the resurrected Jesus, however, it is impossible to use Mark's gospel as a benchmark, for he tells no such stories, and he offers no baseline text. Yet in spite of his silence, perhaps even because of his silence, Mark remains the most authoritative gospel. What he says, or does not say, carries great weight.

Epilogue

Over many centuries the stories told by Matthew and Luke and John about the appearances of Jesus after his death have proved far more popular than the silence and the fear at the end of Mark's gospel. The later stories of the resurrection appearances of Jesus are intriguing and powerful and enduring. They are also, as we have seen, deeply rooted in ancient Hebrew storytelling traditions. Yet the same is also true of the way Mark ends his gospel. The fear and the silence reflect the same awestruck fear we find in the stories of Moses and Elijah and others when they are brought face to face with the powerful mystery of their God.

At the end of his gospel, Mark turns to the traditions of the scriptures as the other gospel writers do, but he uses these traditions differently. He tells of the fearful reaction of witnesses who encounter a mystery, and offers no explanation either of their fear or of the mystery they encounter. For Mark, there is nothing further to say. The mystery of the empty tomb and the fear of the women are enough. They are part of a tradition of unexplained mystery and fear. The other gospel writers go beyond this and, building on Mark's gospel, they tell a variety of elaborate stories to explain more about the mystery, and to ease the fear.

As readers we are faced with this variety of stories about the death of Jesus and about the mysterious events following this death. Each gospel provides a different narrative. All of the gospel stories are honoured in Christian tradition. All of them are also questioned. Such honouring and such questioning are not, and never have been, mutually exclusive.

In writing this book our intention throughout has been to tell some of the stories of Jesus's death and resurrection and to suggest how they are linked to earlier material. In doing so we hope we have both honoured the stories and raised valid and interesting questions about them and how they were written. We do not pretend to have all the answers to these questions, in fact we do not believe that all the questions about these stories and their inter-relationships can be answered. We do believe, however, in trying to learn about all these stories by exploring them with interest, with imagination, or with respect. We also believe that the process of raising questions can sometimes be more important than answering them.

Not everyone will agree with the suggestions we have made nor with the links we have perceived between the gospel stories and other material. We have allowed ourselves to read the material freely and imaginatively. In seeking out the background material to the gospels we have turned to ancient revelations of the divine, to songs of love, to stories of gardens, to cries of despair. We have tried to be open to an intricate and influential web of ancient stories and texts. The influence of much of this material on the gospels is indirect, allusive, haunting. Precise and clearcut lines of descent and dependence cannot always be drawn linking story to story, poem to poem, image to image. Yet for us, the gospels do appear to reflect all of the material we have discussed, sometimes faintly, sometimes tangentially, and sometimes very clearly indeed.

The clear reflections of earlier material in the gospel stories are numerous. To recall only a few of them, the entry of Jesus into Jerusalem on the back of a donkey mirrors a passage in the book of Zechariah. The action of Jesus in the temple recalls the tempestuous actions and words of Jeremiah. The betrayal of Jesus by a friend at a meal echoes other similar betrayals. The thirty pieces of silver in Matthew's gospel is exactly the wage described by the prophet Zechariah. During the trial scenes, Jesus as the silent sufferer is like the suffering servant in Isaiah.

As Jesus is dying on the cross, his words and actions directly recall passages from the psalms. The appearances of the risen Jesus follow a pattern of earlier appearances by God or God's messenger.

These clear connections to other earlier stories or storytelling patterns inevitably bring us back to the question we raised in our introduction. What really happened? Did the gospel writers know from some lost source or through orally transmitted accounts about events in the life of Jesus? Did they then turn to other older stories and discover extraordinary parallels? Or did the gospel writers deliberately mine the older stories to find much of the substance of their accounts of Jesus? Or did the gospels selectively make use of ancient stories to provide a convincing framework for existing stories about Jesus? We do not have definite answers to such questions. Not only is it virtually impossible to say with any degree of certainty what really happened in the life of Jesus, it is also very difficult to say what really happened in the writing of the gospels.

It is, however, possible to say that the reflections of older material in stories about Jesus can be very direct, so direct that the gospel writers are undeniably using the older material to help form their stories of Jesus. It is also possible to say that even when these reflections are no more than faint poetic allusions, taken all together they have a cumulative effect. This effect is, as we suggested earlier, like a hall of mirrors, where images and ideas and bits of story seem to come together from many directions. Analysed individually these can be hard to trace, hard to pin down. Taken together they provide a sense of depth and radical continuity in the stories about Jesus, showing how these stories are profoundly and essentially connected to earlier stories, earlier ideas and images, earlier realities.

These stories about Jesus are robust; their roots lie deep, and their influence is far-reaching. The earliest version of these stories, in Mark's gospel, ends with fear and with mystery; the others end with recognition, reassurance and certainty. The gospel writers all in different ways make use of earlier, very ancient material to tell their stories and to meet the needs of their own times and places. In turn, in our own times and in our own places, we can read these same stories, and we can seek out the same ancient material that lies behind them. Then we can decide for ourselves how it all fits together.

APPENDIX ONE

The End of Mark's Gospel

The abrupt end of Mark at MK.16.8 is acknowledged in most English versions of the Bible. For example:

1611 the AUTHORISED VERSION OR KING JAMES BIBLE ignores the problem; some 20th century reprints acknowledge it.

1881 the REVISED VERSION separates the text and has a note.

1917 the SCOFIELD REFERENCE BIBLE, an annotated edition of the 1611 AUTHORISED VERSION, has a note.

1966 the GOOD NEWS BIBLE separates the text with a heading for an "Old Ending". There is a note.

1973 the NEW INTERNATIONAL VERSION separates the text with a line and a note.

1985 the NEW JERUSALEM BIBLE has a minimal separation of the text. The long note is reluctant but compelling.

1989 the REVISED ENGLISH BIBLE separates the text and has a note.

1989 the NEW REVISED STANDARD VERSION BIBLE separates the text. A series of headings indicate other endings. There are notes.

APPENDIX TWO

Chronology

Note: (i) all dates are BCE unless noted otherwise.
(ii) dates given for documents are approximations of when the documents began to take the form we now know.
(iii) c. means an approximation. ? queries an approximation. ?? means unknown.

Date, People and Events	The Record & Its Date If Known	
date unknown, Lamech and his two wives	Genesis 4.23- 24	c.950-750
? 1850 Abraham to Canaan	Genesis ch.12	c.950-750
1720-1560 Hyksos pharaohs: Hebrews in Egypt	Genesis chh.37-50	c.950-750
c.1725 Hammurabi in Babylon	Hammurabi's code	c.1700
c.1700 Tamar and Judah	Genesis.ch.38	
1290 the building of Pithom and Rameses in Egypt, Hebrews enslaved	Exodus ch.1.6-14	c.950-750
c.1250 the exodus from Egypt, crossing of the Red Sea, Miriam the prophetess	Exodus chh. 1-15 older sources put together	c.625

Date, People and Events	The Record & Its Date If Known	
c.1220 Balaam and his donkey	Numbers chh.22-24, oracles very early indeed	c.950-750
c.1220-1200 Joshua invading Palestine: Rahab, Jericho, crossing of Jordan	Joshua chh. 1-10, older sources put together	c.550
c.1200 the Greeks besiege Troy	Homer's Odyssey	? 800-600
c.1175 the wife of Manoah; Samson	Judges ch.13 older sources put together	±c.650
c.1125 Ruth and Boaz	the book of Ruth	c.625
c.1070 Hannah conceives	1s.chh.1- 2	before c.750
c.1050 death of Eli the priest	1s.ch. 4	
c.1070-1000 Samuel	1s.chh.1- 25	assembled c.625
c.1010 Samuel anoints David as king	1s.ch.16	
c.1010-970 David king, unites the tribes	1s.ch.16 to 1K.ch.2 assembled	± c.625

Date, People and Events	The Record & Its Date If Known	
970-931 Solomon king	1K.chh.1- 12	c.625
temple built	Psalm 72	c.730 re-write c.450
Queen of Sheba visits	Song of Songs	before c.750
		rewrite 450-300
931 the kingdom divides	1K.ch.12	
913-911 Abijam king	1K.ch.15.1- 8	before c.700
	2 Chronicles chh.1- 2	c.350
c.875-850 Elijah the prophet	1K.ch.17 to 2K.2	assembled c.625
c.850-?? Elisha the prophet	2K.ch.2 to 2K.ch.13	assembled c.625
c.750 Hosea, Micah and Amos	Amos, core only	c.730
	Micah, core only	before 700
	Hosea, core only	before 721
740 King Uzziah dies, Isaiah's vision	Isaiah ch.6	
740-698 Isaiah prophet in Jerusalem	Isaiah chh.1-39, core material only	before c.698

Date, People and Events	The Record & Its Date If Known	
734 Isaiah's oracle to Ahaz	Isaiah ch.7	
720 Assyria conquers Samaria, northern kingdom of Israel collapses	2K.17	assembled c.625
c.700 Assyria invades Judah, captures Lachish, besieges Jerusalem	2 K.18-19	
700 Jerusalem pays tribute	2 K.18.13-16	
640-609 Josiah king, 'book of the law' (Deuteronomy) found in the temple	2K.22 Deuteronomy core	c.625 c.650
604-562 Nebuchadnezzar king in Babylon		
610-595 Pharaoh Necho king in Egypt	2K.23.29-34	
16 March.597 Nebuchadnezzar conquers Jerusalem, Jehoiachin & first deportation	2K.24	
587 Nebuchadnezzar destroys Jerusalem, second deportation	2K.25 cp. 2CH.36 & JR.39	c.550 c.350 various dates to 587

Date, People and Events	The Record & Its Date If Known	
c.587-520 Second Isaiah poet in exile	Isaiah chh.40-55	
538 Cyrus of Persia conquers Babylon	Isaiah 44.28 to 45.1	
538-7 Zerubbabel rebuilds altar, foundations laid for second temple	Ezra ch.3	assembled c.350
August 520 second temple, work recommenced	Haggai core	contemporary
October 520 temple rebuilding encouraged	Zechariah core	contemporary
515 completion of second temple	Ezra ch.6	assembled c.350
445-443 new walls built for Jerusalem	Nehemiah 3	
c.400 work on *Law* and *Prophets* and many psalms well advanced		
350 Persia fading, Jerusalem restive, Ezra, Nehemiah and Chronicles started	coins stamped YDH (=Judah)	
348 death of Plato		
336-323 reign of Alexander the Great		

Date, People and Events	The Record & Its Date If Known	
285-246 Pharaoh Ptolemy Philadelphus: Greek version of scriptures started	*Septuagint* work on translation slow	c.250-100
167 Mattathias rebels against Greeks	1M.2.17-25 see also Daniel	c.167
1166-160 Judas Maccabeus leads rebellion. Independence. Treaty with Rome.	1M.	c.100
63 Pompey takes Jerusalem for Rome		
70-19 life of Virgil (Eclogues)		
37-4 Herod puppet king in Jerusalem: massive building includes new temple		
?6 Jesus born (BCE)	Matthew chh.1-2 Luke chh.1-2	c.80 CE c.85 CE
April, 4 BCE Herod dies, revolt in Jerusalem		
6-7 CE Quirinius takes census: revolt	Luke ch.2 Acts ch.5	c.85 CE
c.8 CE Jesus in temple as a youth	Luke ch.2	
c.26 CE Jesus baptised by John Baptist	Luke 3.23	

Date, People and Events	The Record & Its Date If Known	
c.30-32 CE Jesus is killed	Luke ch.23 and all the gospels	
c.33-4 CE conversion of Paul	Acts ch.9	c.85, or earlier
c.38-100 CE Flavius Josephus, Jewish historian		
50-51 CE Paul writes first letter to Thessalonika		
37-69 CE life of Nero, earliest material in Gospel of Thomas		c.60 CE
64 CE persecution of Christians in Rome, Peter and Paul killed		
67 CE Jerusalem rebels		
67-70 CE siege of Jerusalem by Romans	Mark's Gospel	c.70 CE
August 70 CE Jerusalem conquered and destroyed	Josephus: *The Jewish War*	
c.46-119 CE life of Plutarch		
c.80 CE Rabbis using Jamnia as a centre	Matthew's gospel	
c.85 CE Birkhath-ha-Minim	Luke's Gospel	

Date, People and Events	The Record & Its Date If Known
c.95 CE	John's Gospel
c.60-130 CE life span of Papias, a very early bishop	
c.69-? Suetonius, author of *The Twelve Caesars*	
c.140 CE Aquila's Greek translation of the Hebrew Scriptures	
c.150 CE Ptolemy the astronomer	
c.150-200 *Protevangelium of James*	

Surviving New Testament documents and their dates

There are many hundreds of these. They range from very small fragments to nearly complete bibles. A few of these date back to within a century of the writers of the New Testament. For a full list of these and their present locations see Nestle-Aland, *Novum Testamentum Graece*, Deutsche Bibelstiftung, Stuttgart, 1981 pp 684-716; there is an introduction in English.

Index of Biblical References

Note: references given in parentheses are found in footnotes on the page indicated

Bibliography

Alsup, John E., *The Post-Resurrection Appearance Stories of the Gospel Tradition*, SPCK, London, 1974.

Anderson, Janice Capel, "Matthew: Gender and Reading", *Semeia*, Vol. 28: *The Bible and Feminist Hermeneutics*, 1983, pp.3 - 27.

Bousset, Wilhelm, *Kyrios Christos*, translated by John E. Steely, 5th ed., Abingdon Press, New York and Nashville, 1970.

Brown, Raymond E., *The Birth of the Messiah*, Image Books, New York, *1979*.

Brown. Raymond E., *The Gospel According to John*, (2 vols) Anchor Bible #29, Doubleday & Co., Garden City, New York, 1979.

Bruce, F.F., *The Acts of the Apostles: Greek Text with Introduction and Commentary*, William B. Eerdmans, Grand Rapids, Michigan, (Apollos, Leicester, England) first published 1951, third edition 1990.

Buttrick, David G., "Preaching and the Passion Narratives", in *Reformed Liturgy and Music*, 24(1) Winter 1990.

Butts, James R., "Probing the Polling, Jesus Seminar Results on the Kingdom Sayings", in *Foundations and Facets Forum*, Vol.3, No.1, November 1987.

Caird, G.B., *Saint Luke*, Pelican New Testament Commentaries, edited by D.E. Nineham, Penguin Books, first published 1963.

Carrington, Philip, *The Early Christian Church*, 2 Vols., C.U.P., Cambridge, 1957.

Davies, W.D., *The Setting of the Sermon on the Mount*, C.U.P., Cambridge, 1964.

Derrett, J.D.M., *Law in the New Testament*, Darton, Longman and Todd, London, 1970.

Dibelius, Martin, *From Tradition to Gospel*, translated by Bertram Lee Woolf, The Scribner Library, New York, Charles Scribner's Sons, no date.

Donahue, John R., *Are You the Christ? The Trial Narrative in the Gospel of Mark*, Scholar's Press, 1973, [Society of Biblical Literature, Dissertation Series No. 10, Ph.D. 1972, University of Chicago].

Donahue, John R. "From Passion Traditions to Passion Narrative", being the Introduction to:– Kelber, Werner H. (ed), *The Passion in Mark; Studies On Mark 14-16*, Fortress Press, Philadelphia, 1976.

Douglass, James W., *The Nonviolent Coming of God*, Orbis Books; Maryknoll, New York; 1991.

Eisenman, Robert, *Maccabees, Zadokites, Christians and Qumran*, E.J.Brill, Leiden; 1983.

Eusebius, *The History of the Church from Christ to Constantine*, trans. G.A Williamson, revised and edited by Andrew Louth, Penguin Classics edition 1989.

Evans, C.F., *Resurrection and the New Testament*, London, SCM Press, 1970.

Ellis, Peter F., *Matthew: His Mind and Message*, The Liturgical Press, Collegeville, Minnesota, 1974.

Fenton, J.C., *Saint Matthew*, Pelican Gospel Commentaries, Penguin Books, first published 1963.

Fitzmeyer, Joseph A., *The Gospel According to Luke*, Doubleday and Co., Garden City, New York, 1981.

Frazer, James, *The Golden Bough*, 3rd.Ed., c.1910.

Frye, Northrop, *The Great Code; The Bible and Literature*, Academic Press Canada, Toronto, 1982. (U.S. publisher: Harcourt, Brace, Johanovich, New York).

Funk, Robert W. "Poll on the Parables" (Jesus Seminar) in *Foundations and Facets Forum*, 2.1, 1986.

Funk, Robert W., Scott, Bernard Brandon, & Butts, James R., *The Parables of Jesus, Red Letter Edition; A Report of the Jesus Seminar*, Polebridge Press, Sonoma, California, 1988.

Funk, Robert W. & Smith, Mahlon H., *The Gospel of Mark, Red Letter Edition*, (Jesus Seminar Series), Polebridge Press, Sonoma, California; 1991.

Gaston, Lloyd, *Paul and the Torah*, University of British Columbia Press, Vancouver, 1987.

Goulder, M.D., *Luke: A New Paradigm* (2 Vols.), JSOT Press, Sheffield, England, 1989.

Goulder, M.D., *Midrash and Lection in Matthew*, SPCK, London, 1974.

Goulder, M.D., *The Psalms of the Sons of Korah*, JSOT Press, Sheffield, England, 1982.

Goulder, M.D., *The Prayers of David*, JSOT Press, Sheffield, England, 1990.

Guilding, Aileen, *The Fourth Gospel and Jewish Worship*, Clarendon Press, Oxford, 1960.

Hahn, Ferdinand, *The Titles of Jesus in Christology*, translated by H.Knight and G.Ogg, Lutterworth Press, London, 1969.

Hartman, L., *Prophecy Interpreted: The Formation of Some Jewish Apocalyptic Texts and of the Eschatological Discourse Mark 13 Par.*, Coniectanea Biblica, NT Series 1, Lund, 1966.

Hastings, James, ed., *A Dictionary of the Bible*, (4 volumes); Charles Scribner's Sons, New York, 1902.

Hamerton-Kelly, R.G., ed, *Violent Origins: Ritual Killing and Cultural Formation,* Stanford University Press, Palo Alto, California, 1987.

Harvey, A.E., ed., *Alternative Approaches to New Testament Studies*, A.E. Harvey ed., SPCK, London, 1985.

Hendrick, Herman, *Resurrection Narratives,* Geoffrey Chapman, London, 1984.

Hendrick, Herman, *Passion Narratives*, Geoffrey Chapman, London, 1984.

Hennecke, E. tr., *New Testament Apocrypha*, edited by W. Schneemelcher, Lutterworth Press, London. 1963.

Holtz, Barry W., *Back to the Sources*, Summit Books, New York, 1984.

Horsfield, Margaret, *The Birth Narratives*, CBC Radio, Toronto: IDEAS transcript, prepared and presented by Margaret Horsfield, 1987.

Horsfield, Margaret, *Crucified, Dead and Buried*, CBC Radio, Toronto: IDEAS transcript, prepared and presented by Margaret Horsfield, 1989.

Horsfield, Margaret, *The Book of Job*, CBC Radio, Toronto: IDEAS transcript, prepared and presented by Margaret Horsfield, 1991.

Horsfield, Margaret, & Horsfield, Peter, *Beyond Bethlehem,* CBC Enterprises, Toronto, 1989.

Horsley, Richard A., and Hanson, John S., *Bandits, Prophets, and Messiahs: Popular Movements in the Time of Jesus*, Seabury, Minneapolis, Chicago, New York, 1985.

Houlden, J.L., *Backward Into Light: The Passion and Resurrection of Jesus According to Matthew and Mark*, SCM Press, London, 1987.

Jeremias, Jaochim, *The Eucharistic Words of Jesus*, translated by Norman Perrin, 3rd. revised edition, London, S.C.M. Press, 1966.

Josephus, Flavius, *The Jewish War,* edited by Gaalya Cornfeld, Zondervan Publishing House, Grand Rapids, Michigan, 1982.

Josephus, Flavius, *The Jewish War*, tr. G.A. Williamson, 1959, Penguin Classics edition, London, New York &c, 1981.

Josephus, Flavius, *The Works of Flavius Josephus*, trans. William Whiston, The Excelsior Edition, Edinburgh, no date.

Justin (Martyr), *The Dialogue with Trypho*, trans. A. Lukyn Williams, SPCK, London, 1930.

Kee, Howard Clark, *Community of the New Age; Studies in Mark's Gospel*, The Westminster Press, Philadelphia, 1977.

Lane, Eric & Brenson, Ian, *The Complete Text in English, The Oberammergau Passion Play,* with an introduction by Eric Lane and Ian Brenson, Dedalus, London, 1984.

Lane, William L., *The Gospel According to Mark* in the series "New International Commentaries on the New Testament", William B. Eerdmans, Grand Rapids, 1974.

Lindars, B., *New Testament Apologetic*, Westminster Press, Philadelphia and London, 1961.
Maccoby, H., *Judas Iscariot and the Myth of Jewish Evil*; Peter Halban; London; 1992.
Mack, Burton L., *A Myth of Innocence*, Fortress Press, Philadelphia 1988.
Mack, Burton L. "The Kingdom Sayings in Mark", in *Foundations and Facets Forum, 3(1)*, March 1987.
Mack, Burton L., *Wisdom and the Hebrew Epic; Ben Sira's Hymn in Praise of the Fathers*, The University of Chicago Press, Chicago and London, 1985.
Mann, C.S., *Mark*, The Anchor Bible, Doubleday, New York, 1986.
Matera, Frank J., *The Passion Narratives and Gospel Theologies,* Paulist Press, New York, 1986.
Metzger, Bruce M., *A Textual Commentary of the Greek New Testament: A Companion Volume to the United Bible Societies' Greek New Testament*, (third edition), United Bible Societies, 1971.
Morris, Leon, *The Gospel According to John*, in the series "New International Commentaries on the New Testament", William B. Eerdmans, Grand Rapids, Michigan, 1971.
Nelson, Joyce, "Jesus of Montreal: Culling the Living Flower", *THIS Magazine*, (Arts Column; "Art and Soul") Vol.23, #6, Toronto, Jan.-Feb. 1990.
Nineham, D.E., *The Gospel of St. Mark*, Pelican New Testament Commentaries, Penguin, London, 1963.
Nineham, Dennis, *The Use and Abuse of the Bible*, SPCK, London, 1976.
O'Collins, Gerald, *The Easter Jesus,* Darton, Longman and Todd, London, 1973.
Origen, *Contra Celsum*, H. Chadwick tr., Cambridge University Press, 1953 & 1979.
Passion Play of the Community of Oberammergau, 1990, Spielleitung Christian Stuckl.
Perkins, Pheme, *Resurrection,* Geoffrey Chapman, London, 1984.
Perrin, Norman, "The Creative Use of the Son of Man Traditions by Mark", *Union Seminary Quarterly Review*, XXIII (1968).
Plutarch, *The Lives of the Noble Grecians and Romans,* trans. John Dryden, The Modern Library, New York, no date.
Sanders, E.P., *Jesus and Judaism*, Fortress Press, Philadelphia, 1985.
Scanzoni, L.D., & Hardesty, N.A., *All We're Meant to Be: Biblical Feminism For Today,* Nashville, Abingdon Press, first pub. 1974, revised 1986.
Schlussler-Fiorenza, Elizabeth, *In Memory of Her: A Feminist Theological Reconstruction of Christian Origins*, Crossroad, New York, 1983.
Senior, Donald, *The Passion of Jesus in the Gospel of Matthew,* (vol.1 of "The Passion Series") Michael Glazier, Wilmington, Delaware; 1985; 2nd. printing 1989.

Struthers Malbon, Elizabeth, "Fallible Followers: Women and Men in the Gospel of Mark" *Semeia*, Vol.28: *The Bible and Feminist Hermeneutics*, 1983, pp.29-47.
Suetonius, *The Twelve Caesars*, trans. Robert Graves, Penguin Classics, 1957.
Temple, William, *Readings in John's Gospel* (first and second series), MacMillan & Co., London; 1947.
Thucydides, *The Peloponnesian War*, trans. Rex Warner, Penguin Classic Edition, Penguin Books, Harmondsworth, Middlesex, England 1954.
Vermes, Geza, *The Dead Sea Scrolls in English*, Penguin, London, 1962.
Vermes, Geza, *Jesus the Jew*, SCM Press (in Canada), Fortress Press (in U.S.A.), 1973.
Vermes, Geza, *Jesus and the World of Judaism*, SCM Press (Canada), Fortress Press (U.S.A.), 1983.
Virgil, *The Aeneid*, trans. W.F.Jackson Knight, Penguin Classics, first published 1956.
Wiener, Aharon, *The Prophet Elijah in the Development of Judaism*, Routledge and Kegan Paul, London, 1978.

Bibles

The Authorized Version, (also known as the King James Bible), 1611.
The Scofield Reference Bible, O.U.P., 1917.
The Revised Version, O.U.P., London, 1881.
The Revised Standard Version, National Council of Churches, U.S.A. 1946 (New Testament), 1952 (Old Testament), 1957 (Apocrypha).
The New English Bible, O.U.P., 1961 (New Testament) and 1970 (Old Testament and Apocrypha).
The New American Bible, first published by Catholic Bible Publishers, Kansas, 1970.
The Jerusalem Bible, Doubleday & Co.; New York; 1966.
Good News Bible, American Bible Society 1966 (New Testament) and 1976 (Old Testament).
The New International Version, International Bible Society, New York, 1978.
The New Jerusalem Bible, Doubleday and Co.; New York, 1985.
The Revised English Bible, O.U.P., 1989.
The New Revised Standard Version, National Council of Churches, U.S.A., 1989.
The Septuagint with Apocrypha: Greek and English., tr. Sir Lancelot C.L.Brenton; Samuel Bagster & Sons; London; 1851; reprinted by Hendrickson Publishers, Peabody, Ma. 1987.
Novum Testamentum Graece (Greek New Testament), Nestle-Aland, Deutsche Bibelstiftung, Stuttgart, 1981.

Index

Any entry followed by (n) refers to a footnote on the page indicated.